HARRY POTTER AND THE BIBLE

HARRY POTTER AND THE BIBLE

The Menace
behind the Magick

Richard Abanes

HORIZON BOOKS

A DIVISION OF CHRISTIAN PUBLICATIONS, INC.

CAMP HILL, PENNSYLVANIA

HORIZON BOOKS

A DIVISION OF CHRISTIAN PUBLICATIONS, INC.

3825 Hartzdale Drive, Camp Hill, PA 17011

Harry Potter and the Bible
ISBN: 0-7394-2733-4

Unless otherwise indicated,
Scripture taken from the
Holy Bible: King James Version

DEDICATION

To my wife, Bri, my best friend, closest ally and truest critic.
Thanks for being patient and waiting yet a little longer
for that vacation I have been promising you.

CONTENTS

✳ PART ONE ✳
THE WORLD OF HARRY POTTER

✳ PART TWO ✳
OUT OF THE DARKNESS

FOREWORD

Spiritual discernment may be at an all-time low in both the Church and in the world. The idea of "spirituality"—now all the rage in our postmodern times—is deemed a subjective, relative, pragmatic pursuit of personal enjoyment apart from considerations of truth, rationality or objective reality. And far too many Christians have failed to develop their critical faculties concerning the enticements of a post-Christian culture. Moreover, in our fallen world, many forms of evil masquerade as innocent, harmless and fun. They are often accepted with little evaluation or criticism, especially when they are popular and entertaining.

Yet Paul calls us to test everything, hold on to the good and avoid every kind of evil (1 Thessalonians 5:21-22). Jesus also warned the undiscerning people of His day to stop judging according to mere appearance and make right judgments (John 7:24). But right judgments about popular culture are all too rare today, even in the Church (Hebrews 5:11-14).

J.K. Rowling's Harry Potter books (soon to be made into major movies, action figures and an entire multimillion dollar industry of spin-offs) have broken sales records, dominated the best-seller lists, triggered near riots at bookstores upon their release and captured the imaginations and dollars of millions of children and adults. They also have been praised by some evangelical leaders who sadly have failed to understand the insidious nature of their message.

In the midst of this "Pottermania," Richard Abanes' much-needed book provides a rare voice of sanity, reason and biblical discernment. Without sensationalism or bigoted ridicule, he deftly and thoroughly documents that this wildly popular series is not just "good fun," nor does it aptly depict "the battle of good versus evil," as many have claimed. Instead, the Potter series is steeped in a thinly disguised occultism; it favors morally flawed, egocentric characters who lie with impunity, practice occultic techniques, use profanity and refuse to repent; and it frequently depicts gratuitous violence.

Stephen King wrote in the *New York Times Review of Books* ("Wild About Harry," July 23, 2000) that the Potter series, which he loves, would provide children with a good introduction to his own gruesome and demonic horror novels when they are old enough to read them. Media hype to the contrary, this is not good news for the children, or adults, of today.

Some celebrate that children are reading the massive Potter books instead of watching television. They need to think again. To be sure, television is, more often than not, a moral, spiritual and intellectual wasteland; but so are the Potter books.

Abanes, a well-published expert in cults and the occult, meticulously inspects the Potter books and reveals their close connection to nearly every facet of the occult—alchemy, astrology, spells, mediumship and other pagan practices. He demonstrates that these books desensitize children and others to the forbidden and dangerous world of pagan magic (Deuteronomy 18:9-14; Galatians 5:20; Revelation 22:15). In fact, many self-proclaimed pagan groups sing the praises of Rowling's books, and some young people have reported their desire to become witches after reading of their spell-casting hero, Harry Potter.

This is serious business. We would do well to remember Jesus' sobering words: "And whoso shall receive one such little child in my name receiveth me. But whoso shall offend one of these little ones which believe in me, it were better for him that a millstone were hanged about his neck, and that he were drowned in the depth of the sea" (Matthew 18:5-6).

Fortunately, Abanes is not content merely to chronicle spiritual error and its perils. He provides a solid biblical perspective on the occult and explains how followers of Jesus Christ should wisely resist this encroachment of darkness into our increasingly paganized culture. Lovers of Christ can walk in the Spirit's wisdom and strength, even as they tackle the many spiritual counterfeits that assail our culture (1 John 4:4). Nor does Abanes condemn all fantasy literature, as his chapter on the writings of C.S. Lewis and Tolkien makes clear. He gives a hard-hitting but well-balanced assessment on all counts.

This is an important book for parents, grandparents, educators and pastors who want to discern the spirit of the times, walk in the light, repel the darkness and take a well-informed stand for God's truth in our day.

Douglas Groothuis, Ph.D.,
Associate Professor of Philosophy
Denver Seminary

PUBLISHER'S PREFACE

Richard Abanes and I go back a few years. I first saw his byline in *Christianity Today* and decided to track him down. Out of that first contact came an earlier book in this series, *Embraced by the Light and the Bible*. That was in 1995. Now fast forward several years. It is the spring of 2000. The Harry Potter phenomenon is getting heavy media coverage and the glorification of witchcraft is proceeding apace. In my mind, that called for another in our popular apologetic *"and the Bible"* series.

When Richard called me and suggested this title, I told him it had been on my mind as well and I had been wondering to which author I might turn. Richard Abanes was my choice.

It is some months later now and Abanes has presented us an unusual text—*Harry Potter and the Bible*. He has been a relentless researcher and as this volume has moved through to completion, there is no doubt in my mind that he is offering a significant contribution to the international excitement focused on J.K. Rowling's Harry Potter fictional character.

The chapter which compares the Potter material to the writings of Tolkien and C.S. Lewis is invaluable and could be used as a stand-alone article. It is my intention in due course to urge its inclusion in the 2001 edition of *The Alliance Academic Review* published by this house.

Speaking from the perspective of having been involved in the extrication of various persons from occult subjection and bondage over many years, I have to say that Abanes has made his point. The Harry Potter series is loaded with occult references and given the vulnerability of children and the capacity for contagion in occult matters, he is not at all overstating "the menace behind the magick." I find myself wanting to affirm this text repeatedly.

This book is a helpful tool in the kingdom of God. My prayer is that it will find many avenues of usefulness.

K. Neill Foster, Publisher
Christian Publications/Horizon Books

ACKNOWLEDGMENTS

A word of appreciation must first go to K. Neill Foster, president of Christian Publications/Horizon Books, for his unshakeable faith in this book project. I pray that God will continue to bless your ministry in the book publishing industry. I am also indebted to my editor David Fessenden. Wow, are you good! I'm going to have to start calling you "eagle-eye" Fessenden. Additionally, I am thankful for the endless stream of polite assistance that flowed from the entire Christian Publications/Horizon Books staff.

As always, I received invaluable support, encouragement and resources from various ministries. The Christian Research Institute, Answers in Action, Watchman Fellowship, Christian Answers for the New Age and the Centers for Apologetic Research have been of particular help over the last several months. I needed all of you.

Finally, thanks goes to my friends at church who kept me in prayer throughout the writing of this volume. I am especially grateful for the prayers of my friend and music pastor Rick Muchow, the staff members of Saddleback Church and my fellow music ministers in Saddleback's Vocal Worship Ministry.

INTRODUCTION

Any time the dark side of the supernatural world is presented as harmless or even imaginary, there is the danger that children will become curious and find too late that witchcraft is neither harmless nor imaginary. In a culture with an obvious trend toward witchcraft and New Age ideology, parents need to consider the effects that these ideas may have on young and impressionable minds.

Lindy Beam[1]
Focus on the Family

The literary world has been bewitched by a series of four best-selling books: *Harry Potter and the Sorcerer's Stone*, *Harry Potter and the Chamber of Secrets*, *Harry Potter and the Prisoner of Azkaban* and *Harry Potter and the Goblet of Fire*. And just who is Harry Potter? He is merely the lead character found in these children's novels, each of which was written by Scottish author Joanne Kathleen Rowling. Nevertheless, this fictional boy, brought to life through the magic of prose, has mesmerized millions of people worldwide. No one could have imagined that the stories, which detail Harry's mystical adventures as a wizard-in-training, would break numerous publishing records, and in so doing, bestow fame and astonishing wealth upon Rowling (a previously unknown author). But that is exactly what happened via a book-buying frenzy from which a stunned retail industry has yet to recover.

As of December 2000, the ongoing craze over Harry Potter had put 1 million audio versions of the four volumes into circulation. The total number of books in print had reached more than 40 million copies, in over 40 languages, in 130 countries. And Scholastic, Rowling's U.S. publisher, had cleared well over $200 million. Rowling herself has become the highest paid woman in Britain.[2]

"Pottermania" began in June 1997 with the publication in England of Rowling's first novel, *Harry Potter and the Philosopher's Stone*. When it landed on American shores in September 1998 as *Harry Potter and the Sorcerer's Stone*[3], it quickly took up residence on the *New York Times* best-seller list. This same destiny awaited *Harry Potter and the Chamber of Secrets* (Book II, June 1999), *Harry Potter and the Prisoner of Azkaban* (Book III, September 1999) and *Harry Potter and the Goblet of Fire* (Book IV, July 2000). The release of Book IV granted Rowling the top four slots on the best-seller lists of several publications, including *USA Today* and the *Wall Street Journal*. No author had ever accomplished such a stupendous feat.

Diane Roback, children's book editor for *Publishers Weekly*, remarked: "The Harry Potter phenomenon is unprecedented in children's literature."[4] Jean Feiwel, a representative from Scholastic, agreed: "It's mind-boggling. It would be easy to attribute Harry Potter's success to some form of magical intervention."[5]

Hollywood, ever mindful of the public's changing interests, jumped into the picture via a deal between Warner Bros. and Rowling. The legendary movie-making company will produce seven films, one for every volume in Rowling's series. The first movie, due in late 2001, will coincide with the release by Mattel and Hasbro of Harry Potter action figures, trading cards, role-playing games similar to Dungeons & Dragons, assorted "high-tech" toys (such as voice-changing devices), a line of clothing (e.g., invisibility cloaks, T-shirts, caps), video games, computer games, book bags and candies based on the wild-tasting "Every Flavor Beans" (e.g., grass, snot, sardine and vomit) eaten by Harry and his companions. These products alone could generate upward of $1 billion.

Rowling's books, for the most part, have been widely touted as the best fantasy literature produced since the C.S. Lewis and J.R.R. Tolkien era. However, many individuals (mostly Christians) have been less than elated over the popularity of her novels, which tell the story of a boy-wizard and his experiences as he is trained in the art of wizardry. For instance, at www.letusreason.org (an evangelical web site), one article states: "There are numerous books written on witchcraft and the occult, but none is more ingeniously packaged to attract the kids like this one."[6]

Such concerns have been especially disturbing to parents whose children are in public schools where the Harry Potter books are being read to students during class time. This has become an extremely common occurrence. Moreover, several teachers enamored with the books have redecorated their classrooms to look like locations in Potter's world, designed learning exercises based on Rowling's writings and encouraged students to create Harry Potter games/activities.[7]

Major publishers have even released study-books and classroom discussion guides so teachers can lead their students through "the origins and mysteries of Harry's world," including its occult themes.[8]

The *Exploring Harry Potter* sourcebook (Beacham Publications), for example, supplies an internet resource companion web page that gives a "Reading for Research" section, which lists the book *Drawing*

Down the Moon: Witches, Druids, Goddess-Worshippers and Other Pagans in America Today by Margot Adler, a neopagan and leading spokesperson for contemporary paganism and witchcraft (see Chapter Seven).[9] Beacham's online resource page for teachers/parents also provides numerous Internet web sites for children, including www.witchvox.com ("The Witches' Voice"), a web site dedicated to teaching the basics of witchcraft.[10]

It is not surprising that Karen Gounaud, president of Family Friendly Libraries (an organization that monitors inappropriate reading material) would see Rowling's books as unacceptable for classrooms. According to Gounaud, they contain "a great deal of symbolism, language, and activities honoring witchcraft."[11] Many conservative organizations, parents and school administrators agree. Paul Ford, professor of theology and liturgy at St. John's Seminary in Southern California, explains: "Rowling refers to the dark arts as if they're trivial. I don't know if you can treat it so benignly."[12]

One man interviewed by the *Baptist Press* explained: "[There is] a general nastiness underneath the mantle of cuteness. The kids [in these novels] lie, they steal, they take revenge. This is a disturbing moral world, and it conflicts with what I am trying to teach my children."[13]

Concerned parents have responded by lodging protests with schools and children's libraries. Some have even filed lawsuits. As of November 2000, the books had been challenged more than 400 times in over twenty-five school districts in nineteen states. According to the American Library Association's Office for Intellectual Freedom (OIF), Rowling's books topped the 1999 list of most frequently challenged books in America due to their "focus on wizardry and magic."[14] (A "challenge" as defined by the OIF, is any "attempt to remove or restrict materials [from a school's curriculum or library], based upon objections of a person or group.")[15]

This controversy has even spread to England. Carol Rookwood—head teacher for a Church of England primary school—has banned the books from her educational institution because in her opinion they promote what the Bible clearly condemns, i.e., witchcraft and sorcery. "Our ethos on teaching comes from the Bible," she told *The Times* (London). "The Bible is clear about issues such as witchcraft, demons, devils and the occult. It says clearly and consistently from Genesis to Revelation that they are real, powerful and dangerous. Throughout it insists that God's people should have nothing to do with them."[16]

Others have voiced an entirely different viewpoint. Judy Corman, senior vice president for Scholastic, says Harry Potter is "not about witchcraft. It is about the power of imagination."[17] Rowling herself dismisses the objections, saying, "I am not trying to influence anyone into black magic. That's the very last thing I'd want to do. . . . My wizarding world is a world of the imagination. I think it's a moral world."[18]

Interestingly, several prominent Christians and conservative organizations have sided with Rowling. In an article for the Roman Catholic journal *First Things*, Alan Jacobs of Wheaton College described the novels as "a great deal of fun." He further stated that their magic was "charming."[19] During a 1999 radio interview, Jacobs had commented that they promote "a kind of spiritual warfare, a struggle between good and evil." He additionally remarked, "[There is] in books like this the possibility for serious moral reflection."[20]

Born-again Christian Chuck Colson (founder of Prison Fellowship and former Special Counsel to President Richard M. Nixon) also has painted the fantasy tales as relatively harmless. During a November 2, 1999 radio commentary, he said that

Rowling's characters, especially Harry Potter, demonstrated "courage, loyalty, and a willingness to sacrifice for one another—even at the risk of their lives. Not bad lessons in a self-centered world."[21]

An even more positive review of Rowling's material appeared in the influential evangelical magazine *Christianity Today*: "Rowling's series is a *Book of Virtues* with a preadolescent funny bone. Amid the laugh-out-loud scenes are wonderful examples of compassion, loyalty, courage, friendship and even self-sacrifice. No wonder young readers want to be like these believable characters. That is a Christmas present we can be grateful for."[22]

What are we to believe? Are the Potter books harmless fantasy novels fit for adults and children alike? Or do they contain spiritually dangerous material that could ultimately lead youth down the road to occultism? Does J.K. Rowling present a "moral" world consistent with Christianity? Or do her novels promote unbiblical values and unethical behavior, camouflaged beneath a whimsical mask? Is the success behind Rowling's books just a result of good writing and media hype? Or is there an unseen spiritual force of darkness possibly driving the craze? How should parents respond, especially Christian parents? These are some of the questions I hope to answer in *Harry Potter and the Bible*.

Part 1 of this volume examines Rowling's books in the order they were published. Each of her works is given two successive chapters—the first provides "A Brief Summary" of the book being examined, while the second takes "A Closer Look" at the volume. Consequently, Chapters 1 and 2 deal with Rowling's first book, Chapters 3 and 4 cover her second book, and so on.

The odd-numbered chapters in Part 1 explain the plot of the particular book being covered. (This is especially important for parents and educators still unfamiliar with Rowling's novels.) Every even-numbered chapter in Part 1 begins by discussing the real-world occultism present in the volume being examined, then moves on to detail the following aspects of her fantasy tales:

- **Potterethics** shows the morally confusing messages presented throughout the Harry Potter series.
- **Ages 6 and Up?** not only covers the many instances where J.K. Rowling's humor is rather twisted and child-inappropriate, but also discusses the places where she includes what some may feel are scenes of unnecessary violence, gore and cruelty. (In a BBC interview, Rowling admitted that some of her material is "not suitable" for six-year-olds. Nevertheless, she also stated, "But you can't stop them from reading it.... My parents never censored what I read so I wouldn't say don't read them to a six-year-old, just be aware some of it does get uncomfortable."[23])

Part 2 of *Harry Potter and the Bible* provides an overview of the many issues relating to Rowling's books: occultism in society, the place of fantasy in Christian literature (e.g., C.S. Lewis and J.R.R. Tolkien) and the controversies surrounding the use of Harry Potter in public schools. Most importantly, Part 2 clearly explains why God is so against occultism and where it is condemned in Scripture.

Many of us have already been, and will continue to be, affected by the Potter phenomenon. A recent Gallup poll found that almost one-third of all parents with kids under eighteen years old have children who have read a Harry Potter novel.[24] *USA Today* rightly noted that since the release of *Harry Potter and the Sorcerer's Stone*, a bespectacled, orphaned son of a murdered witch and wizard has been "the soul mate of millions of children around the world."[25]

If the Harry Potter series is indeed harmful, then that is something worthy of exposing. If, on the other hand, the books are benign, then that also is something in need of clear articulation. Either way, all of us will be seeing a great deal more of Rowling's creations as time passes, especially since several Harry Potter movies will be produced in the near future along with three more books.

ENDNOTES

1. Lindy Beam, "Exploring Harry Potter's World," *Teachers in Focus*, December 1999, available online at www.focusonthefamily.org.
2. Reuters, "From Hogwarts to Easy Street," August 21, 2000, available online at www.abcnews.com; cf. Morgan Murphy, "Magic Coins," *Forbes Magazine*, March 20, 2000, available online at www.forbes.com. According to Reuters, Rowling's income exceeded $30.5 million in 1999.
3. Book I of Rowling's series was originally titled *Harry Potter and the Philosopher's Stone*. The title was changed to *Harry Potter and the Sorcerer's Stone* for book-buyers in the United States because Rowling's publishers felt that Americans would be more familiar with the word "sorcerer."
4. Diane Roback, quoted in Deirdre Donahue, "Harry Potter's Appeal: Poof Positive," *USA Today*, December 2, 1999, available online at www.usatoday.com/life/enter/books/book293.htm.
5. Elizabeth Mehren, "Despite Sales, Some Not Wild About Harry Books," *Los Angeles Times*, October 22, 1999, available online at www.latimes.com.
6. Mike Oppenheimer, "Harry Potter: A Sorcerer's Tale," Let Us Reason Ministries, available online at www.letusreason.org.
7. Guy Walters, "Harry Potter: Why So Popular?," *The Times* (London), June 29, 2000, available online at www.the-times.co.uk.
8. Elizabeth D. Schafer, *Beacham's Sourcebook: Exploring Harry Potter* (Osprey, FL: Beacham Publishing, 2000), Section VI, available online at www.beachampublishing.com; cf. "Harry Potter Can Help Parents and Teachers Educate Kids, Children's Book Expert Says," *PR Newswire*, August, 17, 2000, available online at www.northernlight.com.
9. Schafer, www.beachampublishing.com. (For ease of reference, an abbreviated citation has been used throughout the book in place of the traditional *Ibid*.)
10. Schafer.
11. Karen Jo Gounaud, quoted in Phyllis Shafley, "Beware of Bewitching Books," *Eagle Forum*, December 1999, available online at www.eagleforum.org.

12. Paul Ford, quoted in Richard Scheinin, "Harry Potter's Wizardly Powers Divide Opinion," *Fort Worth (TX) Star-Telegram*, December 3, 1999, available online at www.arlington.net.

13. Ken McCormick, quoted in Art Toalston, "Latest Harry Potter Book Meets Cautionary Response from Christians," *Baptist Press*, July 13, 2000, available online at www.cesnur.org/recens/potter_044.htm.

14. "Harry Potter Tops List of 'Most Challenged Books,'" *Library Journal*, February 7, 2000, available online at www.ala.org/news/archives/v5n12/99bookchallenges.html.

15. American Library Association definition found at http://www.ala.org/alaorg/oif/reporting.html.

16. Conal Urquhart and Ruth Gledhill, "School Puts Ban on 'Evil' Harry Potter," *The Times* (London), March 29, 2000, available at www.the-times.co.uk/news/pages/tim/00/03/290timnwsnws01029.html.

17. Jim Galloway and Chris Burritt, "School Lets Hero Off Hook," *Atlanta Journal-Constitution*, October 13, 1999, www.accessatlanta.com.

18. J.K. Rowling, quoted in Michele Hatty, "Harry Potter Author Reveals the Secret to Getting Kids to Read as Children's Book Week Kicks Off," *USA Weekend Online*, November 14, 1999, available online at www.usaweekend.com/99_issues/991114/991114potter.html.

19. Alan Jacobs, "Harry Potter's Magic," *First Things*, January 2000, available online at www.firstthings.com/ftissues/ft0001/reviews/jacobs.html.

20. Alan Jacobs, interview on *Mars Hill Audio* (vol. 40, September/October 1999), audio cassette, side 2.

21. Chuck Colson, "Witches and Wizards: The Harry Potter Phenomenon," *BreakPoint Commentary*, November 2, 1999, available online at www.breakpoint.org.

22. "Why We Like Harry Potter," *Christianity Today*, January 10, 2000, available online at www.christianityonline.com/ct/current/9c13/9c13a.html.

23. J.K. Rowling, "Potter Author's Content Warning," BBC, News online edition, September 29, 2000, available online at http://news6.thdo.bbc.co.uk/hi/english/entertainment/newsid%5F944000/944728.stm.

24. Chuck Colson, "Harry Potter and the Existence of God," *BreakPoint Commentary*, July 14, 2000, available online at www.cbn.org/Newsstand/commentary/colson-000721.asp.

25. Deirdre Donahue, "Harry Potter 'Fire' Sale Casts a Spell Tonight," *USA Today*, July 7, 2000, available online at www.usatoday.com.

PART
ONE

THE WORLD OF
HARRY POTTER

ONE

SORCERY IN A STONE:
A BRIEF SUMMARY

It is good to see that the best selling series of books in the west-ern world is such a positive tale about witches and wizards.

The Children of Artemis[1]
Witchcraft & Wicca web site

Harry Potter and the Sorcerer's Stone, Book I in J.K. Rowling's fantasy novel series, lays the foundation for all her other volumes. It not only introduces most of the books' main characters, but also acquaints readers with many unique terms exclusively used by Rowling in her imaginary world (e.g., Muggles, Quidditch, Gryffindor). The series, scheduled to include seven volumes, revolves around the adventures of an orphan named Harry Potter and his struggles against the wickedest of wizards, Lord Voldemort (a.k.a. "He-Who-Must-Not-Be-Named").

Book I begins in the home of Vernon Dursley, his wife, Petunia, and their newborn son, Dudley. Mr. Dursley, who works at a drill manufacturing company called Grunnings, is portrayed as nothing but a big, loud brute with a hot temper, a cruel nature and a terrible sense of fairness. Mrs. Dursley, although not nearly as boisterous as her husband, is certainly as unlikable. She is a beady-eyed, long-necked busybody, whose most grati-fying pastimes are spying on neighbors and gossiping. Both of them adore their overindulged son, Dudley, who in their eyes can do no wrong. The Dursleys, a thoroughly detestable threesome, proudly proclaim that they are "perfectly normal" people.[2]

But this family has an embarrassing secret. Petunia's sister (Lily Potter) is a witch and her "good-for-nothing" husband (James Potter) is a wizard. Harry, their one-year-old baby, also is a wizard, having a magical nature like his parents. Neither family socializes with the other because the Dursleys view Lily and James as "abnormal." The Dursleys, in fact, hate the Potters. Magical talent is especially loathsome to Petunia. In one tirade, she squawks: "I was the only one who saw her for what she was—a freak! But for my mother and father, oh no, it was Lily this and Lily that, they were proud of having a witch in the family!"[3]

Vernon and Petunia plod along in their ordinary, non-magical lives until one day they notice some odd things happening. A cat is reading a map on the street where they live. There is a shower of shooting stars. Hundreds of owls are flying around during the day. And a lot of weird-looking, strangely dressed people seem to be everywhere. Then, without any warning, the Dursleys find little Harry in a basket on their doorstep. He has been delivered to them by Albus Dumbledore, the headmaster of Hogwarts School of Witchcraft and Wizardry. Clutched in Harry's tiny hand is a note explaining what happened.

It seems James and Lily were murdered by the most powerful of all dark sorcerers, the evil Voldemort. This Lord of the Black Arts tried to kill Harry, too. But for some unknown reason, Harry survived. His only wound is a lightening-shaped scar on his forehead. Because he is the only person ever to have survived an attack by Voldemort, Harry is famous (at least among witches and wizards). Voldemort, on the other hand, has disappeared from sight, critically injured by his own death curse, which inexplicably rebounded back to him from Harry. The entire wizard/witch world is celebrating. A very nasty wizard has been defeated. Harry, however, must now live with the Dursleys because his parents are dead.

We next see Harry just before his eleventh birthday. He has no idea that he is a wizard, nor does he know that his parents were magical. He does not even know how his mother and father really died. Thanks to Vernon and Petunia, Harry believes that his parents were killed in a car accident and that the scar on his forehead is from an injury he sustained during the deadly collision. The Dursleys detest Harry, who for ten years has been forced to sleep with spiders in a cupboard under the stairs, and wear Dudley's hand-me-down clothes. He has no friends, knows no other relatives and receives no love. Occasionally, however, complete strangers on the street seem to recognize him. "A tiny man in a violet top hat had bowed to him once while out shopping. . . . A wild-looking old woman dressed all in green had waved merrily at him once on a bus. A bald man in a very long purple coat had actually shaken his hand . . . and then walked away without a word."[4]

Things quickly change when Harry begins receiving letters in the mail. Mr. Dursley tries to keep him from reading these mysterious missives and succeeds in doing so, until the night of Harry's eleventh birthday, when Hagrid—a giant of a man—appears on the scene with one more note. Hagrid is Keeper of the Keys and Grounds at Hogwarts. He also is the one who, at the command of Dumbledore, rescued Harry from the ruins of the Potter home, which was destroyed by Voldemort during his homicidal assault. The letter Hagrid delivers turns out to be an invitation for Harry to become a wizard-in-training at Hogwarts, the "finest school of witchcraft and wizardry in the world."[5] At last, Harry knows he is a wizard. He also learns that his parents were killed by Voldemort, the mighty sorcerer who went "bad" and took many followers over to the "Dark Side" of magic in a quest for greater powers.

Another bit of information directly relates to Uncle Vernon, Aunt Petunia, Dudley and everyone else he has ever known. All of them are "Muggles"—i.e., humans with no magical abilities whatsoever; totally "non magic folk."[6] Muggles are consistently portrayed by Rowling as a narrow-minded and callous group of persons unable to grasp the glory of magic.[7] They also are incredibly slow when it comes to perceiving truth, although as one witch puts it, "they're not completely stupid."[8] Muggles are mostly an embarrassment to witches and wizards, as one of Harry's friends indicates by saying: "I think Mom's got a second cousin who's an accountant, but we never talk about him."[9]

Not surprisingly, Vernon and Petunia do not want Harry going to Hogwarts. But he is able to attend anyway, thanks to Hagrid's persistence in the matter. However, before going off to become a wizard-in-training, Harry must first visit Diagon Alley, which is a sort of wizard's outdoor market featuring shops that sell everything any wizard or witch might need: spellbooks, wands, magical creatures, cauldrons, robes, potions, parchments and more.

Hagrid sees to it that Harry acquires all the supplies listed in his letter from Hogwarts. He also takes Harry to Gringotts, a wizard's bank. There, Harry discovers that he is quite wealthy in terms of wizard money (gold Galleons, silver Sickles and bronze Knuts). His parents, who also attended Hogwarts, left him this small fortune to be used for his education. He further discovers that they not only were highly adept at magic, but also were renowned and greatly loved by most wizards and witches (except evil ones).

Harry finally arrives at Hogwarts—a "vast castle with many turrets and towers."[10] Along with all other first-year students, he must put on the "Sorting Hat," which is an ancient wizard's hat that speaks. After being placed on a student's head, it chooses and announces where that student will live during his or her seven years at Hogwarts. Four possible houses (i.e., fraternity-like dormitories) are available: Gryffindor, Hufflepuff, Ravenclaw and Slytherin. The names reflect those of the two greatest witches (Helga Hufflepuff and Rowena Ravenclaw) and two greatest wizards (Godric Gryffindor and Salazar Slytherin) who founded the school a thousand years earlier.

Gryffindor students are described as "brave at heart." Those in Hufflepuff tend to be "just and loyal." Ravenclaw dwellers are known for their "wit and learning." And students in Slytherin are "cunning folk" who will use any means to "achieve their ends."[11] The house of Slytherin also happens to be where Voldemort lived when he was a student. Only the most black-magic-inclined children go there. In fact, every single wizard or witch who went over to the dark side with Voldemort had come from Slytherin. Harry does not care where he is placed, as long as it is not there. Making him even more apprehensive about Slytherin is an encounter with Draco Malfoy, a fellow first-year student obviously destined for the darker house. He is mean-spirited, arrogant and deceitful. He instantly becomes a kind of nemesis to Harry, who thankfully lands in Gryffindor.

Two of Harry's new acquaintances, Ron Weasley and Hermione Granger, are likewise placed in Gryffindor. This trio ends up trying to solve a mystery that lasts the entire school year. It involves the world's only existing "Sorcerer's Stone," which is being kept in a restricted-to-students corridor beneath a trapdoor that is guarded by a room-sized, three-headed hellhound. The Sorcerer's Stone, as it turns out, is being sought by none other than Voldemort. He wants it because only a Sorcerer's Stone can create the "Elixir of Life," which bestows immortality. This is how Voldemort plans to return to full power.

However, there is a problem. Voldemort no longer has a body. So, in order to accomplish his goal, he possesses the body of Professor Quirrell, Hogwarts' "Defense Against the Dark Arts" teacher. No one suspects Quirrell. But Harry finally discovers what has been going on when he meets Quirrell trying to steal the Stone. Voldemort is there, too—but not in any form that Harry could have imagined in his wildest imagination or most frightening nightmare:

> Quirrell reached up and began to unwrap his turban. . . . The turban fell away. . . . Then he turned slowly on the spot. . . . Where there should have been a back to Quirrell's head, there was a face, the most terrible face Harry had ever seen. It was chalk white with glaring eyes and slits for nostrils, like a snake. . . . "See what I have become?" the face said. "Mere shadow and vapor. . . . [O]nce I have the Elixir of Life, I will be able to create a body of my own."[12]

By this time, Harry already has the Stone in his pocket, and Voldemort knows it. But before taking it from him, he tells Harry how his parents died: "I killed your father first, and he put up a courageous fight . . . but your mother needn't have died . . . she was trying to protect you. . . . Now give me the Stone, unless you want her to have died in vain."[13] Young Potter screams, "NEVER," and Voldemort promptly commands Quirrell to grab Harry, take the Stone and then "KILL HIM! KILL HIM!"[14]

Quirrell seizes Harry, but immediately cries out in pain. For some reason, Harry's skin causes horrible blisters to break out all over Quirrell's hands. He tries again to grab Harry, but cannot hold on to him without his hands burning. Quirrell then begins to cast a death spell. Fortunately, Dumbledore—whose power has always been equal to, if not greater than, Voldemort's—arrives in time. Harry is saved, the Stone is retrieved (and subsequently destroyed), and Voldemort's life essence again flees into the cosmos, leaving Quirrell to die. Afterward, Harry asks Dumbledore why Quirrell could not harm him. Dumbledore answers:

> Your mother died to save you. If there is one thing Voldemort cannot understand, it is love. He didn't realize that love as powerful as your mother's for you leaves its own mark. Not a scar, no visible sign ... to have been loved so deeply, even though the person who loved us is gone, will give us some protection forever. It is in your very skin.[15]

Book I ends with Harry being congratulated and honored. Moreover, because he and his friends—Hermione and Ron—uncovered Voldemort's plot, Gryffindor is awarded 160 merit points, which enables their dorm to win the coveted "House Cup." Sadly, though, the semester is over, which means Harry must return to live with the Dursleys until the following school year.

ENDNOTES

1. Statement available online at www.witchcraft.org.
2. J.K. Rowling, *Harry Potter and the Sorcerer's Stone* (New York: Scholastic Press, 1997), 1.
3. Rowling, *Sorcerer's Stone*, 53.
4. Rowling, *Sorcerer's Stone*, 30.
5. Rowling, *Sorcerer's Stone*, 58.
6. Rowling, *Sorcerer's Stone*, 53.
7. Rowling, *Sorcerer's Stone*, 2, 3, 4, 22.
8. Rowling, *Sorcerer's Stone*, 10.
9. Rowling, *Sorcerer's Stone*, 99.
10. Rowling, *Sorcerer's Stone*, 111.
11. Rowling, *Sorcerer's Stone*, 118.
12. Rowling, *Sorcerer's Stone*, 293-294.
13. Rowling, *Sorcerer's Stone*, 294.
14. Rowling, *Sorcerer's Stone*, 295.
15. Rowling, *Sorcerer's Stone*, 299.

TWO

SORCERY IN A STONE:
A CLOSER LOOK

He'll be famous—a legend—I wouldn't be surprised if today was known as Harry Potter day in the future—there will be books written about Harry—every child in our world will know his name!

Professor Minerva McGonagall[1]
Harry Potter and the Sorcerer's Stone

J.K. Rowling came up with the idea for her books in 1990 while traveling on a train. Without any warning, she suddenly just saw Harry "very, very clearly" in her mind. His visible image actually popped into her thoughts from out of nowhere as a "fully formed individual."[2] During one interview, Rowling stated: "The character of Harry just strolled into my head. . . . I really did feel he was someone who walked up and introduced himself in my mind's eye."[3]

Rowling confesses that she has no idea why he chose to "come to her" when he did.[4] According to her account, Harry just stood there looking very much like he now does on the cover of her books, complete with black hair and spectacles. She somehow perceived that he was a wizard, and knew that he did not know he was a wizard. Soon afterward, she began thinking about how this could possibly be, and before long, was writing about a young boy who did not know he had magical powers.[5] Thus, Harry Potter was born.

Most fans of the Potter series believe that nearly everything in the books are mere products of Rowling's fertile imagination. To these Potter supporters, all of the negative and controversial talk about actual occultism being in Rowling's novels is ridiculous. For example, Dr. Christopher Beiting of the Ave Maria Institute (a Roman Catholic institution of higher education in Michigan), feels that Rowling's creation of Hogwarts is harmless because it exists "in a fantasy world." He continues: "I have heard the interviews with Rowling; she says she doesn't take any interest in the occult and hasn't studied it for her novels. I feel these are just things she has made up in her own head and it is just a device to tell a story."[6]

Christianity Today has taken a similar position, forcefully deriding any concerns about witchcraft: "[T]he literary witchcraft of the Harry Potter series has almost no resemblance to the I-am-God mumbo jumbo of Wiccan circles."[7] (Wicca is the name given to the official religion of Witchcraft founded within the last century by Gerald Gardner [1884-1964].)

Sustaining this notion have been the numerous remarks by Rowling about her complete disinterest in witchcraft and her disbelief in magic. In a July 2000 Associated Press article, for instance, she said: "I truly am bemused that anyone who has read the books could think that I am a proponent of the occult in any serious way. I don't believe in witchcraft, in the sense that they're talking about, at all."[8] In an online interview, she explained that when it comes to the kind of magic that appears in her series, she "does not believe in magic in that way."[9] In another online venue, she remarked, "I don't believe in magic in the way I describe it in my books. I mean, I don't believe in the wand waving sort of magic."[10]

Many people have completely overlooked the obvious quali-
fiers in these statements. Rowling says she does not believe in
witchcraft "in the sense" her critics talk about it, and rejects the
"wand waving sort of magic" that appears in her books. The
questions arise: Is there another "sense" in which Rowling *does*
believe in witchcraft? What brand, of all the different forms of
magic that exist that are *not* the wand waving sort of magic,
might she embrace? Are there any bits and pieces of paganism
with which she may agree?

Interestingly, Rowling has stated that she believes the number seven "is a magical number, a mystical number."[11] Her
ex-husband, Jorge Arantes, confirmed this in London's *Daily
Express*, saying that Rowling "had planned the full series of
seven books because she believed the number seven has magical
associations."[12] And in the introduction to Beacham Publications' educational resource book, *Exploring Harry Potter*, Walter Beacham makes a similar remark: "Ms. Rowling has spoken
extensively about her plans for future Potter novels, and stated
that the magical number seven will see the conclusion of
Harry's education at Hogwarts."[13]

More significant is the fact that not everything in the Potter
series is imaginary. During a 1999 interview, Rowling admitted
that she had studied mythology and witchcraft in order to write
her books more accurately, stating, "I do a certain amount of research. And folklore is quite important in books. So where I'm
mentioning a creature, or a spell that people used to believe genuinely worked—of course, it didn't . . . then, I will find out exactly what the words were, and I will find out exactly what the
characteristics of that creature or ghost were supposed to be."[14]
Rowling goes on to say that roughly one-third of the sorcery-
related material appearing in her books "are things that people
genuinely used to believe in Britain."[15]

What Rowling fails to mention is that a vast amount of the occult material she has borrowed from historical sources *still* plays a significant role in modern paganism and witchcraft. Consequently, her writings merge quite nicely with contemporary occultism. This could easily present a spiritual danger to children and teens, or even adults, who are either leaning toward occultism or who may be vulnerable to its attractions. Also, it is noteworthy that some of the information Rowling uses is not widely known by persons other than those who are actually involved in occultism. She, in fact, has an extremely well-developed and sophisticated knowledge of the occult world, its legends, history and nuances.

In fact, Rowling's thorough understanding of occultism's intricacies is so obvious in her books that during one radio call-in interview show, a self-professed "magus" (a male practitioner of magick) excitedly asked Rowling if she herself was a member of the "Craft" (i.e., Wicca). When Rowling answered no, the caller seemed shocked and replied, "[Well], you've done your homework quite well." This particular caller went on to express his love for the Harry Potter series not only because it contained so much occultism, but because its positive portrayal of magick had served to make his daughter more comfortable with his own practices as a witch-magickian.[16]

Rowling seamlessly weaves into her novels countless references to ancient *and* modern occultism, sometimes hiding them in people's names or disguising them in minor characters. Such inclusions certainly do not teach the precise doctrines of witchcraft, nor do they explicitly instruct children to purchase a step-by-step guide to Wicca. But the allusions could easily stir a child's curiosity about occultism—perhaps enough for that child to one day dabble in it.

The very title of Book I, *Harry Potter and the Sorcerer's Stone*, hearkens back to a set of occultic beliefs about the "Philosopher's

Stone." (Rowling's first volume was originally released in England as *Harry Potter and the Philosopher's Stone*.) In the *Encyclopedia of Occultism and Parapsychology*, the Philosopher's Stone is described as a legendary substance that supposedly enabled medieval alchemists to turn base metals into gold or silver. But unlike the literal stone sought for in Rowling's novel, the stone coveted by real alchemists was an essential powder of some kind, often designated "Powder of Projection."[17] The author of a *Treatise on Philosophical and Hermetic Chemistry*, published in 1725, wrote:

> It is necessary then to proceed first to purge the mercury with salt and with ordinary salad vinegar, to sublime it with vitriol and saltpetre, to dissolve it in aquafortis, to sublime it again, to calcine it and fix it. . . . This is the first operation in the grand work. For the second operation, take in the name of God one part of gold and two parts of the spiritual water, charged with the sal-ammoniac, mix this noble confection in a vase of crystal of the shape of an egg: warm over a soft but continuous fire, and the fiery water will dissolve little by little the gold; this forms a liquor which is called by the sages "chaos" containing the elementary qualities—cold, dryness, heat and humidity. Allow this composition to putrefy until it becomes black; this blackness is known as the "crow's head" and the "darkness of the sages," and makes known to the artist that he is on the right track. . . . It must be boiled once more in a vase as white as snow; this stage of the work is called the "swan," and from it arises the white liquor, which is divided into two parts—one white for the manufacture of silver, the other red for the manufacture of gold. Now you have accomplished the work, and you possess the Philosopher's Stone.[18]

But alchemists were far more than metal-workers. They were spiritual-minded individuals who pursued their science as a means of purifying the soul and achieving an unclouded understanding of their own divine nature. Transmuting base metals into gold was merely a process used to transform themselves and obtain what they called the "fifth element," which was thought to be God's "creative power" by which all things received life.[19]

Consequently, alchemists also believed that creating the Philosopher's Stone produced a sort of natural by-product of the chemical procedure: the Elixir of Life. As Rowling writes in her book, "The stone will transform any metal into pure gold. It also produces the Elixir of Life, which will make the drinker immortal."[20] This is not the only parallel between Rowling's stone and the stone sought by medieval alchemists. In Book I, Harry and his friends learn that the Philosopher's Stone they are seeking (the only one ever made) was created by Dumbledore's partner in alchemy, Nicholas Flamel.[21]

Nicholas Flamel really existed. He was a French alchemist who allegedly succeeded in making the Philosopher's Stone in the late 1300s. According to historical documents and occult tradition, Flamel learned how to make the Philosopher's Stone through the esoteric *Book of Abraham the Jew*. This text, supposedly written by the Jewish Patriarch, contained various directions in hieroglyphic form. Alchemists throughout the centuries have believed that after deciphering these drawings, Flamel did indeed create the Philosopher's Stone, and by doing so, never died.[22]

Rowling also mentions Flamel's wife, Perenelle. Again, this is not fictitious. Nicholas' wife, in agreement with the Potter "fantasy" novel, was named Perenelle (also spelled Petronelle). Rowling even correctly identifies the approximate era of their lives. Book I takes place in late 1991-1992 (a school year cycle), a date easily discerned by calculating subtle time markers in Book II (*Harry Potter and the Chamber of Secrets*). In *Sorcerer's Stone*, Flamel is 665 years old. This number subtracted from

1991/92 comes to the year 1326/27 for Flamel's birth (as recorded by Rowling). In the real world, Flamel was born in 1330, give or take a few years.[23]

Book I goes so far as to add some of Flamel's religious beliefs about death. Toward the book's conclusion, after Nicholas and Perenelle know they will die, Dumbledore tells Harry that they are not afraid because to them dying will simply be "like going to bed after a very, very long day." Dumbledore continues: "After all, to the well-organized mind, death is but the next great adventure."[24] The book *Magicians, Seers, and Mystics* reports that Flamel, in fact, felt this way: "Nicholas Flamel, after his discovery of the Philosopher's Stone, would have had no temptation to evade death; for he regarded death merely as the transition to a better state."[25]

Such a position echoes current pagan/Wiccan thinking. Anthony Kemp, in *Witchcraft and Paganism Today*, writes: "The one who has departed has left for the Summerlands, the fairy realm in the west where he or she will be refreshed before the cycle of rebirth [reincarnation] starts again. . . . Death as we know it is but a transition—an initiation."[26] Celebrated witch, Starhawk, declares: "Death is not an end; it is a stage in the cycle that leads on to rebirth. After death, the human soul . . . grows young and is made ready to be born again."[27]

To Christians, of course, this is an inaccurate and spiritually dangerous view of death. Christians believe that only those who die "in Christ" (i.e., those who have received Jesus Christ as their personal Lord and Savior) will enjoy eternal bliss (Romans 10:9; 1 John 5:11-13). Others will suffer eternal separation from God (Luke 16:19-30; John 3:16; Revelation 20:11-15). Reincarnation too stands at odds with Christianity. Hebrews 9:27 says we are created to die once and then to experience our judgment before

God. There are no second, third or fourth chances after death. "Now is the day of salvation" (2 Corinthians 6:2).

Flamel and his Sorcerer's Stone are only two examples of how Rowling mixes reality with fantasy in her series. Book I also refers to Paracelsus,[28] a Swiss alchemist who lived from 1493-1541. He was "one of the most striking and picturesque figures" in occultism.[29] Another individual Rowling mentions is Adalbert Waffling, author of *Magical Theory*, which is included on Harry's list of required reading. Again, we have a fictional character having a real-world counterpart: Archbishop Adalbert of Magdeburg (eighth century).

Adalbert was a French pseudo-mystic who claimed he could foretell the future and read thoughts. The *Encyclopedia of Occultism and Parapsychology* reveals that "[H]e was in the habit of giving away parings of his nails and locks of his hair as powerful amulets [charms used to drive away evil]. He is said to have even set up an altar in his own name." Adalbert eventually showed followers a letter supposedly sent to him by Christ via St. Michael. He also invoked demons using mystical prayers he had composed. The Church convicted him of sorcery in 744-745 A.D., and condemned him to perpetual imprisonment in the monastery of Fulda.[30]

A sympathetic discussion of Adalbert's plight can be found in the writings of Helena Petrovna Blavatsky (1831-1891), founder of Theosophy, an occult blending of metaphysical thought, spiritualism, channeling, science, Eastern philosophy, Transcendentalism and mental healing. Blavatsky, who greatly helped to spread the concepts of Buddhism and reincarnation in America, wrote the following about Adalbert in her article "Star-Angel-Worship":

> In the middle of the VIIIth century of the Christian era the very notorious Archbishop Adalbert of Magdeburg, fa-

mous as few in the annals of magic, appeared before his judges. He was charged with, and ultimately convicted—by the second Council of Rome presided over by Pope Zacharia—of using during his performances of ceremonial magic, the names of the "seven Spirits"—then at the height of their power in the Church—among others, that of URIEL, with the help of whom he had succeeded in producing his greatest phenomena. As can be easily shown, *the church is not against magic proper*, but only against those magicians who fail to conform to her methods and rules of evocation. However, as the wonders wrought by the Right Reverend Sorcerer were not of a character that would permit of their classification among "miracles by the grace, and to the glory of God," they were declared *unholy*.[31]

Interestingly, these pro-Adalbert sentiments expressed by Blavatsky sound remarkably similar to those voiced by Albus Dumbledore in a speech he gives to students at Hogwarts—which, coincidentally, was founded at approximately the same time Adalbert and others were being convicted by the Church (i.e., 1991 minus approximately 1,000 years [800-1,000 A.D.]). Dumbledore explains:

> You all know, of course, that Hogwarts was founded over a thousand years ago—the precise date is uncertain—by the four greatest witches and wizards of the age. . . . They built this castle together, far from prying Muggle eyes, for it was an age when magic was feared by common people, and witches and wizards suffered much persecution.[32]

An equally odd connection that seems to exist between Rowling and Theosophy can be found in a play on names in Book III (*Harry Potter and the Prisoner of Azkaban*). On page 53 Rowling mentions a book titled *Unfogging the Future* by a Cassandra Vablatsky. Could Vablatsky be an anagram for Blavatsky? I believe so. An anagram, of course, is a word or phrase formed by transposing the letters of another word or phrase. And this is exactly the kind of word games Rowling plays throughout her novels.

For example, in one scene from Book II (*Harry Potter and the Chamber of Secrets*), we learn that it was a boy named Tom Riddle who eventually became Lord Voldemort. Riddle unveils this mystery using an anagram to taunt Harry:

> He [Riddle] pulled Harry's wand from his pocket and began to trace it through the air, writing three shimmering words:
>
> TOM MARVOLO RIDDLE.
>
> Then he waved the wand once, and the letters of his name rearranged themselves:
>
> I AM LORD VOLDEMORT.[33]

Another anagram, this time in Book I, shows up when Harry finds a mirror in which he sees images of his family. Inscribed above the looking glass are these words: *Erised stra ehru oyt ube cafru oyt on wohsi*.[34] Written backward, they read: *Ishow no tyo urfac ebutyo urhe arts desire*. The phrase still makes no sense. But splice the letters together in a different combination and suddenly we get: *I show not your face but your heart's desire*. It is not only an anagram, but a backward anagram! In my opinion, a similar trick is used to disguise Blavatsky as Vablatsky.

Pagan and mythological characters play an important role in *Sorcerer's Stone* as well. One of Harry's teachers, Minerva McGonagall, is named after the Roman goddess of agriculture, navigation, spinning, weaving and needlework.[35] Hogwarts' caretaker, Argus Filch,[36] is named after the Greek mythological giant with a hundred eyes. We also have Harry's best friend, Hermione, who shares her name with the daughter of Helen of Troy in Greek mythology.

From Homer's *Odyssey*, Rowling borrows the name Circe.[37] In the Greek classic tale, Circe is a witch who can transform men into animals. Even the first name of Harry's nemesis, Draco Malfoy, is significant. It refers to astrology. Draco, which means dragon, is the ancient astrological term for the constellation that "used to hold special significance as the location of the pole star, but due to the Earth's precession, the pole has shifted to Polaris in Ursa Minor. The Dragon is usually associated with guardians of the temples and treasures."[38]

And then there are references to Morgana and Merlin taken from the Arthurian legends. Merlin is Arthur's wizard-mentor. Morgana is the evil half-sister of Arthur. She seduces Arthur in order to give birth to Mordred, who eventual destroys the king. Morgana is said to be heavily based on "Morrighan," an ancient Celtic goddess. "Those who see her washing out bloody linen are normally warriors whose vision of her presages their pending death in battle."[39] Morrighan is also known as the battle goddess, queen of witches, the goddess of magick—and the goddess of death.[40]

Perhaps most interesting, though, is Rowling's passing reference to the Druid/Celtic goddess Cliodna,[41] who is still worshiped today by contemporary pagans and witches. According to The Circle of the Ancient Ways (COTAW), an independent group of witches who focus mainly on the Wiccan path, "the names of Gods and Goddesses in the Celtic beliefs are probably the most well known and often used in modern Paganism and Wicca."[42]

Cliodna (also Cliodhna) is Ireland's pagan goddess of beauty. It was believed that through her the magic of "blarney" or the "gift of gab" came to the Celts.[43] She is a Banshee (also Bean Sidhe), which in Scotland is referred to as the wailing woman spirit (Behn Nighe) who lives in the hills and glens. In Irish folklore, this spirit or fairy foreshadows death by wailing:

> She visits a household and by wailing she warns them that a member of their family is about to die. When a Banshee is caught, she is obliged to tell the name of the doomed. The Bean Sidhe has long, streaming hair and is dressed in a gray cloak over a green dress. Her eyes are fiery red from the constant weeping. When multiple Banshees wail together, it will herald the death of someone very great or holy. Aiobhill is the Banshee of the Dalcassians of North Munster, Cliodna of the MacCarthys and other families of South Munster.[44]

Finally, *Sorcerer's Stone* plainly introduces astrology through the words of two Centaurs named Bane and Firenze.[45] (A Centaur is a mythological beast with the torso and head of a man, but the hindquarters of a horse.) Bane says, "Remember, Firenze, we are sworn not to set ourselves against the heavens. Have we not read what is to come in the movements of planets?"[46] Firenze replies, "Do you not see that unicorn? . . . Do you not understand why it was killed? Or have the planets not let you in on that secret?"[47] Astrology is clearly being discussed, given the fact that Hagrid refers to the two Centaurs as "stargazers,"[48] another name for astrologers.

Such occult themes are numerous in Book I. Also plentiful are Rowling's many references to various demonic entities deeply connected to magic, witchcraft and sorcery. However, before taking a closer look at these demonic beings (see Chapter 4), we must touch upon another set of problems within the Potter series—moral ambiguity and ethical confusion.

POTTERETHICS

Countless articles, both Christian and non-Christian, have applauded the admirable morals and ethical behavior of Rowling's characters. According to more than one reviewer, Harry and his companions are brave, true, just, kind, insightful, unselfish and noble. In a January 2000 article written for the Roman Catholic journal *First Things*, Wheaton College literature professor Alan Jacobs saluted the first three books (the fourth had not yet been published), noting: "Rowling's moral compass throughout the three volumes is sound—indeed, I would say, acute."[49] Similarly, a 1999 Knight-Ridder news article reported that Harry Potter is the perfect role model to teach children lessons about endurance, kindness, wisdom and love.[50]

Harry is far from perfect. The morals and ethics in Rowling's fantasy tales are at best unclear, and at worst, patently unbiblical. It is true that there are fleeting moments throughout her stories where the good characters actually behave in a way consistent with being "good." But on many other occasions, these same characters act quite contrary to the biblical definition of "goodness." This is most apparent in Harry.

His image as a "good" boy begins disintegrating early in Book I when he disobeys Madame Hooch, the instructor hired by Hogwarts to teach students broom-riding technique. She directly tells her students, including Harry, not to ride their brooms while she takes an injured student to the infirmary. But Harry, in reaction to Draco Malfoy's jeers, grabs a broom and streaks into the sky. He is caught by Professor McGonagall, but instead of being punished, is rewarded by being put on Gryffindor's Quidditch team.[51] (Quidditch is a wizard's soccer-like sport that is played with self-propelled airborne balls and flying brooms.)

On the same day that Harry ignores Hooch's directive, he breaks two more rules by agreeing to fight Draco in a "wizard's duel" at midnight in the school's trophy room. Fighting, especially fights in which spells are used, are against Hogwarts' rules. Moreover, students are to be in their dorms at night. Nevertheless, Harry sneaks out with his favorite rule-breaking companion, Ron Weasley.

The lone dissenter is Hermione, Ron and Harry's acquaintance. She reminds Harry that every time a student is caught breaking a rule, merit points are taken away from the dorm in which they live. She tries to reason with the two boys: "[Y]ou *mustn't* go wandering around the school at night, think of the points you'll lose Gryffindor if you're caught, and you're bound to be. It's really very selfish of you."[52]

But Harry responds: "[I]t's really none of your business."[53]

During this scene, we also see Ron casting integrity to the wind as he instructs Harry in the art of wizard dueling. Both Harry and Draco have agreed to the terms: "Wands only—no contact."[54] But just before Harry and Ron sneak out at night, Harry asks, "[W]hat if I wave my wand and nothing happens?" In direct contradiction to the promise given to Draco, Ron answers, "Throw it away and punch him on the nose."[55]

Draco never shows up, but the school's caretaker does. In fact, he almost catches Harry and Ron. They manage to avoid capture, however, by slipping into an off-limits corridor that houses a monstrous, three-headed hellhound guarding a trapdoor leading to the Philosopher's Stone. But where Rowling could have demonstrated how breaking the rules can be harmful, she ignores the rule breaking and instead begins the next chapter: "Harry and Ron thought that meeting the three-headed dog had been an excellent adventure, and they were quite keen to have another one."[56]

Next a very serious regulation is broken by Harry when he sneaks into the library, yet again at night, to have a peek at the Dark Magic books kept in the school's restricted section. No student is allowed to look at any of these texts unless they have a request form signed by a teacher. But Harry feels he has a good reason to ignore this rule: he must find out about Nicholas Flamel. Again, rather than following any objective standard of right and wrong (i.e., Hogwarts' rules), Harry lets his own self-interests and subjective rationalizations determine his actions.

Something else happens on this same evening. He finds the mirror of Erised (a.k.a. Desire), which shows him movie-like images of his dead family smiling and waving back at him. This is indeed a touching scene. But it only serves to cause Harry's "moral compass" to go further awry. He sneaks out of his dorm on two subsequent nights in order to go back to the mirror. On the third night, he gets caught by Albus Dumbledore, Hogwarts' Headmaster. Does he punish Harry, or even chastise him for being where students should not be in the middle of the night? No! He simply explains to him about the Mirror of Desire, then sends little Harry scurrying back to bed.[57] So far Harry has disobeyed Hogwarts' codes at least seven times without suffering any consequences.

By page 225 of Book I, Harry is doing just about whatever he wants to do, making decisions for himself based on what he feels is best for him. He even follows Professor Snape—the Potions teacher—into the "Forbidden Forest" (a dangerous wooded area beside Hogwarts that is off-limits to all students).[58] Only Hermione, an oft-ridiculed student, seems bothered by all the rule-breaking. Again and again she tries to explain why following school directives is important. Harry's responses are consistently negative:

Chapter 9
Hermione: "Don't you *care* about Gryffindor, do you *only* care about yourselves, *I* don't want Slytherin to win the house cup, and you'll lose all the points I got from Professor McGonagall . . ."
Harry: "Go away."[59]

Chapter 10

Hermione: "So I suppose you think that's a reward for breaking rules?"

Harry: "I thought you weren't speaking to us?"

Ron: Yes, don't stop now, it's doing us so much good."[60]

Rowling herself, throughout the narrative portions of Book I, refers to Hermione as "hissing . . . like an angry goose," having a "bad temper" and being a "bossy know-it-all."[61]

Sadly, Hermione succumbs to peer pressure after overhearing Ron and Harry say she is disliked at the school and that "she's a nightmare."[62] Hermione endears herself to them by telling a "downright lie" to a teacher in order to cover up for the boys: "Harry was speechless. Hermione was the last person to do anything against the rules, and here she was, pretending she had, to get them out of trouble."[63] This morally troubling scene concludes with Hermione and the boys becoming friends.[64]

In an equally tragic tweak on morality, a small boy named Neville Longbottom tries to correct Ron and Harry and is basically ridiculed for it. "Don't you call me an idiot," Neville says. "I don't think you should be breaking any more rules! And you were the one who told me to stand up to people." Ron's answer perfectly illustrates the message Rowling seems to be communicating: "Yes, but not *us*."[65]

When Neville tries to prevent Ron and Harry from again sneaking out of the dorm, Hermione (now as much a rule-breaker as her friends), puts a full "Body-Bind" spell on him: "Neville's arms snapped to his sides. His legs sprang together. His whole body rigid, he swayed where he stood and then fell flat on his face, stiff as a board."[66]

In yet another scene, Rowling writes: "Excuses, alibis, and wild cover-up stories chased each other around Harry's brain, each more feeble than the last. He couldn't see how they were going to get out of trouble this time."[67] The option of simply telling the truth never even crosses Harry's mind, but he cannot come up with a lie either. Significantly, this one instance in which Harry's knack for lying does not work quickly enough is the one instance that he and his companions are punished with detention after school hours.

The adults in Book I hardly act any better. They not only break other people's rules, but also break their own rules. Consider Hagrid (Hogwarts' Keeper of the Keys and Grounds). He consistently performs spells even though he is not supposed to do magic. (He was expelled from Hogwarts during his third year, which means he never graduated to the level of full wizard.)[68] He also ignores legal statutes applicable to the entire wizard world. For instance, he raises an "illegal" dragon against the 1709 Warlock's Convention law prohibiting dragon breeding in Britain.[69]

Even worse, Hagrid consistently asks Harry and his friends not to tell anyone about his disobedience. On page 64, he makes this request: "If I was ter—er—speed things up a bit, would yeh mind not mentionin' it at Hogwarts?" Harry replies, "Of course not," because he is eager to "see more magic."[70] Later in the book, Hagrid actually asks Harry, Ron and Hermione to smuggle his illegal dragon out of Hogwarts, with the help of Ron's brother, Charlie (a Hogwarts graduate), and some of Charlie's older, postgraduate friends.[71]

Professor McGonagall even persuades Headmaster Dumbledore to allow her to break school rules by allowing Harry to have his own flying broom and to play on Gryffindor's Quidditch team—privileges not granted to first-year students. Why dismiss these rules? Because Harry is a natural-born broom-rider, and as such, is bound to be an excellent Quidditch player. Since Gryffindor has not won the championship in years, the course of action is clear: put Harry on the team.

The threefold moral message that Rowling presents through her characters is clear: 1) rules are made to be broken if they do not serve one's own self-interests; 2) rules need not be obeyed if no good reason seems to exist for them; and 3) lying is an effective and acceptable means of achieving a desired end. This latter lesson is implied in one student's explanation for why he is half-Muggle: " 'Me dad's a Muggle. Mom didn't tell him she was a witch 'til after they were married. Bit of a nasty shock for him.' The others laughed."[72]

Judith Krug of the Chicago-based American Library Association has stated,

> The storyline is wonderful. . . . We have Harry Potter as an orphan. There's no one always telling him what to do, and what young person hasn't at one point said, "Oh, if they'd only leave me alone." Or: "I wish that I didn't have parents." They don't mean this in a mean way. It's just that parents get in the way.[73]

In the real world, parents do indeed "get in the way," especially when a child misbehaves, or when a child needs loving guidance away from harmful activities. But children, because they are children, often do not want to be disciplined. It is no wonder they like the Potter books so much. As one eleven-year-old girl told me, "I like Harry because he can do whatever he wants to do."

Although he may have benevolent motives (e.g., wanting to keep someone from taking the Philosopher's Stone, or trying to keep Draco from hurting a student), Harry ultimately is simply following his own self-interests. This is consistent with modern Wicca, as the Wiccan Creed says: "If it harm none, do what you will." The creed would apply to such things as unbiblical sexual encounters, use of illegal drugs and lying. Starhawk, founder of Covenant of the Goddess, plainly says, "In witchcraft, we do not fight self-interest, we follow it."[74]

Whether Rowling realizes it or not, she is promoting witch-craft/occultism/Wicca in the form of ethical and moral subjectivism.

AGE 6 AND UP?

During a National Public Radio interview with Diane Rehm, J.K. Rowling explained that she did not necessarily write her books for children. She actually penned them as novels that she herself, as an adult, would enjoy reading.[75] Rowling also mentioned that she kept in mind the kind of book she might have wanted to read as a little girl. Interestingly, Rowling has stated: "When I was quite young, my parents never said books were off limits. . . . As a child, I read a lot of adult books. I don't think you should censor kids' reading material. It's important just to let them go do what they need to do."[76]

Rowling apparently feels that adult-oriented material is perfectly suitable for children, which may explain why forty-three percent of her books sold in 1999 were to readers older than fourteen. And according to the N.D. Group, a leading market research firm that tracks book-buying in 12,000 households, nearly thirty percent of Harry Potter purchases were made for readers thirty-five or older. Some adult readers are so captivated by Harry that they have begun concocting their own "fan-written" Potter adult stories.

For example, there is "Harry Potter and the Paradigm of Uncertainty," which can be found on the Internet at e-Groups. Lori Summers, author of this narrative in progress, describes it as a PG-13 story for adult fans of the Harry Potter series. It takes place twelve years in the future, is extremely romantic in nature, and puts Harry living in one big dorm with several other witches (females) and wizards (males). Summers stresses it is not for children.[77]

But adult Harry Potter fans need not scan the Internet for "mature" material, especially when it comes to scenes involving gratuitous violence, gruesome images, cruelty and humor that often borders on perversity. One of the most grisly characters to come from Rowling is a ghost named "Nearly Headless Nick" who lived 500 years earlier and died on a Halloween night by being struck on the neck forty-five times with a blunt ax.[78] He first appears in Chapter 7 of Book I:

> "I know who you are!" said Ron suddenly. "My brothers told me about you—you're Nearly Headless Nick!"
>
> . . . "Nearly Headless?" [asked Seamus Finnigan]. "How can you be nearly headless?"
>
> "Like *this*," he said irritably. He seized his left ear and pulled. His whole head swung off his neck and fell onto his shoulder as if it was on a hinge. Someone had obviously tried to behead him, but not done it properly.[79]

Then, in Chapter 15, readers are treated to a horrible scene featuring Professor Quirrell, who is possessed by Voldemort:

> [O]ut of the shadows, a hooded figure came crawling across the ground like some stalking beast. . . . The cloaked figure reached the unicorn, lowered its head over the wound in the animal's side, and began to drink its blood.[80]

Scenes less gory, but equally disturbing, are those wherein cruelty/vengeance are presented as acceptable. Hagrid, for instance, performs an illegal spell against Harry's cousin, Dudley. (He gives Dudley an extremely painful pig's tail that has to be surgically removed.) This is not done because Dudley himself acts improperly toward Hagrid. It is done to punish Mr.

Dursley for insulting Dumbledore.[81] Rather than attacking Mr. Dursley, Hagrid turns his revenge against Dudley (an innocent individual) as a way of more gravely hurting the father.

Revenge also appears in a Diagon Alley scene, where Harry finds *Curses and Countercurses (Bewitch Your Friends and Befuddle Your Enemies with the Latest Revenges: Hair Loss, Jelly Legs, Tongue-Tying and Much, Much More)* by Professor Vindictus Viridian. When Hagrid drags Harry away so they can stay on their time schedule, Harry says: "I was trying to find out how to curse Dudley." Instead of correcting Harry and pointing him in a better direction, Hagrid replies: "I'm not sayin' that's not a good idea, but yer not ter use magic in the Muggle world except in very special circumstances."[82]

A display of similar attitudes by other "good" characters throughout the Potter series creates a running theme that is not difficult to discern: It is appropriate to return evil for evil, and treat others well only if they treat you well. As Rowling herself has stated about her main character: "Harry wants to get back at Dudley. . . . [A]nd we readers want him to get back at Dudley. And, in the long run, trust me, he will."[83] Contrast this approach with what Scripture says regarding enemies and our treatment of them:

- Thou shalt not avenge. . . . [L]ove thy neighbour as thyself. (Leviticus 19:18)
- Recompense to no man evil for evil. . . . If it be possible, as much as lieth in you, live peaceably with all men. . . . Be not overcome of evil, but overcome evil with good. (Romans 12:17-18, 21)
- Love your enemies, do good to them which hate you, bless them that curse you, and pray for them which despitefully use you. (Luke 6:27-28)

In yet another scene, Professor Snape—the disliked potions teacher—is seen limping due to some sort of injury to his leg. Harry wonders what is wrong with Snape, and Ron bitterly replies: "Dunno, but I hope it's really hurting him."[84] Again, the Bible reads very differently: "Rejoice not when thine enemy falleth, and let not thine heart be glad when he stumbleth" (Proverbs 24:17).

Clearly, Rowling's books include a great deal of material that is inappropriate for children as well as inconsistent with Christian values.

Despite these flaws, Book I has become a best-seller around the world. According to an ABCnews.com report, it is because Rowling's books "show the complexities of children, and the ambiguities of childhood—the delights and fears of separation and exploration."[85] But as we have seen, these volumes also contain material that is both unsuitable and harmful to children. Rowling's second volume, *Harry Potter and the Chamber of Secrets*, is just as problematic.

ENDNOTES

1. J.K. Rowling, *Harry Potter and the Sorcerer's Stone* (New York: Scholastic Press, 1997), 13.
2. J.K. Rowling, interview on *The Diane Rehm Show*, WAMU, National Public Radio, October 20, 1999, available online at www.wamu.org.
3. J.K. Rowling, quoted in Reuters, "Harry Potter 'Strolled into My Head,' " July 17, 2000.
4. J.K. Rowling, *The Diane Rehm Show.*
5. J.K. Rowling, *The Diane Rehm Show.*
6. Dr. Christopher Beiting, quoted in Kate Ernsting, "Is Harry Potter's Magic Kid-Friendly?," *Credo*, November 15, 1999, available online at www.credopub.com.
7. "Why We Like Harry Potter" (editorial), *Christianity Today*, January 10, 2000, available online at www.christianityonline.com.
8. J.K. Rowling, quoted in Audrey Woods, "Success Stuns Harry Potter Author" (Associated Press), July 6, 2000.
9. J.K. Rowling, quoted in Judy O'Malley, "Talking with J.K. Rowling," *Book Links* (Vol. 8, No. 6, pp. 32-36: Online Version), available online at www.northernlight.com.

10. J.K. Rowling, AOL Online Chat, May 4, 2000. Transcript available through America Online.

11. J.K. Rowling, quoted in Elizabeth Nehren, "Upward and Onward Toward Book Seven," *Los Angeles Times*, October 25, 2000. Available online at www.latimes.com/living/20001024/t000101702.html; also see J.K. Rowling, radio interview, October 12, 1999, *Talk Connection*, WBUR (Boston).

12. Peter Fearon, "A Dark Flashback in 'Potter' Author's Tale," *New York Post*, July 11, 2000, available online at www.newyorkpost.com.; also available online at www.foxnews.com.

13. Walter Beacham, editor's introduction for Elizabeth D. Schafer, *Beacham's Sourcebook: Exploring Harry Potter* (Osprey, FL: Beacham Publishing, 2000), statement available online at www.beachampublishing.com.

14. J.K. Rowling, *The Diane Rehm Show*.

15. J.K. Rowling, *The Diane Rehm Show*.

16. WBUR interview with J.K. Rowling, October 12, 1999, available online at www.wbur.org.

17. Leslie A. Shepard, ed., *Encyclopedia of Occultism and Parapsychology* (Detroit: Gale Research, 1991), 2:1282.

18. Shepard.

19. Kurt Seligmann, *Magic, Supernaturalism, and Religion* (New York: Pantheon, 1948; 1971 edition).

20. Rowling, *Sorcerer's Stone*, 220.

21. Rowling, *Sorcerer's Stone*, 219.

22. Maurice Magre, *Magicians, Seers, and Mystics* (Kila, MT: Kessinger Publishing, 1997; transl. Reginald Merton), available online at www.alchemylab.com.

23. Shepard, 1:594.

24. Rowling, *Sorcerer's Stone*, 297. Children are not simply reading such comments and giving no thought to what they mean. In a letter to www.yabooks.com, a fifteen-year-old wrote the following comment in reference to Rowling's books: "They deal with death, but in a positive way—in the first book, Dumbledore tells Harry, Ron, and Hermione that death is just like a rest after a very long day" ("Young Adult 'Save Harry Potter' Comments: Page 1," available online at http://yabooks.about.com/teens/yabooks/bl_potter2.htm).

25. Magre, available online at www.alchemylab.com.

26. Anthony Kemp, *Witchcraft and Paganism Today* (London: Brockhampton Press, 1993; 1995 edition), 129.

27. Starhawk, *The Spiral Dance* (San Francisco: Harper San Francisco, 1979; 1989 edition), 41.

28. Rowling, *Sorcerer's Stone*, 103.

29. Shepard, 2:1250.

30. Shepard, 1:6-7.

31. Helena Petrovna Blavatsky, "Star-Angel-Worship in the Roman Catholic Church," *Lucifer*, July 1888, available online at www.blavatsky.net/blavatsky/arts/StarAngel WorshipInTheRomanCatholicChurch.htm (Blavatsky Net Foundation).

32. J.K. Rowling, *Harry Potter and the Chamber of Secrets* (New York: Scholastic, 1999), 150.

33. Rowling, *Chamber of Secrets*, 314.

34. Rowling, *Sorcerer's Stone*, 207.

35. Thomas Bullfinch, *The Age of Fable* (Garden City, NY: Doubleday, 1948), Chapter 14, available online at www.bullfinch.org.

36. Rowling, *Sorcerer's Stone*, 132.

37. Rowling, *Sorcerer's Stone*, 103

38. No author. "Draco," available online at www.astronomical.org.

39. Terry McCombs, (no title), available online at the Pagan Homesite (www.pagan-home.com).

40. Statement available at http://www.cyberphile.net/~taff/taffnet/mabinogion/gods.html.

41. Rowling, *Sorcerer's Stone*, 103.

42. Statement available online at http://www.darkcastle.net/COTAW/celtic.htm.

43. Dira's Online Pagan Files, available at http://www.concentric.net/~qempa/goddess/cc3.htm#Cliodhna.

44. Statements available online at www.irishclans.com and www.loggia.com/myth/ireland.html.

45. Astrology, one of the most ancient occultic means of predicting the future, rests on the assumption that the movement and position of celestial bodies (i.e., the sun, moon, stars and planets) not only affect individual lives, but also nations and even humanity as a whole (see Shepard, 1:102). It is an extremely popular belief system. A 1997 poll found that only twenty percent of Americans completely disbelieve in astrology, while forty-eight percent say that astrology is "probably or definitely valid" (Kenneth Miller, "Star Struck," *LIFE*, July 1997, 40). Another 1997 poll published in *USA Today* gave a slightly lower figure of thirty-seven percent for those who believe in astrology, but also revealed that this percentage had risen dramatically from seventeen percent in 1976 (Matt Nisbet, "New Poll Points to Increase in Paranormal Belief," available online at www.csicop.org).

46. Rowling, *Sorcerer's Stone*, 257.

47. Rowling, *Sorcerer's Stone*.

48. Rowling, *Sorcerer's Stone*, 254.

49. Alan Jacobs, "Harry Potter's Magic," *First Things*, January 2000, available online at www.firstthings.com.

50. Quoted in Richard Scheinin, "Harry Potter's Wizardly Powers Divide Opinion," *Fort-Worth (TX) Star-Telegram*, December 3, 1999, available online at www.arlington.net.

51. Rowling, *Sorcerer's Stone*, 148-152.

52. Rowling, *Sorcerer's Stone*, 154.

53. Rowling, *Sorcerer's Stone*.

54. Rowling, *Sorcerer's Stone*, 153.

55. Rowling, *Sorcerer's Stone*, 154.

56. Rowling, *Sorcerer's Stone*, 163.

57. Rowling, *Sorcerer's Stone*, 207-214.
58. Rowling, *Sorcerer's Stone*, 225-226.
59. Rowling, *Sorcerer's Stone*, 155.
60. Rowling, *Sorcerer's Stone*, 166.
61. Rowling, *Sorcerer's Stone*, 155, 161, 164.
62. Rowling, *Sorcerer's Stone*, 172.
63. Rowling, *Sorcerer's Stone*, 177-178.
64. Rowling, *Sorcerer's Stone*, 179.
65. Rowling, *Sorcerer's Stone*, 273.
66. Rowling, *Sorcerer's Stone*.
67. Rowling, *Sorcerer's Stone*, 242.
68. Rowling, *Sorcerer's Stone*, 59, 64.
69. Rowling, *Sorcerer's Stone*, 230-233.
70. Rowling, *Sorcerer's Stone*, 64.
71. Rowling, *Sorcerer's Stone*, 237.
72. Rowling, *Sorcerer's Stone*, 125.
73. Judith Krug, quoted in "The 'Harry Potter' Books: Craze & Controversy," available online at www.familyhaven.com.
74. Starhawk, 76.
75. J.K. Rowling, *The Diane Rehm Show*.
76. Michael Hatty, "*Harry Potter* Author Reveals the Secret to Getting Kids to Read as Children's Book Week Kicks Off," November 14, 1999 USAWeekend.com, available online at www.usaweekend.com/99_issues/991114/991114potter.html.
77. Laura Miller, "Harry Potter Rumor Watch," Salon.com, available online at www.salon.com/books/log/2000/07/06/potter_rumors/index.html.
78. Rowling, *Chamber of Secrets*, 123.
79. Rowling, *Sorcerer's Stone*, 124.
80. Rowling, *Sorcerer's Stone*, 256.
81. Rowling, *Sorcerer's Stone*, 59, 90.
82. Rowling, *Sorcerer's Stone*, 80.
83. J.K. Rowling, quoted in O'Malley in "Talking with J.K. Rowling," available online at www.northernlight.com.
84. Rowling, *Sorcerer's Stone*, 182.
85. George F. Will, "Magical Mystery Book," ABCnews.com, July 3, 2000, available online at www.abcnews.go.com/onair/thisweek/tw_georgewill_harrypotter000703.html.

THREE

ENTER THE CHAMBER:
A BRIEF SUMMARY

Sure, you are seeing witches in Harry Potter *do things they don't do in real life. But it is positive. They are friendly. They are good. The book might change the way people feel about us.*

Phyllis Curott, witch[1]
ABCnews.com

Harry Potter and the Chamber of Secrets, J.K. Rowling's second fantasy novel, begins toward the end of Harry's first summer away from Hogwarts. He misses being at school so much that it is like "having a constant stomachache." He longs for "the castle . . . his classes . . . the mail arriving by owl, eating banquets in the Great Hall . . . visiting the gamekeeper, Hagrid, in his cabin next to the Forbidden Forest in the grounds, and, especially, Quidditch, the most popular sport in the wizarding world."[2]

The Muggle relatives with whom Harry lives (Uncle Vernon, Aunt Petunia and Cousin Dudley) loathe Harry now more than ever because he knows magic. The mere mention of "the 'm' word" causes them to cower in fright. Consequently, Harry cannot mention Hogwarts or any of his adventures from the previous year. He is not even allowed to do his summer assignments from Hogwarts. In fact, all of his possessions (spellbooks, wand, robes, cauldron and flying broom) have been locked in the cupboard under the stairs. The only reason Harry is not locked up with them is because the Dursleys are terrified of his magical abilities.

Unfortunately, Uncle Vernon intercepts a letter to Harry from the Ministry of Magic (a kind of law enforcement agency within the wizarding world) and learns that wizards-in-training cannot use magic while away from Hogwarts.[3] This is all Mr. Dursley needs to know to muster up enough courage to imprison Harry forever:

> He was bearing down on Harry like a great bulldog, all his teeth bared. "Well, I've got news for you, boy. . . . You're never going back to that school . . . never . . . and if you try and magic yourself out—they'll expel you!"
>
> And laughing like a maniac, he dragged Harry back upstairs. . . . The following morning, he paid a man to fit bars on Harry's window. He himself fitted a cat-flap in the bedroom door, so that small amounts of food could be pushed inside three times a day. They let Harry out to use the bathroom morning and evening. Otherwise he was locked in his room around the clock.[4]

But just when it seems as if Harry will never be able to return to where he belongs and where he is loved, he is rescued by his truest pal, Ron Weasley. Ron arrives in a magical flying car with his two elder brothers, Fred and George. The car is an old Muggle Ford that has been bewitched by Mr. Weasley, who works for the Ministry of Magic. The Weasleys free Harry and whisk him away to remain at their home until the new school year starts.

Harry tells the Weasleys all about his summer and also confides in them about a strange visitor, a "house-elf" named Dobby, who showed up just before Ron and his brothers arrived. Dobby did not bring good news. He told Harry that he must not return to school because he would not be safe. The little elf warned that Harry would be "in mortal danger" because there was "a plot to make most terrible things happen at Hogwarts."[5]

Fred and George theorize that the elf probably was sent by Draco Malfoy, Harry's archrival at school. The explanation sounds plausible. Malfoy would indeed be happy if Harry did not return to Hogwarts. The two boys are competing Quidditch players, and Draco knows that Harry's presence at school almost guarantees a Gryffindor House victory in the yearly tournament. Although this theory makes sense, Harry cannot help but wonder if perhaps the elf was telling the truth.

Harry's fears eventually fade against the backdrop of the Weasley's happy home, where magic is accepted as a normal part of life, and after a few days he forgets all about the warning. We next see him going off to Diagon Alley, this time with the Weasleys, in order to pick up his second-year school supplies. Then, before he knows it, he is back at Hogwarts with Ron, Hermione, Neville, Hagrid, Professor Dumbledore and everyone else. It is a joyful reunion, but the celebratory mood does not last long. Terrible and frightening events plague the school year.

Harry is the first to be affected. Without warning and seemingly from out of nowhere, he begins to hear a voice saying horrible things. While doing some paperwork in a classroom with Professor Lockhart (the new Defense Against the Dark Arts teacher), Harry hears, *"Come . . . come to me. . . . Let me tear you. . . . Let me kill you. . . ."* [6] As he goes up some steps, the voice again speaks: *"rip . . . tear . . . kill . . . soo hungry . . . for so long . . . kill . . . time to kill . . . I smell blood . . . I SMELL BLOOD!"*[7] Harry cannot imagine from whom these dreadful words might be coming.

Then, the unthinkable is discovered. Mrs. Norris, the caretaker's pet, is found hanging by her tail from a torch bracket. She is "stiff as a board, her eyes wide and staring."[8] The cat, although not dead, has been petrified as hard as stone. Only one clue is found. On the wall above where Mrs. Norris is suspended, someone has scrawled a message in foot-high letters: "THE CHAMBER OF SECRETS HAS BEEN OPENED. ENEMIES OF THE HEIR, BEWARE."[9]

Harry learns that this "Chamber of Secrets" was built somewhere under the school by Salazar Slytherin, one of Hogwarts' wizard-founders. He constructed it just as he was going over to the Dark Side. Apparently, Slytherin's journey toward evil started after he disagreed with the other wizard-founders about who should be allowed to attend Hogwarts. The other founders, especially Godric Gryffindor, wanted to enroll any child who showed signs of magic, even if they were not fully magical (e.g., a half-Muggle child, or a wizard/witch child of two Muggle parents).

Slytherin, on the other hand, wanted the school only to admit children from "all-magic families."[10] After a heated argument over the subject with Gryffindor, Slytherin left Hogwarts. But before doing so, he built the chamber and sealed it

> so that no one would be able to open it until his own true heir arrived at the school. The heir alone would be able to unseal the Chamber of Secrets, unleash the horror within, and use it to purge the school of all who were unworthy to study magic.[11]

The reality of the story becomes terrifyingly apparent as students one-by-one begin turning into stone. Fortunately, Professor Sprout, the school's herbologist, knows how to brew a Mandrake root potion that can reanimate petrified individuals. The mandrake roots, however, will not be ripe for several months. Consequently, Hogwarts' students can only hope that the chamber's "monster" will be caught before more victims are claimed. But Harry, Ron and Hermione are not about to wait around for the adults to take care of things. They resolve to find the answers to the probing questions everyone is asking: What is the monster? Where is the chamber? Who is Salazar's heir?

Harry and Ron eventually piece together a very complex puzzle. In doing so, they realize that the beast attacking everyone is a "basilisk," an enormously long snake that can, with one look, kill anyone who stares into its eyes. And for those persons unlucky enough to glance indirectly at it (e.g., through a camera lens or in a mirror's reflection), their fate is to turn into stone.

Harry and Ron find the secret chamber's entrance behind a wall in a girls' bathroom—the very same one haunted by Moaning Myrtle, a young female ghost who is always heard weeping and moaning. As it turns out, Myrtle was a former Hogwarts student who was killed in the bathroom by the basilisk fifty years earlier when the chamber was first opened by Slytherin's heir—Voldemort. Although only a sixteen-year-old at the time, Voldemort was already well on his way to the Dark Side. Meanwhile, Voldemort has returned in a form no one thought possible. He has come back as a sort of holographic image of his teenage self.

This is possible by means of an enchanted diary he created while still a young student at Hogwarts. Within the diary, a sixteen-year-old Tom Riddle (who would eventually become Voldemort) magically placed his living memories and personality. Fortunately for Riddle, the diary was found by Ginny Weasley, Ron's eleven-year-old sister, who had just started going to Hogwarts. By recording her own thoughts, feelings and experiences in the journal, she awakened Riddle's persona, and he was able to write back to her on the book's pages.

As Ginny poured out her soul to Riddle, he grew stronger, eventually being able to possess her body and control her. Ginny even told Riddle about Harry and how he had defeated the adult Voldemort. This fascinated Riddle, who by now was actually starting to reassume physical form. In order to meet Harry and find out how he defeated the adult Voldemort (i.e., Riddle in later years), Riddle/Voldemort kidnaps Ginny. Harry goes into the Secret Chamber looking for Ginny and not only finds her, but also runs into Riddle, who is close to regaining complete physicality. He is nearly able to leave the diary's pages and exist in the real world as a living human rather than just a projected image. Riddle/Voldemort explains the whole unbelievable scenario to a stunned Harry:

> I grew stronger and stronger on a diet of her deepest fears, her darkest secrets. I grew powerful, far more powerful than little Miss Weasley. Powerful enough . . . to start pouring a little of *my* soul back into *her*. . . . Ginny Weasley opened the Chamber of Secrets. She strangled the school roosters and daubed threatening messages on the walls. . . . Of course, she didn't *know* what she was doing at first. . . . I wish you could have seen her new diary entries. . . . *Dear Tom, . . . I think I'm losing my memory. There are rooster feathers all over my robes and I don't know how they got there. Dear Tom, I can't remember what I did the night of Halloween, but a cat was attacked and I've got paint all down my front. . . . There was another attack today and I don't know where I was. . . . I think I'm going mad.* Now, Harry, I'm going to teach you a little lesson.[12]

Then Riddle calls forth the basilisk, and Harry is forced into a bloody battle with the snake. Fortunately, he receives help from Dumbledore's pet phoenix, Fawkes, which magically appears when Harry needs him the most. Thanks to Fawkes and the Hogwarts Sorting Hat, Harry gets his hands on the magical Sword of Gryffindor. Harry ultimately kills the basilisk and is able to impale the diary on one of its fangs: "There was a long, dreadful, piercing scream. Ink spurted out of the diary in torrents, streaming over Harry's hands, flooding the floor. Riddle was writhing and twisting, screaming and flailing and then— He had gone."[13]

After everything is restored to order, some bits of information are pieced together. Earlier we learned that Harry is a "parselmouth"—i.e., one who can communicate with snakes. The murderous voice he heard was actually that of the basilisk as it roamed through the school's plumbing system. Interestingly, being able to communicate with snakes is a rare gift that is supposedly the "mark of a Dark wizard,"[14] just like Voldemort. Hogwarts' Headmaster, Albus Dumbledore, tells Harry, "Unless I'm much mistaken, he transferred some of his own powers to you the night he gave you that scar."[15]

The gift of parseltongue, by the way, is only one of several traits shared by Voldemort and Harry. Both of them carry wands with a core created from identical magical elements (see Book I, p. 85). Both were raised as orphans (see Book IV, p. 646). Both come from similar family backgrounds (see Book IV, p. 646). And Harry bears a physical resemblance to the teenage Lord Voldemort-Tom Riddle (Book II, p. 243). All of this suggests that in future books Harry may face a powerful temptation from the Dark Side, à la Luke Skywalker in *Star Wars*.

Hints of this approaching conflict appear early in Book I, when the Sorting Hat nearly puts Harry in Slytherin. As Harry puts on the hat and begins thinking about how much he does not want to be in Slytherin, he hears the magical cap whispering, "Hmm. . . . Difficult. Very difficult. . . . Not Slytherin, eh? . . . Are you sure? You could be great, you know, it's all here in your head, and

Slytherin will help you on the way to greatness, no doubt about that."[16]

Book II clearly reinforces the possibility that at some point Harry will have to make a decision similar to the one Skywalker made when his father, Darth Vader, asked him to come over to the Dark Side. It is also discovered in Book II that Riddle's diary did not just accidentally fall into the hands of Ginny. Lucius Malfoy, Draco's father, saw to it that the little girl would find the evil journal by placing it into one of her schoolbooks. But because no one is able to actually prove it, Dumbledore can only give Lucius a warning: "I would advise you, Lucius, not to go giving out any more of Lord Voldemort's old school things. If any more of them find their way into innocent hands, I think Arthur Weasley [Ginny's father], for one, will make sure they are traced back to you."[17]

To celebrate the monster's destruction, Hogwarts has a feast the likes of which no one has ever seen. Ginny recovers from her ordeal. Final exams are canceled as a "school treat." And Harry is once more a hero. Even so, the last semester is nearly over, which means that he is soon back in the Muggle world; back living with the Dursleys, until the next school year. Thus ends Book II.

ENDNOTES

1. Phyllis Curott, quoted in Buck Wolf, "Witches Bless Harry Potter," ABC News Online, available online at www.abcnews.go.com/sectons/us/WolfFiles/wolffiles122.html

2. J.K. Rowling, *Harry Potter and the Chamber of Secrets* (New York: Scholastic, 1999), 3.

3. Rowling, *Chamber of Secrets*, 20-21.

4. Rowling, *Chamber of Secrets*, 21-22.

5. Rowling, *Chamber of Secrets*, 13-16.

6. Rowling, *Chamber of Secrets*, 120.

7. Rowling, *Chamber of Secrets*, 137-138.

8. Rowling, *Chamber of Secrets*, 139.

9. Rowling, *Chamber of Secrets*, 138.

10. Rowling, *Chamber of Secrets*, 150.

11. Rowling, *Chamber of Secrets*, 151.
12. Rowling, *Chamber of Secrets*, 310-311, 317.
13. Rowling, *Chamber of Secrets*, 322.
14. Rowling, *Chamber of Secrets*, 199.
15. Rowling, *Chamber of Secrets*, 333.
16. J.K. Rowling, *Harry Potter and the Sorcerer's Stone* (New York: Scholastic Press, 1997), 121.
17. Rowling, *Chamber of Secrets*, 337.

FOUR

ENTER THE CHAMBER: A CLOSER LOOK

With the growing popularity of youth-oriented TV shows on witchcraft—Sabrina, the Teenage Witch; Charmed; Buffy the Vampire Slayer—a generation of children is becoming desensitized to the occult. But with Hollywood's help, Harry Potter will likely surpass all these influences, potentially reaping some grave spiritual consequences.

John Andrew Murray[1]
Headmaster, St. Timothy-Hale Episcopal School

In her article "It's Just a Bunch of Hocus Pocus," teacher Lauren Hill of Eagle School (Madison, Wisconsin) writes, "As for teaching witchcraft, the Potter books certainly don't do this. There is no list of directions on how to perform spells in the books. Also, most spells that are used in the book are completely harmless."[2] Hill may be correct in saying that the Potter books do not technically *teach* "witchcraft." In other words, they do not contain any clearly defined set of doctrinal beliefs associated with Wicca. But as we saw in Chapter 1, the moral relativism rampant at Hogwarts and throughout Harry's wizarding world does reflect the kind of subjective morality found in Wiccan circles.

What about the spells in Rowling's books? Starhawk, a renowned modern-day witch, has stated that spells and the casting of them, is a very "important part of magical training."[3] But according to Hill, this has nothing to do with the Potter series because they do not teach children how to do spells. Again, Hill is only partially correct. Although the novels may not contain true incantations, they do illustrate the importance of spells to occultists and the significance that words play in casting those spells. This happens as Harry and his friends go about learning and using the various words necessary to cause changes in accordance to their will (e.g., opening a door, levitating an object, immobilizing someone, etc.). Such practices are the very definition of magic, as the notorious occultist Aleister Crowley (1875-1947) taught: "Magick is the Science and Art of causing Change to occur in conformity with Will."[4]

Obviously, the nonsensical words used in the Potter books (e.g., *Alomohora! Expelliarmus! Rictusempra! Finite Incantatem!*) are not truly magical. Each spell is nothing but silly babble, humorously latinized by Rowling to impart a sense of mysticality. But noteworthy is the fact that sorcerers of the Middle Ages and ancient Egypt also used gibberish terms.[5] Using secret words and phrases has always been important to those practicing magic. According to the *Encyclopedia of Occultism and Parapsychology*, "The power of the spoken word was implicitly believed in by all primitive peoples, especially . . . if it be in a language or dialect unknown to ordinary people."[6]

Also significant is the process that Hogwarts' students go through to master the words they use in their spells. It is very similar to the procedure actual occultists use to become adept at speaking their magical phrases. Again, the *Encyclopedia of Occultism and Parapsychology* casts light on the issue, stating, "[N]ot only were the formulas [i.e., exact wording] of spells well fixed, but the exact tone of voice in which they were to be *pronounced* was specially taught (emphasis added)."[7]

This is precisely what Harry and his companions learn at Hogwarts. For example, in one scene where Ron and Harry are incorrectly casting a spell, Hermione explains that they are saying the appropriate magic words but are not putting the emphasis in the correct place:

> "Now don't forget the wrist movement we've been practicing!" squeaked Professor Flitwick.... "And saying the magic words properly is very important, too." ...
>
> Ron, at the next table, wasn't having much more luck.
>
> "*Wingardium Leviosa!*" he shouted. ...
>
> "You're saying it wrong," Harry heard Hermione snap. "It's Wing-*gar*-dium Levi-*o*-sa, make the 'gar' nice and long."[8]

Rowling has again blended innocent-looking fantasy with real world occult principles. She also succeeds in blurring the lines between fantasy and fiction by portraying some spells as long-lasting and without end until such time as an antidote potion is given or a counterspell is uttered.[9] Real world occultists believe their magic works the same way. The *Encyclopedia of Occultism and Parapsychology* reveals: "The power of the spell remained until such time as it was broken by an antidote or exorcism. Therefore, it was not a transient thing."[10]

Additionally, Rowling's stories identify magical ability as a sort of gift that is possessed from birth. This mirrors the belief held by occultists, as it says in *Witchcraft & Paganism Today*: "There are those who have a natural affinity for magic and already possess psychic or clairvoyant abilities."[11] These special individuals, like the children at Hogwarts, are gifted with magical talents other mortals lack. Many contemporary occultists have put forth the teaching that "the powers of witchcraft, magic, shamanism, or whatever one likes to call it, are latent in everyone."[12] Celebrated witch Doreen Valiente says that the only thing any of us has to do is properly train our abilities via "techniques which will bring them out and develop them."[13]

Rowling has clearly infused her books with a basic principle of occultism: Persons are born with magical capabilities that must be developed in order to be practical. Perhaps even more interesting is a quote from Rowling herself to a worldwide student audience. In a video prepared by Scholastic, Rowling's U.S. publisher, the Scottish author declares: "It's important to remember that we all have magic inside us."[14]

Clearly, a significant percentage of the Harry Potter material does not come from Rowling's inventiveness. She herself has admitted that approximately one-third of what she has written is based on actual occultism.[15] Some scenes, many of them particularly grisly, are not only based on reality, but often are also described using details taken verbatim from sorcery and witchcraft. A prime example of this in *Chamber of Secrets* (Book II) is Rowling's "Hand of Glory"—a "withered hand on a cushion."[16]

Harry finds this gruesome trinket at a store located in Knockturn Alley, another wizard shopping area similar to Diagon Alley, except for one small difference: Knockturn Alley is devoted to the Dark Arts. In this scene, he is hiding in a large cabinet, where he overhears Lucius and Draco Malfoy speaking to the shop's attendant. Draco suddenly spies the Hand and asks if his father will purchase it for him. "Ah, the Hand of Glory," replies the shopkeeper, Mr. Borgin. "Insert a candle and it gives light only to the holder! Best friend of thieves and plunderers! Your son has fine taste, sir!"[17]

According to occult tradition, the Hand of Glory was "a right hand of a murderer that was severed while the corpse was still hanging from the gallows. It was then used as a charm or in black magic practices after being magically preserved. It is also believed robbers often used the hand when breaking into buildings and homes."[18] The following text, taken from themystica.com, more fully explains the belief Rowling used to color her "fantasy":

> Preferably the hand was cut off during the eclipse of the moon. Afterwards it was wrapped in a shroud, squeezed of blood and pickled for two weeks in an earthenware jar with salt, long peppers and saltpeter. Then it was either dried in an oven with vervain, an herb believed to be able to ward off demons, or laid out to dry in the sun. . . .
>
> When the hand was ready, candles were fitted on it between the fingers. These were called the "dead man's candles" and were made from another murderer's fat, with the wick being made from his hair. Another method of curing the severed and dried hand was to dip it in wax. After this process the fingers themselves could be lit.
>
> The hand with burning candles or fingers was shocking when coming at people. It froze them in their tracks and rendered them speechless. Burglars lit the hand before entering homes. A warning sign was that if the thumb would not light it meant there was someone in the house who could not be charmed or made afraid. It was believed once the hand was lit nothing but milk could extinguish it. . . . Belief in the efficacy of the Hand of Glory persisted as late as 1831 in Ireland.[19]

Surprisingly, several evangelical Christians have chosen to support Rowling's works despite these warning signs of occultism. Chuck Colson, founder of Prison Fellowship, has stated that Rowling "presents evil as evil, and good as good."[20] He also says the following:

> [T]he magic in these books is purely mechanical, as opposed to occultic. That is, Harry and his friends cast spells, read crystal balls, and turn themselves into animals—but they don't make contact with a supernatural world. . . .

> Contrast the mechanical magic in the Potter books to the
> kind of real life witchcraft the Bible condemns—the kind
> that encourages involvement with supernatural evil.[21]

Although sincere in his attempt to support what he believes to be harmless fantasy, Colson fails to comprehend the depth of occultism found in the books and does not understand the relationship that exists between the novels and real world occultism. He is partially correct in saying that Rowling nowhere has "good" characters conjuring up "evil" entities from the supernatural world ("evil" being defined by Rowling's books as anything in league with Voldemort [see Chapter 8 for a discussion of Rowling's "good" and "evil" characters]). And it is also true that Rowling has a sort of battle being waged between the good wizards/witches (Harry et al.) and the evil forces of the Dark Side (Voldemort et al.).

But Colson incorrectly states that Harry and his friends engage only in harmless "mechanical" magic, or behaviors that are mere literary devices (like robots and transporter beams in sci-fi films). In reality, Harry and his companions go far beyond this kind of entertaining hocus-pocus by delving into the realms of divination. This presents an even more straightforward example of how Rowling incorporates actual occultism into her books. Divination is defined as "[w]illful exploration of the future or the discovery of hidden things by various practices. Most common are astrology, dowsing, dreams, cards, crystal-gazing, numerology, palmistry, omens."[22] Many of these techniques are repeatedly mentioned and casually engaged in by Rowling's characters, especially in her third and fourth books.

Furthermore, God's Word does more than forbid "involvement with supernatural *evil*." The Bible condemns *all* forms of communication with the spirit world, except communication with God, through the Holy Spirit, in the name of the Son. In other words, *all* interaction with the spirit world, if it takes place apart from God, is prohibited by Scripture. Yet unbiblical spiritual involvement takes place all through the Potter books, which is why they can be so dangerous for young children.

Rowling's characters are constantly communicating with ghosts, magical creatures and enchanted objects (books, mirrors, etc.). They regularly commune with ghosts, including Professor Binns (one of Hogwarts' teachers), Peeves (a *poltergeist* [malevolent spirit]), Moaning Myrtle (a murdered Hogwarts student) and Nearly Headless Nick (Gryffindor's resident apparition).

Each student dorm, in fact, has its own house-ghost. In Book III (*Harry Potter and the Prisoner of Azkaban*), Headmaster Dumbledore uses these and countless other ghosts to send messages to the students.[23] In occultism, ghosts are defined as the "disembodied spirit or image of a deceased person, appearing to be living. . . . Ghosts are believed to haunt specific localities, either dwellings associated with their earthly life or locales with a tragic history."[24]

Additionally, a ghoul lives with the Weasleys, and the family seems perfectly content having this entity dwell with them as a long-term guest. A ghoul, according to occult legend, is "[a]n evil spirit supposed to rob graves and feed upon human corpses. . . . Amongst Hindus there are similar beliefs of the *vetala*, a demon that haunts cemeteries and animates dead bodies, or the *rakshasas*, a whole order of evil demons that disturb sacrifices, harass devout people, or devour human beings."[25]

Readers of the Potter series will find several examples of animals that give the impression of being a "familiar." (According to Medieval demonology, a familiar was a low-ranking demon that assumed any animal shape: a rat, toad, dog, cat or owl. The small animals, kept as a witch's attendant, were either given by Satan or inherited from another witch.) Mrs. Norris, the cat

owned by the school's caretaker, exhibits some of the characteristics of a familiar. In Book III, Hermione gets her own familiar—a cat named Crookshanks.

These same types of small animals are specifically mentioned as
the only pets that Hogwarts students may keep at school.[26] Again,
Starhawk writes: "Witches also traditionally keep special pets, 'familiars' in part as a source of elemental energy."[27] In *The Rebirth of
Witchcraft*, Doreen Valiente explains: "Witches had 'familiars.'
These could be either animals or birds, or discarnate [i.e., bodi-
less] spirits."[28] And Deva Bluewing, at the Internet's "Bayowolf &
Erzsebet's Wiccan Page," explains that during the Middle Ages,
familiars often were "given names like any household pet."[29]
Christina Hole, author of *English Folklore* and *A Mirror of Witchcraft*, explains the significance of familiars in her book *Witchcraft
in England*:

> No idea was more firmly rooted in the popular mind during
> the later centuries of the witchcraft-belief than the notion
> that all witches possessed familiar spirits which they re-
> ceived from the Devil and by whose aid they practiced divi-
> nation and magic. . . . The familiar was personal to the
> witch. . . . The commonest forms of manifestations were
> cats, dogs, or any small animals."[30]

Obviously Harry and his friends are indeed making contact
with the spiritual world. Rowling is presenting an entirely skewed
picture of the spiritual dimension; one in which "good" spiritual
entities and "evil" spiritual entities await our summoning, the goal
being to interact with the "good" entities.

Also within the Potter series, one can find magical books that
closely parallel texts circulating within the occult community,
each of which is used to help witches/wizards/sorcerers com-

municate in some way with the spirit realm. Consider the following similarities:

HARRY POTTER FANTASY	REAL WORLD OCCULTISM
• *The Standard Book of Spells*[31]	• *Book of Spells* (1997) by Arthur Edward Waite
• *A History of Magic*[32]	• *The History of Magic* (1997) by Eliphas Levi
• *One Thousand Magical Herbs and Fungi*[33]	• *Encyclopedia of Magical Herbs* (1985) by Scott Cunningham
• *Magical Drafts & Potions*[34]	• *Magick Potions: How to Prepare and Use Homemade Oils, Aphrodisiacs, Brews and Much More* (1998) by Gurina Dunwich

Even the "school supplies" that Hogwarts' students are required to use parallel tools commonly used by contemporary witches and sorcerers: wands, black robes, cauldrons. As well, there are the owls in Rowling's novels, which are used to send messages back and forth between witches and wizards. During the Middle Ages in Europe, owls were thought to be the "associate of witches and the inhabitant of dark, lonely and profane places, a foolish but feared spectre."[35] It also was believed that their appearance signaled an imminent death or some nearby evil.

All of this might be less significant if Rowling's story took place in a world far removed from our own. But her fantasy takes place here and now, only a few hours' train ride (albeit a magic train) from major British cities. The separation between reality and fantasy may not be wide enough for some children to draw clear lines in their minds between the two worlds. Even if they can separate Harry Potter from their own lives, there still exists the very tangible possibility that many children will become so enthralled with magic and wizardry that they will seek out the paganism/witchcraft that is available in the real world. In fact, this by-product of Rowling's work is already occurring across England.

According to an August 4, 2000 article that appeared in the British publication *This Is London*, the Pagan Federation has had to appoint a new youth officer to deal with "a flood of inquiries following the success of the Harry Potter books."[36] In the story, titled "Potter Fans Turning to Witchcraft," Pagan Federation media officer Andy Norfolk explained:

> In response to increased inquiries coming from youngsters we established a youth officer. . . . It is quite probably linked to things like *Harry Potter*, *Sabrina the Teenage Witch* and *Buffy the Vampire Slayer*. Every time an article on witchcraft or paganism appears, we have a huge surge in calls, mostly from young girls.[37]

John Buckeridge, editor of *Youthwork*, a British Christian youth ministry magazine, said he has no doubt such stories have inspired widespread curiosity about occultism. "The growing number of books and TV shows like *Harry Potter* and *Sabrina the Teenage Witch* encourage an interest in magic as harmless fun," he further commented. "However, for some young people, it could fuel a fascination that leads to dangerous dabbling with occult powers. So what starts out as spooks and spells can lead to psychological and spiritual damage."[38]

The success of Rowling's novels and the generalized defense of them might be attributable to something the renowned Christian author C.S. Lewis discussed in *The Screwtape Letters*.

In this fictionalized communication between a high-ranking demon ("Screwtape") and his nephew ("Wormwood"), Lewis explores the ways that forces of darkness seek to draw humans away from God. The relevance of Lewis' story to the Harry Potter books has been expertly pointed out by John Andrew Murray in Focus on the Family's *Citizen Magazine*:

> In the 1941 preface of his book, Lewis revealed two of the greatest mistakes in humanity's beliefs about demons. . . . One is to disbelieve in their existence. The other is to believe, and to feel an excessive and unhealthy interest in them. They themselves are equally pleased with both errors and hail a materialist or a magician with the same delight. An even greater error, and the one most valued by Lewis' demonic characters, is the fusion of the two errors. As Screwtape writes to Wormwood: "If once we can produce our perfect work—the Materialist Magician, the man, not using but veritably worshiping, what he vaguely calls 'Forces' while denying the existence of 'spirits'—then the end of the war will be in sight."[39]

In other words, as Murray explains, by disassociating magic from supernatural evil, "it becomes possible to portray occult practices as 'good' and 'healthy,' contrary to the scriptural declaration that such practices are 'detestable to the Lord.' This, in turn, opens the door for less discerning individuals—including, but not limited to, children—to become confused about supernatural matters."[40]

POTTERETHICS

Perhaps the most concise summation to date of the morality and ethics found in Rowling's novels appeared in a July 10, 2000 online story for Salon.com. In an article titled "The Plot Deepens," Charles Taylor stated that Harry Potter learns through his adventures to "balance his sense of what's right and his sense of what's necessary."[41] Taylor could not be more accurate. Like *Sorcerer's Stone* (Book I), *Chamber of Secrets* (Book II) presents a highly subjective and changeable code of right and wrong that both children and adults seem to enjoy. They seem perfectly comfortable with breaking not only minor rules, but highly important regulations as well. Furthermore, some kind of lie is usually told to cover up their actions.

The moral tone of Book II is set on page 30, when Harry discovers that the Weasley brothers rescued him by taking their father's bewitched car without permission. Fred Weasley comes up with a simple way to explain Harry's presence at their home: a lie.[42] But when this plan fails to work because Mrs. Weasley catches the boys coming home, the only thing they must endure is a brief lecture about how they could have been injured. When Mr. Weasley finds out his sons flew the car, his first response is "Did you really? . . . Did it go all right?"[43]

Later in the book, Ron and Harry again fly the magical car over the city without permission, but this time they crash into a tree. The second incident is even worse than the first, however, because both boys are underage wizards, which means they are forbidden to use magic outside Hogwarts. Breaking the "Restriction of Underage Wizardry" law is supposedly a very serious offense, resulting in expulsion. But all Ron and Harry get is "a detention" which, though an unpleasant punishment, is much less severe than having to leave school.

Next, Hermione, Ron and Harry break "about fifty school rules" by using a magic potion to transform themselves to look like three other students.[44] Their disobedience even includes stealing restricted magical ingredients.[45] To make matters more twisted, Rowling flips the usual scenario by making Ron and Harry the apprehensive ones, while Hermione (the more "honest" of the three) becomes the instigator. " 'I never thought I'd see the day when you'd be persuading us to break rules,' said Ron. 'All right, we'll do it.' "[46]

This severe departure from Hogwarts' rules easily eclipses the children's many other infractions (such as when Harry uses magic in a hallway, or when Harry and Ron sneak out of their dorm at night).[47] But by the end of Book II, the number of broken rules simply does not matter, because Harry is a hero. His end justifies his means. As Professor McGonagall admiringly says: "[S]o you found out where the entrance was [to the chamber]—breaking a hundred school rules into pieces along the way, I might add—but how on *earth* did you all get out of there alive, Potter?"[48] A slightly embarrassed Headmaster Dumbledore adds:

> "I seem to remember telling you both that I would have to expel you if you broke any more school rules. . . . Which goes to show that the best of us must sometimes eat our words. . . . You will both receive Special Awards for Services to the School and—let me see—yes, I think two hundred [merit] points apiece for Gryffindor."[49]

As in Book I, the adult characters in Book II break almost as many rules as the children and routinely lie to further their own agenda. For instance, Mr. Weasley, who is portrayed as a positive character, works for the Ministry of Magic in the "Misuse of Muggle Artifacts Office." His job is to prevent wizards from bewitching "things that are Muggle-made" (appliances, books, clothes, etc.). It is a way of protecting Muggles (non-magical mortals) from objects that might prove to be harmful because they are bewitched.[50] To capture wizards/witches who have broken this law, Mr. Weasley conducts various raids and confiscates their illegally bewitched property.

But Mr. Weasley is "crazy about everything to do with Muggles" and has a shed full of Muggle objects. His son, Ron, explains to Harry, "He takes it apart, puts spells on it, and puts it back together again. If he raided *our* house he'd have to put himself under arrest."[51] In short, Mr. Weasley is not only a lawbreaker, but a hypocrite. He then lies to his wife about the extent to which he has bewitched the Muggle car.[52] Rowling even has Mr. Weasley starting a brawl with Lucius Malfoy in a bookstore.[53]

Yet these issues pale in seriousness to the lie that the entire Hogwarts teaching staff seems to tell students through most of Book II. Although every teacher, including Headmaster Dumbledore, knows about the secret chamber and its dangers, they assure students that "there is no Chamber and no monster."[54]

Not surprisingly, when Dumbledore asks Harry if he knows anything about the mysterious events going on at Hogwarts, Harry responds with a lie.[55] In yet another scene where Harry is caught doing something he should not have been doing, Rowling makes a straightforward declaration that typifies her lead character: "Harry lied quickly."[56]

Perhaps all of this unrepentant lying and disobedience can be traced to Rowling's personal belief that children are "innately good unless they've been very damaged."[57] Oddly, she has used these very words to describe her young heroes, saying: "Harry, Ron and Hermione are innately good people."[58] Perhaps Rowling sees sporadic lying, along with varying degrees of rebellion and disobedience, as little more than the natural quirks of "innately good" kids.

However, Scripture teaches that both lying and disobedience is morally wrong and should be avoided (1 Samuel 15:23; Romans 1:30; Colossians 3:9, 20; 2 Timothy 3:2). The Bible also reveals that none of us are innately good (Romans 3:23). We are all born with a sinful nature (Psalm 14:1-3). That, in fact, is why we sin (i.e., do bad things). The validity of these spiritual teachings are daily demonstrated by both adults and children; all of us show unkindness toward each other, ignore what is best for ourselves and others, and rebel against those who seek to guide us in the right way.

Now, thanks to the Harry Potter series and the lessons it teaches, parents may face a much more difficult task as they seek to lead their children through the often complex world of right and wrong. Such a problem might not have existed if only Harry Potter had understood the words of wisdom given to him by Dumbledore: "It is our choices, Harry, that show what we truly are, far more than our abilities."[59]

AGES 6 AND UP?

Book II clearly contains a marked increase of occultism and moral ambiguity. But in addition to these troubling facets of the book, *Chamber of Secrets* more fully illustrates Rowling's dark and sometimes disturbing sense of wit. For example, Rowling apparently finds humor in Moaning Myrtle, the tormented spirit of a murdered Hogwarts student who haunts the bathroom where she was murdered. Myrtle, whom Rowling describes as a fat, pimple-faced girl, not only lived a ridicule-filled life, but also must endure an afterlife marked by depression and rage. According to Hermione, "[I]t's awful trying to have a pee with her wailing at you."[60] Rowling even makes light of the fact that Myrtle's tortured soul longs for relief through suicide:

> "My life was nothing but misery at this place and now people come along ruining my death. . . . I came in here and tried to *kill* myself. Then, of course, I remembered that I'm—I'm—" "Already dead," said Ron helpfully. Myrtle gave a tragic sob, rose up in the air, turned over, and dived

headfirst into the toilet. . . . Hermione shrugged wearily and
said, "Honestly, that was almost cheerful for Myrtle."[61]

Another series of allegedly funny scenes involves Rowling's
macabre descriptions of Professor Sprout's lessons on, and use
of, the mandrake plant. People used to believe that this root,
which looks vaguely like a small human, grew under the gallows
of a hanged man and consequently had magical properties. In *A
Handbook on Witches*, Gillian Tindall explains the historical beliefs which surround this oddly shaped plant, which during the
Middle Ages, was a virtual symbol of witchcraft:

> [I]ts root may be considered—with a little imagination—to
> look like a dead, shriveled baby. It is gnarled, and forked
> into two little "legs." Mandrakes were therefore regarded as
> the progeny of the Devil, said to grow in places where he
> had spilt his seed on the ground (while romping with
> witches?). *They were said to shriek in protest when they were
> drawn out of the earth* [emphasis added]. Nevertheless many
> people, witches included, must have braved this ordeal,
> since mandragora appears in a large number of spells.[62]

Not only does Rowling stress the significance of the mandrake
root for the depetrification potion needed in Book II, but her
storyline details a rather horrifying procedure that involves pulling live "mandrake-babies" out of the ground and growing them
to maturity before "cutting them up and stewing them."[63] To add
a little more color to the story, Rowling has the children wearing
earmuffs to protect them from the mandrake-babies' harmful
screams which ring out whenever they are repotted. This distaste-
ful image is periodically referred to throughout Book II as a sort
of running joke:

> Professor Sprout . . . grasped one of the tufty plants firmly,
> and pulled hard. Harry let out a gasp of surprise. . . .

Instead of roots, a small, muddy, and extremely ugly baby popped out of the earth. The leaves were growing right out of his head. He had pale green, mottled skin, and was clearly bawling at the top of his lungs.

Professor Sprout took a large plant pot from under the table and plunged the Mandrake into it, burying him in dark, damp compost. . . .

"As our Mandrakes are only seedlings, their cries won't kill yet. . . . However, they *will* knock you out for several hours. . . .

Professor Sprout had made it look extremely easy, but it wasn't. The Mandrakes didn't like coming out of the earth, but they didn't seem to want to go back into it either. They squirmed, kicked, flailed their sharp little fists, and gnashed their teeth; Harry spent ten whole minutes trying to squash a particularly fat one into a pot.[64]

There are a number of other places where Rowling not only displays a twisted sense of humor, but also goes so far as to allow some rather cruel comments and actions to go unchallenged. On pages 130-131, she has Fred and George Weasley setting off a "Filibuster firework" (a combination firecracker/ bottle rocket/sparkler) in the mouth of a salamander that emits loud sparks and bangs as it whizzes around the room.[65]

The unkindness permeating Book II continues on page 297, where a handsome teacher named Lockhart derides unattractive people and persons with facial deformities. In this scene, Lockhart tries explaining why in his best-selling books he takes credit for heroic acts done by other witches and wizards: "Do use your common sense. My books wouldn't have sold half as well if people didn't think *I'd* done all those things. No one wants to read about some ugly old Armenian warlock. . . . And the witch who banished the Bandon Banshee had a harelip. I mean, come on—".[66]

This degrading-slang reference to the facial abnormality known as a cleft lip is not only callous, but does little to alter for the better childrens' misperceptions of people with physical deformities. Even though Lockhart is not considered a "likeable" character, it is no excuse for the use of a term which is considered offensive by many people.

In the words of one irate reader, whose letter to the editor appeared in a Pennsylvania newspaper: "If Ms. Rowling knew what these children have to go through with surgery maybe she would not have written this. What would happen if Ms. Rowling replaced harelip with cerebral palsy or some other congenital defect? I'm sure she wouldn't be selling as many books."[67]

Rowling also succeeds in poking fun at obese people in the form of Harry's horrible cousin, Dudley, who hates exercise.[68] He is obnoxious, spoiled, sloppy, mean, violent and "very fat."[69] In Book II, Rowling describes him as "so large his bottom drooped over either side of the kitchen chair."[70] In Book III, we read: "Dudley had spent most of the summer in the kitchen, his piggy little eyes fixed on the [TV] screen and his five chins wobbling as he ate continually."[71] Then, in *Harry Potter and the Goblet of Fire* (Book IV), Rowling tells readers that Dudley has been forced to diet because he has "reached roughly the size and weight of a young killer whale."[72] Vernon Dursley, Harry's terribly cruel uncle, also is "a big, beefy man with hardly any neck."[73] Aunt Marge, yet another despicable character, is "large, beefy, and purple-faced."[74]

Such depictions shamelessly conform to the widespread bias that exists against obese people, especially overweight children, who, according to clinical studies on prejudice, are the persons most often targeted for "ridicule and disgust both by their peers and by the adults in their lives, such as teachers, counselors, and parents."[75] As early as preschool age, children have accepted stereotypes about and developed prejudice against fat people.

For example, when given an opportunity to play with either fat dolls or thin dolls, all children preferred playing with thin dolls.[76] Given pictures of children in a wheelchair, missing a limb, on crutches, facially disfigured or obese, most children said they would least like to play with the obese child.[77] By elementary school, children describe "fat" children as lazy, sloppy, dirty, stupid and ugly.[78] When shown silhouettes of obese and thin figures, nine-year-old children rated the heavy figures as having significantly fewer friends, being less liked by their parents and doing less well at school.[79] A group of six- to ten-year-old boys rated obese children as most likely to be teased.[80]

Sadly, Rowling's characterizations can only serve to strengthen misguided attitudes in the young minds that read her books. But despite these and other unsavory passages, Book II continues to be a best-seller around the world, even within the Christian community.

Roger Sutton, editor of *The Horn Book* (a seventy-five-year-old children's literary digest in Boston), has described the Potter books as a "critically insignificant" series, adding that as literature they are "nothing to get excited about."[81] Reviewers such as Sutton cannot understand why Rowling's works have so bedazzled the reading public. I, too, can only speculate that perhaps her success can be attributed to a combination of: 1) the right amount of publicity; 2) peer pressure among children for the latest fad (similar to the Pokémon trading card phenomenon); and 3) undiscerning reviewers jumping on the Harry Potter bandwagon.

Of course, even if the Harry Potter books are poor literature, that does not make them particularly damaging to children.

Harmful, though, are the many occultic, morally ambiguous and gruesome portions of her novels. Sadly, these occur with greater frequency and intensity in her third book, *Harry Potter and the Prisoner of Azkaban.*

ENDNOTES

1. John Andrew Murray, "The Trouble with Harry," *Citizen Magazine*, available online at www.family.org/pplace/schoolkid/a0009678.cfm.
2. Lauren Hill, "It's Just a Bunch of Hocus Pocus," available online at http://eagleschool.org/e-zine2000/17lh/LHReagle.htm.
3. Starhawk, *The Spiral Dance* (San Francisco: Harper San Francisco, 1979; 1989 edition), 124.
4. Aleister Crowley, *Magick in Theory and Practice* (New York: Dover Publications, 1976), 12.
5. Leslie A. Shepard, ed., *Encyclopedia of Occultism and Parapsychology* (Detroit: Gale Research, 1991), 2:1569.
6. Shepard, 2:1569.
7. Shepard, 2:1569.
8. Rowling, *Sorcerer's Stone*, 171.
9. J.K. Rowling, *Harry Potter and the Chamber of Secrets* (New York: Scholastic, 1999), 192, 226; cf. Rowling, *Sorcerer's Stone*, 217.
10. Shepard, 2:1569.
11. Anthony Kemp, *Witchcraft and Paganism Today* (London: Brockhampton Press, 1993; 1995 edition), 67.
12. Doreen Valiente, *The Rebirth of Witchcraft* (Custer, WA: Phoenix Publishing, 1989), 92.
13. Valiente, 92.
14. J.K. Rowling, video interview for Scholastic Press, available online at www.scholastic.com.
15. J.K. Rowling, interview on *The Diane Rehm Show*, WAMU, National Public Radio, October 20, 1999, available online at www.wamu.org.
16. Rowling, *Chamber of Secrets*, 51.
17. Rowling, *Chamber of Secrets*, 51-52.
18. Alan G. Hefner, "The Hand of Glory," available online at www.themystica.com/mystica/articles/h/hand_of_glory.html; also see Rosemary Elle Guiley, *The Encyclopedia of Witches and Witchcraft* (New York: Facts On File, 1989).
19. Hefner, available online at www.themystica.com/mystica/articles/h/hand_of_glory.html; also see Guiley. An extremely detailed description of exactly how to make a "Hand of Glory" appears in *Secrets merveilleux de la magie naturelle et cabalistique du Petit Albert*, published in 1722. The text is available online at www.witchhaven.com.

20. Chuck Colson, "Witches and Wizards: The Harry Potter Phenomenon," *Break-Point Commentary*, November 2, 1999, available online at www.breakpoint.org.
21. Colson, available online at www.breakpoint.org.
22. Rudolf Steiner Publications, *The Steinerbooks Dictionary of the Psychic, Mystic, Occult* (New York: Rudolf Steiner Publications, 1973), 62.
23. J.K. Rowling, *Harry Potter and the Prisoner of Azkaban* (New York: Scholastic, 1999), 162.
24. Shepard, 1:662.
25. Shepard, 1:664.
26. Rowling, *Sorcerer's Stone*, 67.
27. Starhawk, 148.
28. Valiente, 82.
29. Deva Bluewing, "The Witches Familiar," Bayowolf & Erzsebet's Wiccan Page, available online at http://ftp.rmci.net/idahopyro/0070.htm, or http://www.geocities.com/SouthBeach/Breakers/1965/wiccan.html.
30. Christina Hole, *Witchcraft in England* (New York: Collier, 1947; 1968 edition), 59-60.
31. Rowling, *Sorcerer's Stone*, 66; Rowling, *Chamber of Secrets*, 43.
32. Rowling, *Sorcerer's Stone*, 66; Rowling, *Prisoner of Azkaban*, 5.
33. Rowling, *Sorcerer's Stone*, 66.
34. Rowling, *Sorcerer's Stone*, 66.
35. "Owls in Mythology and Culture," The Owl Pages (Internet Site), available online at www.owlpages.com/mythology/index.html.
36. "Potter Fans Turning to Witchcraft," *This Is London*, August 4, 2000, available online at www.thisislondon.co.uk.
37. Andy Norfolk, quoted in *This Is London*, "Potter Fans Turning to Witchcraft," available online at www.thisislondon.co.uk.
38. John Buckeridge, quoted in *This Is London*, "Potter Fans Turning to Witchcraft," available online at www.thisislondon.co.uk.
39. John Andrew Murray, *Citizen Magazine*.
40. John Andrew Murray, *Citizen Magazine*.
41. Charles Taylor, "The Plot Deepens," Salon.com e-zine, July 10, 2000, available online at www.salon.com/books/review/2000/07/10/potter/.
42. Rowling, *Chamber of Secrets*, 32.
43. Rowling, *Chamber of Secrets*, 39.
44. Rowling, *Chamber of Secrets*, 159.
45. Rowling, *Chamber of Secrets*, 165, 186.
46. Rowling, *Chamber of Secrets*, 166.
47. Rowling, *Chamber of Secrets*, 239, 281.
48. Rowling, *Chamber of Secrets*, 328.
49. Rowling, *Chamber of Secrets*, 330-331.
50. Rowling, *Chamber of Secrets*, 31.
51. Rowling, *Chamber of Secrets*, 31.
52. Rowling, *Chamber of Secrets*, 66.

53. Rowling, *Chamber of Secrets*, 62-63.
54. Rowling, *Chamber of Secrets*, 151.
55. Rowling, *Chamber of Secrets*, 209.
56. Rowling, *Chamber of Secrets*, 128.
57. J.K. Rowling, interview with the BBC, "Harry Potter Fights Back," October 17, 1999, available online at www.bbc.co.uk.
58. J.K. Rowling, quoted in Linton Weeks, *Washington Post*, October 20, 1999, available online at www.northernlight.com; cf. "What Is It About Harry Potter," available online at www.northernlight.com.
59. Rowling, *Chamber of Secrets*, 333.
60. Rowling, *Chamber of Secrets*, 133.
61. Rowling, *Chamber of Secrets*, 156.
62. Gillian Tindall, *A Handbook on Witches* (New York: Castle Books, 1945; 1965 edition), 111-112.
63. Rowling, *Chamber of Secrets*, 234.
64. Rowling, *Chamber of Secrets*, 92-94.
65. Rowling, *Chamber of Secrets*, 130-131.
66. Rowling, *Chamber of Secrets*, 297.
67. Thomas Casey, "J.K. Rowling's Ignorance Is Showing," *Intelligencer Journal* (Lancaster, PA), June 26, 2000, editorial section, available online at www.northernlight.com.
68. Rowling, *Sorcerer's Stone*, 20.
69. Rowling, *Sorcerer's Stone*, 20.
70. Rowling, *Chamber of Secrets*, 2.
71. Rowling, *Prisoner of Azkaban*, 16.
72. J.K. Rowling, *Harry Potter and the Goblet of Fire* (New York: Scholastic, 2000), 27.
73. Rowling, *Sorcerer's Stone*, 1.
74. Rowling, *Prisoner of Azkaban*, 22.
75. Dr. Michael I. Loewy, "Working with Fat Children in Schools," Fall 1988, *Radiance Magazine*, available online at www.radiancemagazine.com/working.htm.
76. S.R. Dyrenforth, D. Freeman, and S.C. Wooley, *Self Esteem, Body Type Preference, and Sociometric Ratings of Peers in Pre-School Children* (1978), unpublished manuscript, Department of Psychiatry, University of Cincinnati College of Medicine. Quoted in Loewy, available online at www.radiancemagazine.com; cf. E.D. Rothblum, "The Stigma of Women's Weight: Social and Economic Realities," *Feminism & Psychology* (Newbury Park: Sage Publications, 1992). Quoted in Loewy, available online at www.radiancemagazine.com.
77. E.D. Rothblum, "I'll Die for the Revolution, but Don't Ask Me Not to Diet: Feminism and the Continuing Stigmatization Of Obesity," as found in S. Wooley, M. Katzman, and P. Fallon, eds., *Feminist Perspectives on Eating Disorders* (New York: Guilford Press, 1993). Quoted in Loewy, available online at www.radiancemagazine.com.

78. M.P. Levine, *How Schools Can Help Combat Student Eating Disorders: Anorexia Nervosa and Bulimia* (Washington, DC: National Education Association of the United States, 1987). Quoted in Loewy, available online at www.radiancemagazine.com.

79. A.J. Hill and E.K. Silver, "Fat, Friendless and Unhealthy: 9-Year Old Children's Perceptions of Body Shape Stereotypes," *International Journal of Obesity* (1995), 19:423-30. Quoted in Loewy, available online at www.radiancemagazine.com.

80. J.R. Staffieri, "A Study of Social Stereotype of Body Image in Children," *Journal of Personal and Social Psychology* (1967), 7:101-104. Quoted in Loewy, available online at www.radiancemagazine.com.

81. Roger Sutton, quoted in Elizabeth Mehren, "Wild About Harry," *Los Angeles Times*, July 28, 2000, available online at www.latimes.com.

FIVE

AZKABAN'S PRISONER: A BRIEF SUMMARY

I was really very lucky growing up—my parents let me read anything and everything. Adult books. The works.

J.K. Rowling,[1]
in response to a child's question

In J.K. Rowling's third book, *Harry Potter and the Prisoner of Azkaban*, the action begins several weeks before Harry starts his third year at Hogwarts, a boarding school for young wizards and witches. His summer holiday has been tremendously unhappy, thanks to the Dursleys (Uncle Vernon, Aunt Petunia and cousin Dudley), his cruel stepfamily. They hate Harry, along with everything that has anything to do with Harry—especially magic.

During this particular summer, Harry's aunt and uncle have been extraordinarily mean. Not only have they locked up all of his magical possessions (e.g., wand, cauldron, spellbooks, etc.), but they have also forbidden him to speak to any neighbors. They will not even allow him to receive phone calls from schoolmates. Harry's best friend, Ron Weasley, tried to call once, but Uncle Vernon hung up on him, warning: "NEVER CONTACT ME AGAIN! DON'T YOU COME NEAR MY FAMILY!"[2]

Harry's frustration and anger reach a boiling point when Uncle Vernon's sister, Aunt Marge, visits. She detests Harry as much, if not more, than the Dursleys do. When Harry was only five years old, she beat him around his shins with a walking stick so he would lose a game of musical statues to Dudley. When Harry was ten years old, he was attacked by Marge's dog, Ripper, who chased Harry up a tree.[3]

After Marge arrives, she immediately begins to abuse Harry verbally, going so far as to make a snide remark in which she subtly refers to Harry's mother as a "bitch."[4] Then, to make matters worse, she flippantly asserts that Harry's parents probably got themselves killed in an accident by driving drunk. Harry protests, "They didn't die in a car crash!" But Marge venomously snaps, "They died in a car crash, you nasty little liar, and left you to be a burden on their decent, hardworking relatives!"[5]

Suddenly, Harry loses control and directs his anger-intensified magic at Marge. She quickly swells like a balloon and floats to the ceiling. Harry then storms from the room and magically bursts open the locked door leading to his possessions. He grabs them up, gathers his other belongings and heads out the door. "I'm going," Harry yells to Uncle Vernon. "I've had enough." Moments later, Harry is wandering the streets. He is stranded, alone, in "the dark Muggle world, with absolutely nowhere to go."[6] Worst of all, he performed "serious magic" in direct violation of the "Restriction of Underage Wizardry" law. He will almost certainly be expelled from Hogwarts.[7]

Harry must now use even more magic in order to light the street where he is stranded. "*Lumos*," he mutters, and a light appears at the end of his wand. Suddenly, from out of thin air comes assistance in the form of "The Knight Bus," an emergency transport system for stranded witches and wizards. Apparently, this service monitors the Muggle world and whenever someone puts their wand out at night, that is a signal for the bus to come and take the wand's owner anywhere he wishes to go. Harry chooses Diagon Alley's Leaky Cauldron, a sort of tavern/inn for wizards and witches.

When he arrives at the inn, Cornelius Fudge (the Minister of Magic) is waiting for him. Harry thinks he is in trouble for all the magic he has performed, but instead Fudge tells Harry he will not be punished, nor will he be expelled from Hogwarts. He is simply supposed to get a room, stay in Diagon Alley and spend the next several weeks preparing for his return to Hogwarts.

It seems Fudge and everyone else in the wizarding world are facing a more serious matter than Harry's rule-breaking. Sirius Black, a viciously wicked wizard with an notably vile background, has escaped from Azkaban (a dungeon-like prison for sorcerers). Sirius allegedly was one of Lord Voldemort's right-hand men who landed in Azkaban soon after the Dark Lord disappeared. Black was captured only after being hunted down by agents from the Ministry of Magic. It was a horrible incident. The street on which Black had been cornered was full of Muggles. But this did not stop Sirius from taking out his wand and "blasting 'alf the street apart."[8] Twelve Muggles were killed, along with one wizard named Peter Pettigrew, who supposedly tried to capture Black single-handedly.

Harry certainly finds the whole account astonishing, but he is subsequently stunned beyond words when he finds out that Sirius used to be best friends with his father, James Potter. Sirius, he learns, was the one who betrayed Harry's parents into the hands of Voldemort. Worse yet, Black is now out to kill Harry. To ensure his safety at school, the Ministry of Magic stations a cadre of "Dementors" (Azkaban guards) around Hogwarts in hopes of capturing Black should he try to enter the area and finish the murderous task that his evil master started. But the black-cloaked, hooded Dementors are not the most enjoyable entities to have around. They are tall, slimy-looking, scabbed creatures that re-semble "something dead that had decayed in water."[9] Their pow-ers are terrible. They cannot be deceived with tricks or disguises, and can even sense someone wearing an Invisibility Cloak. More-over, if they get close to someone, they are able to suck happiness out of that person's soul. This ability, which acts as a sort of para-lyzing weapon, is explained to Harry by Professor Remus Lupin, Hogwarts' new Defense Against the Dark Arts teacher:

> Dementors are among the foulest creatures that walk this earth. They infest the darkest, filthiest places, they glory in decay and despair, they drain peace, hope, and happiness out of the air around them. Even Muggles feel their presence, though they can't see them. Get too near a Dementor and ev-ery good feeling, every happy memory will be sucked out of you. If it can, the Dementor will feed on you long enough to reduce you to something like itself . . . soul-less and evil. You'll be left with nothing but the worst experiences of your life.[10]

But the deadliest weapon these fetid creatures possess is their blood-curdling "Dementor's Kiss." Its use marks the only time Dementors remove their hood. Again, Lupin explains:

> It's what Dementors do when they wish to destroy utterly. I suppose there must be some kind of mouth under there [i.e., under their hood], because they clamp their jaws upon the mouth of the victim and—and suck out his soul. . . . [Y]ou'll have no sense of self anymore, no memory, no . . . anything. There's no chance of at all of recovery. You'll just—exist. As an empty shell. And your soul is gone forever . . . lost.[11]

Lupin eventually reveals that he, too, knew James Potter. In fact, they went to Hogwarts together and were part of a close-knit group of friends that included Lupin, James Potter, Black and a boy named Peter Pettigrew. The foursome were inseparable until Voldemort's enticements drew one of them (allegedly Sirius Black) to the Dark Side. So when Black is at Hogwarts, everyone panics. Security measures are tightened and extra help is brought in to guard the school, but all to no avail. After careful planning, Black lures Harry and his friends to an isolated location, where it looks like Black will finally be able to kill the son of James and Lily Potter.

But there is more to the story than anyone has been told. Instead of killing Harry, Sirius tells him what really happened. As it turns out, Sirius never betrayed James and Lily. The traitor was Peter Pettigrew, who framed Black to make it look as if he had led Voldemort to the Potters. Even the whole terrifying street scene leading up to Black's arrest had been staged by Pettigrew. In reality, it was Black who went after Pettigrew, and it was Pettigrew who had killed all the Muggles with a wand blast. Just before doing so, Pettigrew yelled out to everyone listening that Black had betrayed Lily and James. Then, during the explosion, he transformed himself into a rat and scurried down a drain, leaving Black in the middle of the street as if he was responsible for the carnage.

The real shocker for everyone, however, is that Pettigrew, in rat form, has been living for the last twelve years as Scabbers—Ron Weasley's family pet! This whole story finally comes out, along with the news that Sirius Black also is Harry's true guardian. Finally, after explaining his close relationship to Harry's father, Sirius asks Harry to come and live with him. It is like a dream come true. "Harry's mind was buzzing. He was going to leave the Dursleys. He was going to live with Sirius Black, his parents' best friend. . . . He felt dazed."[12]

But then Pettigrew escapes, and due to various other circumstances, Black still looks guilty. Ultimately, only Dumbledore,

Lupin, Ron, Hermione and Harry know the truth. And the most they can do for Black is to help him escape from his accusers. This is arranged by Harry and Hermione, who go three hours back in time and change a key event that ultimately enables Black to flee Hogwarts before being handed over to wizard authorities who intend for him to endure the Dementor's Kiss.

Book III ends with Sirius Black hiding somewhere in the world, waiting for a time in the future when he can clear his name. Harry, unfortunately, is yet again forced to go back and live with the Dursleys for another summer. His only remaining link to Black is a message he receives by owl. "I believe the dementors are still looking for me," Black writes. "[B]ut they haven't a hope of finding me here. . . . If ever you need me, send word. Your owl will find me. I'll write again soon. Sirius."[13]

ENDNOTES

1. J.K. Rowling, quoted in Mark McGarrity, "A wizard of words puts spell on kids; 'Potter' author visits school in Montclair," *The Star-Ledger* (New Jersey), October 14, 1999, available online at www.montclairkimberley.org/mkasite/jkrowling/buzz.html.
2. J.K. Rowling, *Harry Potter and the Prisoner of Azkaban* (New York: Scholastic Press, 1999), 4.
3. Rowling, *Prisoner of Azkaban*, 18.
4. Rowling, *Prisoner of Azkaban*, 25.
5. Rowling, *Prisoner of Azkaban*, 28-29.
6. Rowling, *Prisoner of Azkaban*, 31.
7. Rowling, *Prisoner of Azkaban*, 31.
8. Rowling, *Prisoner of Azkaban*, 39.
9. Rowling, *Prisoner of Azkaban*, 83.
10. Rowling, *Prisoner of Azkaban*, 187.
11. Rowling, *Prisoner of Azkaban*, 247.
12. Rowling, *Prisoner of Azkaban*, 380.
13. Rowling, *Prisoner of Azkaban*, 432.

SIX

AZKABAN'S PRISONER: A CLOSER LOOK

[I]t is impossible to set aside the fact that in the Bible witch-craft is never viewed positively. Spells, sorcery, divination witches and witchcraft: all these are seen as mere superstitions that do have a dark reality behind them.

Dr. Curt Brannan[1]
Bear Creek School District, Washington

Rev. Rachel Berry of Good Samaritan United Methodist Church (Cupertino, CA) is incensed over all the criticisms that have been leveled at the Harry Potter books. "Lighten up," she suggests in one interview. "The magic is so tongue-in-cheek."[2] Berry's husband, Rev. John Kraps, agrees, stating, "We love Harry Potter, and our whole family is outraged by the opposition of the Christian right."[3] Kraps goes on to say: "There are some distinctly Christian themes in those books, so much so that I'd like to preach a sermon on Harry Potter."[4]

According to Don Compier of the Church Divinity School of the Pacific (the Episcopal seminary at Graduate Theological Union in Berkeley, CA), Rowling's books "stand in the tradition of great British fantasy in which biblical themes and metaphors are wrestling around in powerful ways."[5] Compier believes, for instance, that Potter's magical powers are akin to the "divine gift bestowed by the Holy Spirit at Pentecost." And he draws a rough parallel between Harry and the prophet Samuel: "Pledged to God by his mother, Samuel is raised by strangers and only later learns that he is meant to be a great leader at a crucial junction in history."[6] Compier continues:

> The prophets bring down the rain and stars from heaven. So I am incredulous that people find Harry Potter to be satanic. There's a long-standing Christian tradition that there are powers in the world—powers for good and evil. And in the end, as happens in Harry Potter, the good wins out.[7]

Comparisons such as these are absurd. As previously discussed, the morality presented in Rowling's works has little to do with biblical standards of honesty, integrity and justice. And when it comes to her fantasy battle between "good" and "evil," Rowling does not employ the biblical definitions of "evil" or "good." She has both sides relying on the same power source (magical), both sides resorting to a similar philosophy for discerning right from wrong (subjectivism) and both sides using comparable acts to further their own, albeit different, goals. For example, all the characters (good *and* evil) participate in various forms of occultism when it is necessary, lie when it is expedient and break rules whenever those rules do not serve their needs. From a biblical perspective both sides are technically "evil" or sinful, even though their agendas might be vastly different (see Chapter 8).

This is a spiritually significant truth that the Harry Potter series constantly obscures, especially when it comes to the area of occult involvement. Even a casual overview of the many occult practices accepted in Rowling's books clearly removes her material from anything that might remotely reflect Christian symbolism. Consider the following methods of divination (i.e., the gaining of knowledge about either the unknown or the future) practiced by Harry and other "good" characters in Books I, II and II:

FORTUNE-TELLING/MEDIUMSHIP[8]

Fortune-telling plays a prominent role in *Prisoner of Azkaban* (Book III) through the character of Sibyll Trelawney, Hogwarts' divination teacher. Coincidentally, "Sibyl" was the title given to the women in ancient Greece and Rome who lived in caves and who were "renowned for their gifts of prophecy."[9] During Trelawney's classes, the children study palmistry, reading tea leaves and crystal ball gazing (also called *scrying*).[10] Trelawney pays special attention to scrying, a very old form of divination wherein a person "gazes at a shiny or polished surface to induce a trance-state in which scenes, people, words or images appear as part of a psychic communication. The familiar crystal ball of the gypsy fortune-teller provides the best example; but mirrors, polished metal, coal or bone, and even cups of clear liquid have also been used for scrying."[11]

"Crystal gazing is a particularly refined art," she tells them. "We shall start by practicing relaxing the conscious mind and external eyes . . . so as to clear the Inner Eye and the superconscious."[12]

This is exactly what scryers do when they enter a trance and attempt to contact the spiritual dimension to gain knowledge about the future. The *Encyclopedia of Occultism and Parapsychology* explains that crystal gazing is a form of self-induced hypnosis which helps free one's telepathic powers.[13] In other words, we have a fantasy character giving realistic scrying instructions. Moreover, Trelawney *accurately* predicts: 1) Hermione's dropping of a class; and 2) the escape of Peter Pettigrew.[14]

The manner in which Trelawney gives her prediction about Pettigrew is especially disturbing. Without knowing what is happening, Trelawney becomes momentarily possessed by someone (or something) which, through her mouth, speaks using a loud,

harsh voice described as "quite unlike her own."[15] This scene occurs when Harry and Trelawney are engaged in scrying. Suddenly,
Trelawney goes "rigid in her armchair; her eyes were unfocused
and her mouth sagging."[16] From her gaping jaws, the voice (which
Rowling never identifies) declares, "IT WILL HAPPEN TONIGHT."
The voice continues to make its prophecy, while Trelawney remains transfixed, completely unaware of what is going on:

> THE DARK LORD LIES ALONE AND FRIENDLESS, ABAN-
> DONED BY HIS FOLLOWERS. HIS SERVANT HAS BEEN
> CHAINED THESE TWELVE YEARS. TONIGHT, BEFORE MID-
> NIGHT ... THE SERVANT WILL BREAK FREE AND SET OUT
> TO REJOIN HIS MASTER. THE DARK LORD WILL RISE
> AGAIN WITH HIS SERVANT'S AID, GREATER AND MORE TER-
> RIBLE THAN EVER HE WAS. TONIGHT ... BEFORE MID-
> NIGHT ... THE SERVANT ... WILL SET OUT ... TO REJOIN ...
> HIS MASTER ...[17]

Trelawney's head then falls forward onto her chest, and she
makes "a grunting sort of noise" as if she is exhausted. This incident is nothing less than full mediumship (i.e., demon possession). The history of spiritualism is filled with mediums, who have
always held prominence in occultism as persons "qualified in
some special manner to form a link between the dead and the living."[18] According to the *Encyclopedia of Occultism and Parapsychology*, "[t]he essential qualification of a medium is an abnormal
sensitiveness, which enables him or her to be readily 'controlled'
by disembodied spirits."[19] Trelawney's episode of possession is
perhaps the clearest contradiction of the assertion that characters
in Rowling's novels "don't make contact with a supernatural
world."[20]

A final prediction in Book III is made by none other than Harry
as he takes his final scrying examination. While looking into a

crystal ball, he accurately predicts that one of Hagrid's pets will be set free and fly away. Rowling's actual text suggests that Harry is making the whole thing up, and yet his prediction does come true. The accuracy of his words is our first hint that Harry is one of those rare "True Seers" who has inherited what Trelawney calls the "Gift granted to few" (see chapter 8, pp. 121-122).[21]

HERBOLOGY/POTIONS

Magical potions made from various herbs and fungi play an extremely important role in the education of Harry and his friends.[22] Early in Book I, we read: "Three times a week they went out to the greenhouses . . . where they learned how to take care of all the strange plants and fungi, and found out what they were used for."[23] Hogwarts' students also must take a class on brewing potions. The potions teacher, Professor Snape, states: "I don't expect you will really understand the beauty of the softly simmering cauldron with its shimmering fumes, the delicate power of liquids that creep through human veins, bewitching the mind, ensnaring the senses. . . . I can teach you how to bottle fame, brew glory, even stopper death."[24]

In *The Rebirth of Witchcraft*, modern-day witch Doreen Valiente explains that medieval witches did indeed have a "very extensive and specialized knowledge of herbs, plants and trees."[25] She also writes that "[m]ost country witches would have an herb garden and use its products in their spells. . . . [with] all sorts of plants, twigs, leaves or fungi of which any magical use was made."[26]

As we have seen, Rowling tends to blend fantasy with reality, and her potion/herbology references are no exception to this rule. In Book I, for instance, the potions professor speaks of adding "powdered root of asphodel to an infusion of *wormwood*," which creates a Draught of Living Death.[27] In the real world, wormwood is used to make *absinthe*, a hallucinogenic liqueur that has been illegal for sale or use in America since 1915. Its many harmful symptoms include delirium, paralysis, convulsions, brain damage, renal failure and death.

In *Sorcerer's Stone*, we also find Harry looking up "Dittany" in *One Thousand Magical Herbs and Fungi*. This plant, too, plays an important role in witchcraft. Dittany is the ritual herb used by witches on Samhain/Halloween. It also aids witches in astral projection,[28] an occult practice which allegedly entails the separation of one's conscious self from the body, thereby enabling one to visit other locations in our world freely or pass through the cosmos to other dimensions of reality.

Rowling's depiction of potions and mixtures might easily cause a child to try making his own Potter-potions based on ingredients available to him. This is not as farfetched as it may sound. Recently, an individual who had read about absinthe decided to make his own cocktail from a wormwood extract that was obtained on the Internet. This person ended up in the hospital with renal failure.[29]

PALMISTRY/TEA LEAVES/FIRE OMENS

As was mentioned before, the character of Sibyll Trelawney, the divination teacher, also teaches *palmistry* to her students.[30] This pseudoscience, based on the lines and markings on a person's palm, supposedly can reveal an individual's future. It dates back as early as the ancient Brahmins of India and was known to Aristotle (384-322 B.C.). Palmistry usually is mentioned by Rowling in connection with reading tea leaves and interpreting omens.[31] Reading tea leaves is done by swirling the dregs of a tea cup three times, then dumping it out on to a saucer. The pattern of leaves remaining in the cup is then interpreted. Fire omens (pyromancy) are read as an occultist gazes at the movement of flames while throwing leaves, twigs or incense into a fire. Changes in the coloring and intensity of the flames are then interpreted as omens of things to come.

ARITHMANCY

This form of divination, studied by Hermione in Book III (pp. 57, 111, 295, 316), dates back to the ancient Greeks and Chaldeans. According to the *Dictionary of Mysticism and the Occult*, the Greeks used this precursor to numerology as a means of discerning the winner of a battle. They would analyze the names of opponents and try to predict the victor by the numerical value of each combatant's name. The Chaldeans linked their arithmancy to the seven planets then known to exist in the solar system.

NUMEROLOGY

Page 315 of Book III reveals that in addition to arithmancy, Hermione also studies numerology. This form of divination "analyzes the symbolism of numbers and ascribes numerical values to the letters of the alphabet."[32] Neville Drury's *Dictionary of Mysticism and the Occult* traces the popular origins of numerology back to the magician/astrologer Cornelius Agrippa (1486-1535). This German occultist is best known for his three-volume defense of magic titled *De occulta philosophiae* (written c. 1510, published 1531). Interestingly, Rowling briefly mentions an "Agrippa" in Book I.[33]

ANCIENT RUNES

According to Book III, the Study of Ancient Runes is one Hermione's many classes.[34] Runes (ancient Germanic characters) can be used for writing things which one does not want others to be able to read. . . . [Runes] can also be written or inscribed for magickal workings . . . can also be cut into staves, and then cast down as a form of divination . . . [and] can also be used to inscribe the name of an object, such as a weapon or armor. These names take on magickal meanings, and both the naming of the object and the encryption of that name are very important.[35]

CHARMS

Throughout the Potter series, Rowling has her characters either studying or working "charms."[36] A charm is basically an incantation of some kind that is designed to bring about a positive effect. These incantations also can be used to endow any object (an amulet or talisman) with magical power.[37]

In addition to these forms of divination, Book III contains many examples of phrases, names and legends that have counterparts in actual occultism.[38] For instance, the names of two characters (*Albus* Dumbledore, *Rubeus* Hagrid) and a password (*Fortuna Major*) are directly taken from astrological *geomancy*,[39] yet another kind of divination that "had its heyday in the Renaissance during Western Europe's transition from the medieval to the modern world."[40] At the Internet's New Age Access site, Anthony Louis describes the practice as follows:

Geomancy is any system of divination (an attempt to get in touch with the divine) related to manipulation of the earth. . . . It is similar to the casting of lots referred to in the Latin and Greek classics. . . . [G]eomancy is akin to horary astrology. In fact, the same philosophical principle—cosmic sympathy—underlies both geomantic divination and horary astrology.[41]

A prominent segment of *Prisoner of Azkaban* has to do with the appearance of several *boggarts* at Hogwarts. These, too, are characters taken from occult mythology. Folk-Tales.com gives an excellent description of these entities:

> Boggarts, in their tattered and filthy clothing, are nasty household spirits. They are usually recognized due to the unusual number of mishaps, sometimes fatal in nature, that occur while a boggart is in the house. No way is known to eliminate the boggart, except leaving the house, although sometimes this doesn't even work, as boggarts are some-times transported with household items.[42]

Even more pivotal in Book III is the *Grim*, a death omen in the form of a large black dog that Trelawney sees stalking Harry. The divination teacher observes this omen in Harry's tea leaves. "The Grim, my dear, the Grim!" she cries. "The giant, spectral dog that haunts churchyards. My dear boy, it is an omen—the worst omen—of *death*!"[43]

In British and Scandinavian folklore, the word *grim* is a generic name for "a spirit which associates with humanity and human dwell-ings. The church grim . . . haunts churches and graveyards. . . . [T]he church grim normally takes the form of a huge black dog . . . [that] will not leave its designated churchyard."[44] The origin of this legend probably derived from the belief that "the first person to be buried in a churchyard would have to guard any subsequent inhumed souls."[45] But in order to free the first individual from this duty, a dog would be sacrificed and buried in the yard before any human being was laid to rest on the church grounds. This dog, usually an all-black one, would then become the cemetery's guardian instead of the first human bur-ied on the site.[46]

One character in Book III, Sirius Black, actually turns out to be a wizard who is able to transform himself into a huge, black canine. Interestingly, Sirius (the brightest star in the sky) is known in most mythologies throughout the world as the "Dog Star." In other words, Black's name literally means "black dog." Again, we see pagan mythology playing a significant role in Rowling's fantasy.

It is obvious that Rowling has pulled a great deal of material from actual occult legends, beliefs and history. More significant, however, are her many references to contemporary occult practices, which means that the "magic" in her books would more properly be considered "magick." This word "magick" was popularized by the infamous occultist Aleister Crowley (1875-1947), who stated, "Magick is the Science and Art of causing Change to occur in conformity with Will."[47] He deliberately added the "k" to magic primarily to differentiate his rituals from those practiced by other occultists of his day, but the spelling is now widely used to distinguish *any* form of occult magic from sleight-of-hand tricks performed by stage magicians.[48]

All occultists use this spelling in reference to their rites, ceremonies, spells and incantations. It is an exclusively *religious* word, as noted at Fingle's Cave, an Internet resource site for "Celtic Wicca in Northern New England."[49] According to this witchcraft site, "Wicca is a religion that embraces magick as one of it's basic concepts. In Wicca, as in many other religions, magick is a religious practice. . . . 'Magick is the projection of natural energies to produce needed effects.'"[50]

Although Rowling may spell the word magic without a "k" throughout her books, the occult activities she describes are certainly more than stage illusions or sleight-of-hand tricks. They clearly are references to magick practices that are part of the contemporary religion of witchcraft (e.g., palmistry, astrology, mediumship/channeling). Nevertheless, her fantasy series continues to be read in public school classrooms throughout America.

POTTERETHICS

In a 1999 article published by Gospel Communications, Terry Mattingly wrote, "No one wants to be reactionary. But we have to take issues of good and evil seriously and we just can't endorse the kind of moral ambiguity that we see in these books."[51] Yet, numerous individuals continue to overlook this very serious flaw in Rowling's material. In August 2000, for instance, officials of the famous eleventh-century cathedral in Gloucester, England granted Warner Brothers permission to use the historical church as Hogwarts School of Witchcraft and Wizardry in the upcoming Harry Potter movie. The Dean of Gloucester, the Very Reverend Nicholas Bury, defended the decision, stating: "[I]n the Potter books goodness, honesty and integrity overcome lies and deceit."[52]

But in fact, the books clearly present far too much moral subjectivity and patently unbiblical actions to be of any ethical value. Moreover, when it comes to *Prisoner of Azkaban* (Book III), there is a marked increase in the unbiblical attitudes and actions among the characters. For example, in addition to lying and rule-breaking, which continue unabated in Book III, we have drunkenness, crude language and swearing—all done by "good" characters.

Although these latter behaviors exist in Books I and II, they are more prevalent in Book III. Consider the common insult used by Rowling's characters: the British slang "git." According to *A Dictionary of Slang*, "git" is a derogatory term for "an idiot or contemptible person."[53] The online *British-American Lexicon* describes a git as a "stupid person, jerk, also nasty person, real bastard."[54] In the slang dictionary at Princeton University's web site, under the heading "Exclamations, Crudity & Insults (Rough Slang)," is found this definition: "*git*—jerk, bastard (v. strong)."[55]

This term, however, is used by Hagrid in Book I on page 141 ("Harry and Ron were delighted to hear Hagrid call Filch 'that old git' ") and page 303 ("I told the evil git how ter get past Fluffy!" Ron Weasley uses it in Book II on page 163 ("That's because he's a brainless *git*") and page 303 ("I'm okay—this git's not, though"). And in Book III, George Weasley calls Draco Malfoy, "That little git" (p. 97). At one point during Book III, Rowling even has a student screaming, "YOU CHEATING SCUM! . . . YOU FILTHY, CHEATING B —" He is stopped from swearing only by the presence of Professor McGonagall. But the word he intimates is obvious to child readers.[56]

Less specific, but more open to the imagination, are comments in Book II such as "Dean swore loudly" (p. 253) and "Ron swore" (p. 259). In Book III, the word "damn" is used on page 23 and "bitch" on page 25 (although, in fairness, this is spoken by an "evil" character). But the most offensive language (to Christians, at least) appears on page 113 of Book III, where Draco Malfoy uses God's name in vain, shouting, "God, this place is going to the dogs."

Also troublesome are Rowling's consistent and positive references to adults drinking to the point of drunkenness in front of children. (In fact, Harry's best adult friend, Hagrid, could be considered an alcoholic—he constantly turns to strong drink when either depressed *or* joyful. In a scene from Book III, one of the children even has to take charge and tell him he's had enough.)

Consider the following instances of excessive alcoholic consumption:

Sorcerer's Stone:

> Harry watched Hagrid getting redder and redder in the face as he called for more wine, finally kissing Professor McGonagall on the cheek. (p. 203-204)

"Hagrid told that stranger how to get past Fluffy . . . it must've been easy once he'd got Hagrid drunk." (p. 266)

Chamber of Secrets:

Dumbledore led them in a few of his favorite [Christmas] carols, Hagrid booming more and more loudly with every goblet of eggnog he consumed. (p. 212)

Prisoner of Azkaban:

"I think you've had enough to drink, Hagrid," said Hermione firmly. She took the tankard from the table and went outside to empty it. (p. 121)

It was Hagrid, making his way up to the castle, singing at the top of his voice, and weaving slightly as he walked. A large bottle was swinging from his hands. . . .

They watched Hagrid meander tipsily up to the castle. (p. 405)

When it comes to lying and rule-breaking, Book III continues in the same vein as Books I and II. Rowling's "good" characters, in fact, resort to so much deceitful behavior in Book III that they actually seem to be promoting it as a valuable tool for successful living. Although such was presented in a rather disguised way in Books I and II, *Prisoner of Azkaban* flaunts the deception used by Harry and his friends, clearly establishing it as amusing and beneficial.

On page 34 of Book III, Harry lies to a bus driver. On page 155, he lies to Professor Lupin, who is supposed to be his friend. On page 246, Harry lies again to Lupin—and this time he lies "quickly." Harry then lies to Professor Snape on pages 283-285. Ron also lies to Snape on page 289. Then, in order to "cover up" for Harry and Ron, Lupin lies to Snape on pages 289-290. It is further revealed on page 353 that when

Dumbledore first became Headmaster, he lied to his staff, the students, their parents and local townspeople so that Lupin—a werewolf—could attend Hogwarts when he was still a young boy. And to repay Dumbledore, Lupin broke the rules by wandering off school grounds as a wolf, which nearly caused the deaths of several innocent people. Lupin, who now regrets his youthful actions, explains how easily he dismissed his guilt:

> I sometimes felt guilty about betraying Dumbledore's trust. . . . [H]e had no idea I was breaking the rules he had set down for my own and others' safety. . . . But I always managed to forget my guilty feelings every time we [James, Sirius, and Peter] sat down to plan our next month's adventure.[57]

On page 326, we find that Hermione is "flattered" because Harry and Ron are astounded over her punching another student and walking out on a teacher. Their admiration is set in contrast to an earlier episode in which Ron had scathingly rebuked Hermione, saying, "Why didn't you lie, Hermione? You should've said Neville did it all himself" (p. 129).

Readers finally find out in *Prisoner of Azkaban* why Harry seems so bent toward rule-breaking and lying. His father, James Potter, also "didn't set much store by rules."[58] In reference to Sirius Black and James Potter, Professor McGonagall remembers: "Black and Potter. Ringleaders of their little gang. Both very bright, of course—exceptionally bright, in fact—but I don't think we've ever had such a pair of troublemakers."[59]

Lupin, who was a close friend of James', reveals that Harry's father and two other Hogwarts students (Sirius Black and Peter Pettigrew) secretly and illegally became animagi—i.e., wizards who can turn themselves into animals. Moreover, they were supposed to register with the Minister of Magic, but remained unregistered, again contrary to wizard law.[60] Of course, as always, actions such as these rarely have negative consequences.

In Book III Rowling has Harry inheriting a "Marauders Map" from George and Fred Weasley. This map magically shows all the corridors in Hogwarts and displays the movements of teachers and students. The map—originally made by James Potter, Sirius Black, Peter Pettigrew and Remus Lupin—was stolen by the Weasley brothers from a drawer marked "Confiscated and Highly Dangerous." To activate the map, George taps it, saying, "*I solemnly swear that I am up to no good.*"[61] As Fred gives it to Harry, he solemnly sighs about the map's makers: "Noble men, working tirelessly to help a new generation of lawbreakers."[62]

Rowling's message is simple: If someone is "good" and he has good intentions, or if he is particularly clever, or exceptionally bright, or somehow more special than others, then he can break rules, lie and steal. On page 40 of Book III, Rowling herself writes: "He, Harry, had broken wizard law just like Sirius Black." But how do wizard authorities respond to Harry breaking a prime directive about underage wizards not using magic in the Muggle world? Page 45 of Book III, which contains a conversation between Harry and Cornelius Fudge (Minister of Magic), reads,

> "I broke the law!" Harry said. "The Decree for the Restriction of Underage Wizardry!"
>
> "Oh, my dear boy, we're not going to punish you for a little thing like that!" cried Fudge, waving his crumpet impatiently.

Even Harry's friends understand that he is special and gets special treatment. His best friend, Ron Weasley, responds to Fudge's leniency by saying, "Famous Harry Potter and all that. I'd hate to see what the Ministry'd do to *me* if I blew up an aunt."[63] Ultimately, Rowling's characters seem to share an unspoken admiration for Harry's willingness to do his own thing. As Headmaster Dumbledore articulates in Book II, Harry has those rare qualities common to Slytherin House students, including resourcefulness, determination and "a certain disregard for rules."[64]

This "disregard for rules" does not seem to bother Dumbledore. In fact, usually the only individuals who *ever* seem to care about following rules are evil characters like the Dursleys, or mean characters like Professor Snape and Hogwarts' caretaker, Argus Filch. Rowling writes: "Filch burst suddenly through a tapestry to Harry's right, wheezing and looking wildly about for the rule-breaker."[65] In Book II, Snape legitimately complains, "Professor Dumbledore, these boys [Harry and Ron] have flouted the Decree for the Restriction of Underage Wizardry, caused serious damage to an old and valuable tree—surely acts of this nature—"[66] But neither Ron or Harry are appropriately punished. They are merely given a token penalty of light detention. In the end, Snape is the one who does not get his way (also see Chapter 7).

Such negative depictions of disciplinarians, coupled with positive depictions of deceitfulness, may be part of what is drawing children to the Potter series. It is fun for them to read about kids being "bad" and getting away with it, while stupid adults seem either unable or unwilling to punish them. One seven-year-old wrote to a newspaper in Britain, "I like Harry Potter because he is rather cheeky—he isn't always good."[67] Another nine-year-old said: "I think all the characters are very well described, especially Harry and his friends Ron and Hermione. Together they are very mischievous."[68] Eleven-year-old Megan Campanelle told the *New York Times* she likes reading the Potter series because it's "like we're reading about ourselves.... They like to do stuff like we like to do. They like to get in trouble."[69]

Amazingly, many parents steadfastly maintain that in Rowling's books, Hogwarts "promotes studious students and obedience to the rules."[70]

AGE 6 AND UP?

Children love to be "grossed out," as they say. Anyone who knows anything about kids will testify to this widespread phenomenon. Crude jokes and coarse things are fun for them to read about, look at, hear and discuss. It just seems to be part of being young. And Rowling's series is filled with end-on-end images that cater to this juvenile sense of humor. In Book I, for instance, there are references to "troll boogers" (p. 177) and jelly bean-like candies with tastes ranging from vomit to ear wax (pp. 104, 300-301).

Book II continues exploiting this approach to humor in various ways. For example, there is a description of one potion that turns "the khaki color of booger" (p. 216). Another scene has Ron accidentally cursing himself, which in turn causes him to begin belching up hundreds of slugs.[71] Additionally, *Chamber of Secrets* includes a game of Head Hockey, in which a group of a dozen headless horsemen play a sort of polo match with the head of one of the ghosts.[72]

Book III merrily trundles down the same path, its humor reminiscent of contemporary horror/comedy films such as *Beetlejuice* and *The Adams Family*. On page 50, Rowling describes a wizard game called Gobstones in which "stones squirt a nasty-smelling liquid into the other player's face when they lose a point."[73] Page 138 tells of a single, bloody eyeball that transforms into a severed hand and creeps along the floor like a crab. And in a kind of nightmarish twist on *Willy Wonka and the Chocolate Factory*, Rowling has a wizard candy shop that has an Unusual Taste section featuring blood-flavored lollipops and Cockroach Clusters.[74]

Book IV, *Harry Potter and the Goblet of Fire*, pushes the bounds of crass humor even farther. For example, during one divination class where students are studying the planets, a girl named Lavender Brown discovers an unexpected planet. Professor Trelawney explains, "It is Uranus, my dear." Ron Weasley jokes, "Can I have a look at Uranus too, Lavender?"[75] In another scene, an elderly wizard complains about having to trade his loose-fitting robe in for pants, saying: "I'm not putting them on. . . . I like a healthy breeze 'round my privates, thanks."[76]

Gruesome images also abound in *Goblet of Fire*. A shy child, for instance, is forced to "disembowel a barrel full of horned toads."[77] And Harry jokingly predicts "his own death by decapitation."[78] This latter image fits well with Rowling's ongoing references to Nearly Headless Nick, the Gryffindor House resident ghost. He is the apparition of Sir Nicholas De Mimsy-Porpington, who died on Halloween in 1492 after being partially decapitated in a botched execution. Now, although he struggles to keep his head on, it often flops off in front of students, only to dangle from an inch or so "of ghostly skin and muscle that still attached it to his neck."[79]

Finally, Book IV supplies several stupendously "gross" scenes involving bubotubers, which are black, squirming plants that fourth year students must squeeze in order to harvest the vegetation's "pus" into bottles. This foul substance is used as "[a]n excellent remedy for more stubborn forms of acne." Rowling writes:

> Squeezing the bubotubers was disgusting, but oddly satisfying. As each swelling was popped, a large amount of thick yellowish-green liquid burst forth, which smelled strongly of petrol. They caught it in the bottles as Professor Sprout had indicated, and by the end of the lesson had collected several pints.[80]

Rowling obviously understands what children like to read and has delivered it to them. But are these images appropriate for children? Parents must ask themselves if this is the kind of humor that a child should be encouraged to develop. Aren't there other books that present more wholesome avenues of entertainment?

The questionable content has not stopped Rowling's first three volumes from becoming mega-best-sellers. Their sales, however, pale in comparison to those racked up by Rowling's fourth book, *Harry Potter and the Goblet of Fire*. It is to this 734-page tome, one of the longest children's books ever written, that we now turn.

ENDNOTES

1. Curt Brannan, "What About Harry Potter," available online at www.tbcs.org/papers/article04.htm.
2. Rev. Rachel Berry, quoted in Richard Scheinin, "Trouble with Harry? The Exploits of the Books' Boy Hero Reflect Christian Values, Say Fans from a Diverse Group of Denominations," *San Jose (CA) Mercury News*, November 13, 1999, available online at www.newslibrary.com.
3. John Kraps, quoted in Scheinin.
4. Kraps, quoted in Scheinin.
5. Don Compier, quoted in Scheinin.
6. Compier, quoted in Scheinin.
7. Compier, quoted in Scheinin.
8. Interestingly, Rowling presents two contradictory messages about divination in her books. Several comments seem to suggest that fortune-telling is not a very reliable form of gaining knowledge. On page 109 of *Prisoner of Azkaban*, for instance, Professor McGonagall says, "Divination is one of the most imprecise branches of magic." But this statement, more than a criticism of divination, implies that other "branches of magic" *are* precise and are therefore acceptable. An even more telling comment follows: "True Seers are very rare." This second remark, which greatly qualifies McGonagall's earlier reproach, legitimizes divination by revealing that its imprecision is due only to the fact that "True Seers" are rare. Far from denouncing fortune-telling, McGonagall is endorsing it.
9. Nevill Drury, *Dictionary of Mysticism and the Occult* (San Francisco: Harper & Row, 1985), 238.
10. J.K. Rowling, *Harry Potter and the Prisoner of Azkaban* (New York: Scholastic, 1999), 103-104, 296.
11. Drury, 241.
12. Rowling, *Prisoner of Azkaban*, 297.

13. Leslie A. Shepard, ed., *Encyclopedia of Occultism and Parapsychology* (Detroit: Gale Research, 1991), 1:285.

14. Rowling, *Prisoner of Azkaban*, 148, 299, 324.

15. Rowling, *Prisoner of Azkaban*, 324.

16. Rowling, *Prisoner of Azkaban*.

17. Rowling, *Prisoner of Azkaban*.

18. Shepard, 2:1066.

19. Shepard.

20. Chuck Colson, "Witches and Wizards: The Harry Potter Phenomenon," *Break-Point Commentary*, November 2, 1999, available online at www.breakpoint.org.

21. Rowling, *Prisoner of Azkaban*, 103.

22. Rowling, *Prisoner of Azkaban*, 124.

23. J.K. Rowling, *Harry Potter and the Sorcerer's Stone* (New York: Scholastic, 1997), 133.

24. J.K. Rowling, *Sorcerer's Stone*, 137.

25. Doreen Valiente, *The Rebirth of Witchcraft* (Custer, WA: Phoenix Publishing, 1989), 83.

26. Valiente, 87.

27. Rowling, *Sorcerer's Stone*, 137 (emphasis added).

28. Listings of use for "dittany" in witchcraft can be found at www.paganism.com/ag/herbs/d.html.

29. "Thujone," available online at www.chem.orst.edu/ch331-7t/ch335/MOTD120.htm.

30. Rowling, *Prisoner of Azkaban*, 103, 296.

31. Rowling, *Prisoner of Azkaban*, 104.

32. Drury, 196.

33. Rowling, *Sorcerer's Stone*, 102. Agrippa's numerical symbolism was as follows: One—the origin of all things (God); Two—marriage and agreement and/or division and evil; Three—the Trinity, wisdom; Four—solidarity, permanence, foundation; Five—justice; Six—creation, labor, service; Seven—life; Eight—fullness, balance; Nine—cosmic significance; and Ten—completeness. Agrippa further gave each letter of the alphabet a number. Using these numbers in conjunction with various formulas, the numerologist supposedly is able to discern knowledge about a person's present state or their future (Drury, 196).

34. Rowling, *Prisoner of Azkaban*, 57.

35. Crystal Miller, "Runes and Their Meaning," available online at www.witchhaven.com. The term "rune," which comes from a root word meaning "mystery" or "secret," refers to any set of secret symbols or letters used as either a magical inscription or as a means of divination.

36. Rowling, *Sorcerer's Stone*, 133; Rowling, *Chamber of Secrets*, 20.

37. Doreen Valiente, *An ABC of Witchcraft* (New York: St. Martin's Press, 1973), 22.

38. Another individual whose name is taken from history is "Rosmerta," Rowling's barmaid character in Book III (pp. 202-207). In Gaulish Celtic mythology, "Rosmerta was the goddess of fire, warmth, and abundance. A flower queen and hater of marriage, Rosmerta was also the queen of death. [She was] a Celtic goddess of fertility and wealth,

whose cult was widely spread in Northeast Gaul" (Todd Gavelek, "Rosmerta," available online at www.pantheon.org/mythica/articles/r/rosmerta.html).

39. Albus Dumbledore appears often in the Potter books, as does Hagrid, whose first name only appears in Book III, on page 93. Fortuna Major is used as a password in Book III, page 94. In astrological geomancy, Albus, which means "white," as in the white hair of the wise old prophet, is associated with ideas of "wisdom, clear thought, news, and communication. Albus is a positive symbol." Rubeus, which means "red," is the color of Mars and of blood spilled in violence. "Rubeus is a negative symbol, the dark side of Scorpio and Mars, associated with danger, lust, addiction, passion, fire, aggression, and destruction. It is generally unfortunate, except where a show of force or eroticism is needed." Fortuna Major, which means "major fortune," usually shows significant good fortune.

40. Anthony Louis, "Astrological Geomancy," available online at www.accessnewage.com/articles/astro/TLOUIS4.htm.

41. Louis, available online at www.accessnewage.com/articles/astro/TLOUIS4.htm.

42. Cat Eldridge, ed. "Anglo-Celtic Folktales," *The Green Man Review*, available online at www.folk-tales.com/anglo_celtic_folktales.html.

43. Rowling, *Prisoner of Azkaban*, 107.

44. Graeme Davis, "Black Dogs, Church Grims, and Hell Hounds: Supernatural Canines in British Folklore," *Roleplayer* #30, January 1993, available online at www.sjgames.com/gurps/Roleplayer/Roleplayer30/GhostDogs.html; cf. Coamhin O'Dubhfaigh, "Another Shaggy Dog Story," *Talking Stick*, No. 11, 1993.

45. O'Dubhfaigh.

46. Davis; cf. O'Dubhfaigh.

47. Aleister Crowley, *Magick In Theory and Practice* (New York: Dover Publications, 1976), 12.

48. See discussion on Crowley at: http://www.netmeg.net/faq/people/esoterica/alt.magick/kreeeping-ooze/01.html; also see Crowley, *Magick In Theory and Practice*.

49. Statement available online at http://homepage.fcgnetworks.net/pmather/wicca/index.html.

50. http://homepage.fcgnetworks.net/pmather/wicca/ index.html.

51. Terry Mattingly, "Harry Potter: Is He Safe?," Gospel Communications Network, October 27, 1999, available online at www.gospelcom.net/tmattingly/1999/col/col.10.27.99.html.

52. "Cathedral Says OK to Harry Potter," Religion News Service, August 12, 2000, available at www.religionnews.com.

53. *Online Dictionary of Slang*, available online at www.peevish.co.uk/slang/g.htm.

54. *British-American Online Lexicon*, available online at www.peak.org/~jeremy/dictionary/lexe-a.html.

55. *Princeton Online Slang Dictionary*, available online at www.eeb.princeton.edu/~ben/vocab/vocab.html.

56. Rowling, *Prisoner of Azkaban*, 310.

57. Rowling, *Prisoner of Azkaban*, 355-356.

58. Rowling, *Prisoner of Azkaban*, 284.
59. Rowling, *Prisoner of Azkaban*, 204.
60. Rowling, *Prisoner of Azkaban*, 351-352.
61. Rowling, *Prisoner of Azkaban*, 192.
62. Rowling, *Prisoner of Azkaban*, 193.
63. Rowling, *Prisoner of Azkaban*, 56.
64. Rowling, *Chamber of Secrets*, 333.
65. Rowling, *Chamber of Secrets*, 125.
66. Rowling, *Chamber of Secrets*, 81.
67. Jasmine Wark, letter to the editor, *London Times*, June 29, 2000, available online at londontimes.co.uk.
68. Anastasia Wark, letter to the editor, *London Times*, June 29, 2000, available online at londontimes.co.uk.
69. Megan Campanelle, quoted in Jodi Wilgoren, "Don't Give Us Little Wizards, The Anti-Potter Parents Cry," *New York Times*, November 1, 1999, available online at www.nytimes.com.
70. Angela, "Harry Potter Novels and the Bible (Commentary)," *Children's Express*, March 2000, 41, available online at http://www.cenews.org/comments/feedback00.htm.
71. Rowling, *Chamber of Secrets*, 116, 118.
72. Rowling, *Chamber of Secrets*, 136-137.
73. Rowling, *Prisoner of Azkaban*, 50.
74. Rowling, *Prisoner of Azkaban*, 197.
75. J.K. Rowling, *Harry Potter and the Goblet of Fire* (New York: Scholastic, 2000), 201.
76. Rowling, *Goblet of Fire*, 84.
77. Rowling, *Goblet of Fire*, 209.
78. Rowling, *Goblet of Fire*, 223.
79. Rowling, *Goblet of Fire*, 182.
80. Rowling, *Goblet of Fire*, 195. Rowling brings up "bubotuber pus" again on page 541.

SEVEN

GOBLET OF DEATH:
A BRIEF SUMMARY

[T]his is the book in which the deaths start. I always planned it this way. It's become a bit of an idée fixe with me. I have to follow it just the way I wanted to write it and no one is going to knock me off course.

J.K. Rowling[1]

J.K. Rowling's fourth book, *Harry Potter and the Goblet of Fire*, answers many questions about Voldemort, his evil servants and the mysterious years immediately following the murder of Harry's parents. Book IV also finds Harry and his friends approaching adolescence, which allows for hints of sexuality to appear in the plot. Additionally, Book IV sets the storyline direction for the final three books in Rowling's seven-volume series (scheduled for publication by 2003).

Goblet of Fire begins in the dilapidated Riddle House, located on a hill overlooking the sleepy village of Little Hangleton. Fifty years earlier, the house had been regarded as "the largest and grandest building for miles around."[2] At that time, the mansion served as home to the elderly Mr. and Mrs. Riddle, and their adult son, Tom. But everything changed one morning when all three Riddles were found dead "with their eyes wide open."[3] Oddly, none of them had been "poisoned, stabbed, shot, strangled, suffocated or . . . harmed at all."[4] They had died of fright!

The only stranger seen nearby at the time of the murders was a teenage boy.[5] This boy was young Tom Riddle, the Hogwarts student who would eventually become Lord Voldemort (see *Chamber of Secrets*). As it turns out, the elderly couple was the boy's grandparents, and their adult son, also named Tom, was the boy's estranged father. Voldemort-Tom had tracked them all down and killed them for revenge, as Voldemort himself explains:

> My mother, a witch who lived here in this village, fell in love with [my father]. . . . But he abandoned her when she told him what she was. . . . He didn't like magic. . . . He left her and returned to his Muggle parents before I was even born . . . and she died giving birth to me, leaving me to be raised in a Muggle orphanage . . . but I vowed to find him. . . . I revenged myself upon him, that fool who gave me his name . . . *Tom Riddle*.[6]

Now, fifty years later, the only resident of the property is seventy-seven-year-old Frank Bryce, the gardener who continued living alone in the servant's quarters. One night he sees lights on in the old mansion, and investigates, thinking the intruders are mischievous children. But Frank is wrong. Upon entering the home, he overhears two men in one of the mansion's rooms. The first voice belongs to Peter Pettigrew, the traitor in *Prisoner of Azkaban* who escaped from Sirius Black and Remus Lupin (see Chapter 5). Pettigrew is with Voldemort, or rather, what is left of him.

The Dark Lord is nothing but a slimy, hairless creature. His skin, far from anything recognizable as skin, is a dark, raw, reddish-black mass of scales. His legs are thin and feeble, and his face is "flat and snake-like, with gleaming red eyes."[7] This hideous monstrosity is the last thing Frank ever sees. As the old man screams in horror, Voldemort raises his wand and mutters, *Avada Kedavra!*," the death curse. Frank is "dead before he hit[s] the floor."[8]

At that very moment, Harry, who lives miles away, wakes up from a frightful dream. Moreover, the lightning bolt-shaped scar on his forehead, which only hurts when Voldemort is near, burns with pain. The "dream" featured Pettigrew, Voldemort and a dying old man. Harry also heard Voldemort talking about someone he had murdered (a woman named Bertha Jorkins) as well as someone he was going to murder. And that someone was going to be Harry. Obviously, the nightmare actually was a vision of what had transpired at the rundown Riddle house. But because Harry believes it is only a dream, he tells no one about it.

All of this takes place two weeks before Harry is supposed to start his fourth year at Hogwarts. Although he still lives with the Dursleys (his cruel stepfamily), things have not been nearly as bad as usual because the Dursleys know that Harry's godfather is Sirius Black, the infamous mass murderer. Harry, of course, knows that Black is innocent, but keeps this information to himself because he realizes that fear of Black is the only thing keeping the Dursleys from verbally and physically abusing him.

Finally, Harry gets a note from the mother of his best friend, Ron Weasley. It is an official invitation for Harry to stay with the Weasley family for the rest of the summer. Moreover, Ron and his family have tickets to the see the Quidditch World Cup match between Ireland and Belgium. This championship game is akin to America's Super Bowl or Europe's World Cup soccer match. (Quidditch however is a sport played by wizards/witches on flying broomsticks.)

When Harry moves in with the Weasleys, all goes well until the Quidditch championship. The game itself, attended by 100,000 wizards, is a fun-filled and exhilarating event. But afterward, amid thousands of wizard families, post-game violence erupts. Hooded

Death Eaters (followers of Voldemort) appear suddenly and terrorize everyone. Worst of all, into the night sky is beamed the Death Mark, "a colossal skull, comprised of what looked like tiny emerald stars, with a serpent protruding from its mouth like a tongue . . . blazing in a haze of greenish smoke."[9]

Thirteen years earlier, this was the same sign Voldemort and his followers projected into the sky over the bodies of those whom they had murdered. It was one of the bleakest periods in wizard history, one that even affected Muggles, as Mr. Weasley tells his son, Ron:

> [Voldemort] and his followers sent the Dark Mark into the air whenever they killed. . . . The terror it inspired . . . you have no idea, you're too young. Just picture coming home and finding the Dark Mark hovering over your house, and knowing what you're about to find inside. . . . Everyone's worst fear . . . the very worst. . . . Half the Muggle killings back when You-Know-Who was in power were done for fun.[10]

Voldemort's reign of terror also is remembered by Sirius Black, who on pages 526-527 of *Goblet of Fire*, gives his own impressions of this terrifying era in wizard history:

> Imagine that Voldemort's powerful now. You don't know who his supporters are, and you don't know who's working for him . . . you know he can control people so that they do terrible things without being able to stop themselves. You're scared for yourself, and your family, and your friends. Every week, news comes of more deaths, more disappearances, more torturing . . . the Ministry of Magic's in disarray, they don't know what to do, they're trying to keep everything hidden from the Muggles, but meanwhile, Muggles are dying too. Terror everywhere . . . panic . . . confusion . . . that's how it used to be.[11]

The Death Eater incident makes the whole wizarding world exceedingly nervous. Is Voldemort back? Who is secretly supporting him? Is anyone trying to help him return to power? These are the questions that everyone is asking as Hogwarts' new school year begins. Fortunately, a thrilling announcement momentarily eclipses the unpleasant atmosphere: Hogwarts will host a Triwizard Tournament, a contest between Europe's three top wizard schools. In a speech to his students, Hogwarts' Headmaster—Albus Dumbledore—stresses that this is no ordinary competition:

> The Triwizard Tournament was first established some seven hundred years ago as a friendly competition between the three largest European schools of wizardry: Hogwarts, Beauxbatons, and Durmstrang. A champion was selected to represent each school, and the three champions competed in three magical tasks. The schools took it in turns to host the tournament once every five years, and it was generally agreed to be a most excellent way of establishing ties between young witches and wizards of different nationalities—until, that is, the death toll mounted so high that the tournament was discontinued.[12]

To ensure that none of the students die during the tournament, the Ministry of Magic and the headmasters of all three schools decide to place a minimum age of seventeen on the competitors. Younger students, they fear, will not have the physical strength or magical training to avoid fatal injuries. This prevents Harry (who is only fourteen) from putting his name into the "Goblet of Fire," a magical artifact that chooses the three students most worthy of representing their schools.

Although the goblet itself cannot discern students' ages, Dumbledore enforces his restriction by encircling the goblet with a magical "Age Line" that can only be crossed by someone older than seventeen. Those meeting the age requirement must write their name and school on a piece of parchment and drop it into the goblet. Then, at a ceremony marking the end of this submitting period, the goblet chooses the champions by shooting their parchments out into the air, where they are collected and read.

At a subsequent ceremony, three parchments, each containing the name of one student from a different school, fires out of the goblet's flame. A boy named Viktor Krum is chosen champion for Durmstrang, a girl named Fleur Delacour is champion for Beauxbatons, and for Hogwarts, the champion is Cedric Diggory. At the joint ceremony, all three schools roar in ecstatic enthusiasm for their champions until the oddest thing happens. The goblet spits out another parchment. Dumbledore grabs the paper, and to his astonishment, it reads: Harry Potter.

Everyone is shocked and believes that Harry blatantly disregarded the rules. But after further inquiries and discussions among the headmasters of each school, it is agreed that Harry is not responsible. Someone secretly put his name into the magical goblet. Why? No one knows. One thing, however, is certain. Harry *must* compete in the dangerous contest because anyone chosen by the goblet immediately enters into an invisible, "[b]inding magical contract."[13]

As the story continues, we learn that the three magical tasks comprising the tournament are scheduled for various days throughout the school year, and they are to be watched as one might watch the Olympics. There is even a point system used by the judges to determine who completed their task in the most efficient, resourceful and honorable way. Then, to finally ascertain the winner, these scores are tallied. The student with the highest total score wins, thus bringing honor to his or her school. They also receive a prize: one thousand gold coins.

The first magical task pits the four champions against a dragon guarding a giant, golden egg. Each student must use their wizarding skills to get past the dragon and steal the egg. The second task involves diving deep into the lake beside Hogwarts to rescue a friend taken captive by the underwater dwellers of the lake (i.e., the merpeople). The third task has the four champions running to the center of a maze, where the Triwizard's Cup has been placed. But this is not just any maze. It is booby-trapped with various monsters, riddles to solve and assorted other dangers to be overcome.

The final task culminates when Harry and Cedric Diggory reach the Triwizard's Cup simultaneously. They decide to share the glory and grab the prized object together. But suddenly they are transported to a graveyard outside Little Hangleton. A traitor had turned the Triwizard's Cup into a "Portkey"—i.e., an object used to transport wizards from one location to another. It was all a trap. Waiting at the Portkey's destination location is Peter Pettigrew.

Before either Harry or Cedric realize what is happening, Harry hears *Avada Kedavra!* echo loudly through the night air as a blast of green light bursts forth all around him. Cedric falls dead to the ground, his mouth half-open, and his eyes staring upward, "blank and expressionless as the windows of a deserted house."[14]

The next thing Harry knows, he is being bound to a marble tombstone that reads: TOM RIDDLE. This is the grave of Voldemort's father. Pettigrew then rolls forward a huge, man-sized cauldron and lights a fire beneath it. Next, he brings forth a small bundle of twitching robes, out of which emerges Voldemort, who is too withered even to walk on his own. It is a ghastly sight as Pettigrew lifts up Voldemort's shriveled shell of a body and heaves it into the concoction now churning within the cauldron.

The worst is yet to come when Pettigrew begins an incantation. *"Bone of the father, unknowingly given, you will renew your son."*[15] At these words, the ground covering Riddle's grave splits open and a trickle of dust rises into the air. It falls into the cauldron's magical solution, turning it a "poisonous-looking blue."[16]

Stammering with fright, Pettigrew continues: *"Flesh—of the servant—w-willingly given—you will—revive—your master."*[17] Harry is horrified as Pettigrew stretches out his own right hand, and using a huge dagger, cuts it off. His screams pierce the darkness, blood splatters everywhere, and then Harry hears the "sickening splash" of the hand being thrown into the seething potion, which reacts by turning red.[18]

Although racked with excruciating pain, Pettigrew crosses to Harry and proceeds with his unholy assignment, saying: *"B-blood of the enemy . . . forcibly taken . . . you will . . . resurrect your foe."*[19] Nothing can be done to stop Pettigrew from using his dagger to slash open Harry's arm, releasing a flow of blood that is caught in a small vial and poured into the cauldron. The potion then turns a brilliant white color and begins emitting sparks in the sky.

Once the sparks fade, a surge of white steam billows from the depths of the cauldron, and out of the smoke appears "the dark outline of a man, tall and skeletally thin. . . . [His face] whiter than a skull, with wide, livid scarlet eyes and a nose that was flat as a snake's with slits for nostrils."[20] Lord Voldemort had finally arisen more powerful than ever before, just as Harry's divination teacher, Madam Trelawney, had predicted in *Prisoner of Azkaban*.

But this is not the end of Book IV. Having felt his resurrected presence, the remaining Death Eaters begin appearing near Voldemort to again pledge their allegiance. There are not many of them left, but the small band of evil witches and wizards that materialize will be enough for the Dark Lord to begin another reign of terror.

After the last evil servant arrives, Voldemort decides to finish the deed he failed to complete thirteen years earlier: killing Harry. He has nothing to fear now, sneering: "I wanted the blood of the one who had stripped me of power thirteen years ago . . . for the lingering protection his mother once gave him would then reside in my veins too."[21] But before committing this heinous crime, Voldemort unbinds Harry, gives him back his wand, and cruelly "duels" with him, knowing a mere boy could never defend himself against his vastly superior powers.

In an agonizing scene, Voldemort tortures Harry using the Cruciatus Curse, an outlawed spell that causes indescribable pain:

> [B]efore Harry could do anything to defend himself . . . he had been hit again by the Cruciatus Curse. The pain was so intense, so all-consuming, that he no longer knew where he was. . . . White-hot knives were piercing every inch of his skin, his head was surely going to burst with pain, he was screaming more loudly than he'd ever screamed in his life. . . . And then it stopped. Harry rolled over and scrambled to his feet; he was shaking as uncontrollably as Wormtail [Pettigrew] had done when his hand had been cut off; he staggered sideways into the wall of watching Death Eaters, and they pushed him away, back toward Voldemort. "A little break," said Voldemort, the slit-like nostrils dilating with excitement, "a little pause. . . . That hurt, didn't it, Harry? You don't want me to do that again, do you?"[22]

By the time Voldemort chooses to end his game of torture, Harry also has made a decision: He is going to die fighting, just like his father. Harry steps out from his hiding place, lifts his wand, and shouts one of the few spells he knows: *Expelliarmus!* (a basic defensive spell that merely disarms an opponent of their wand). At the exact same moment, Voldemort thunders the dreaded words: "*Avada Kedavra!*" It looks as if Harry will surely die.

But then, a most remarkable thing happens. The fatal jet of green light shooting from Voldemort's wand and the stream of red light shooting from Harry's wand meet in midair. This creates a third band of golden light that effectively fuses the two wands together, and to the astonishment of the Death Eaters, levitates both Harry and Voldemort high off the ground.

As their wands remain connected, "a golden, dome-shaped web, a cage of light," forms around both of them.[23] Then Harry notices that a bead of light is moving along the golden beam connecting them. Although he does not know what this bead is, or why it is there, he somehow knows what he must do. By concentrating on it, Harry forces the bead along the golden ray until it touches Voldemort's wand. This in turn causes the wand to emit screams, after which the wand's tip produces, in reverse order, the images of the last several people murdered by Voldemort.

The first image is that of Cedric. Next to appear is Frank Bryce, the gardener. An apparition of Bertha Jorkins then comes out of the wand, followed by Harry's father and mother. Each of these individuals give Harry words of encouragement, while whispering taunts to Voldemort. Harry's mother imparts a final word of instruction: "When the connection is broken, we will linger for only moments . . . but we will give you time . . . you must get to the Portkey, it will return you to Hogwarts."[24]

When Harry hears his father yell, "NOW!," he breaks the connection and is able to run to the Portkey. He grabs hold of Cedric's limp hand, touches the Triwizard's Cup, and both he and his slain friend are transported back to Hogwarts, where shocked onlookers still have no idea why the boys disappeared. Cedric's body, however, tells them that something terrible has happened. But at least Voldemort's plan to kill Harry has failed.

The remainder of Book IV reveals that the plan against Harry had been in the works for a long time, and that it was made possible by a traitor within Hogwarts. Also explained is the unexpected interaction between Voldemort's wand and Harry's wand. It seems that both wands share the same magical core; one tail feather from the same phoenix—Dumbledore's phoenix, to be precise (cf. *Chamber of Secrets*)—and apparently, when a wand meets its brother, they both malfunction. According to Dumbledore, if the owners force the wands to do battle, "[o]ne of the wands will force the other to regurgitate spells it has performed—in reverse."[25]

Goblet of Fire concludes with Dumbledore informing Hogwarts' students, and the students from Durmstrang and Beauxbatons, that Lord Voldemort killed Cedric. Unfortunately, Cornelius Fudge—the Minister of Magic—refuses to believe that Voldemort is back, and for politically expedient reasons, blames the death of Cedric on an escaped Death Eater from Azkaban. What of Harry's eyewitness account? Fudge dismisses it as an hallucination brought on by stress.

Dumbledore firmly tells Fudge he is wrong and outlines the steps he feels the Ministry of Magic must take to prepare for the horrors that will surely accompany Voldemort's return. But Fudge will not listen. "It seems to me that you are all determined to start a panic that will destabilize everything we have worked for these last thirteen years!" he exclaims. Dumbledore responds: "You are blinded . . . by the love of the office you hold. . . . Fail to act—and history will remember you as the man who stepped aside and allowed Voldemort a second chance to destroy the world we have tried to rebuild."[26]

But these warnings are ignored by Fudge, who storms away, content to discount the obvious. Dumbledore then takes matters into his own hands by spreading the bad news and dispatching various individuals on important missions that will hopefully prepare the wizarding world for the "good vs. evil" war that will no doubt begin in the near future.

Thus ends a very eventful year at Hogwarts. And as Harry returns to live with the Durlseys for yet another summer, Book IV concludes with him accepting the fact that life will soon become very difficult.[27]

ENDNOTES

1. J.K. Rowling, interview, *The Times* (London), June 30, 2000, available online at www.thetimes.co.uk.
2. J.K. Rowling, *Harry Potter and the Goblet of Fire* (New York: Scholastic, 2000), 1.
3. Rowling, *Goblet of Fire*, 2.
4. Rowling, *Goblet of Fire*, 4.
5. Rowling, *Goblet of Fire*, 3.
6. Rowling, *Goblet of Fire*, 646.
7. Rowling, *Goblet of Fire*, 640.
8. Rowling, *Goblet of Fire*, 15.
9. Rowling, *Goblet of Fire*, 128.
10. Rowling, *Goblet of Fire*, 142-143.
11. Rowling, *Goblet of Fire*, 526-527.
12. Rowling, *Goblet of Fire*, 187.
13. Rowling, *Goblet of Fire*, 278.
14. Rowling, *Goblet of Fire*, 638.
15. Rowling, *Goblet of Fire*, 641.
16. Rowling, *Goblet of Fire*.
17. Rowling, *Goblet of Fire*.
18. Rowling, *Goblet of Fire*, 642.
19. Rowling, *Goblet of Fire*.
20. Rowling, *Goblet of Fire*, 643.
21. Rowling, *Goblet of Fire*, 657.
22. Rowling, *Goblet of Fire*, 660-661.
23. Rowling, *Goblet of Fire*, 664.
24. Rowling, *Goblet of Fire*, 667.
25. Rowling, *Goblet of Fire*, 697.
26. Rowling, *Goblet of Fire*, 707-708.
27. Rowling, *Goblet of Fire*, 734.

EIGHT

GOBLET OF DEATH:
A CLOSER LOOK

*[P]arents expecting a respite from the violence in popular cul-
ture will be surprised by the amount of violence that Rowling
introduces into her tales. I cannot think of any classic children's story that has as much of it. Rowling is a clever writer,
and she has assimilated just about every basic bit of business
you might encounter in an action movie.*

Lee Siegel, reviewer[1]
The New Republic

Goblet of Fire*, unlike Rowling's first three novels,
drifts deeply into the realm of adult fiction. It is
more violent, contains harsher images and has an
overall tone that is significantly darker than Books I, II or III. Especially noticeable in Book IV is the intensified blur between
Rowling's so-called "fantasy" magic and actual occultism. As
noted earlier, Rowling herself admits, "[Y]es, I have done research
on witchcraft and wizardry, but I tend only to use things when
they fit my plot."[2] Examples of these "things" are not difficult to
spot in Book IV.

For instance, in *Prisoner of Azkaban* (Book III), Rowling
merely suggests that Harry is a "True Seer" who has the gift of
divination (see Chapter 5). But this aspect of Harry's character is
clearly confirmed in Book IV through his visions of Voldemort

and Pettigrew (pp. 17, 576-577). These supernatural episodes are textbook illustrations of clairvoyance (i.e., the "paranormal faculty of seeing persons and events which are distant in time or place, and of which no knowledge can reach the seer through the normal sense channels"[3]). As Professor Trelawney says to Harry after he has one of his visions, "My dear, you were undoubtedly stimulated by the extraordinary clairvoyant vibrations of my room."[4]

Trelawney's own credibility as a True Seer, which is somewhat obscured in Book III, also is solidified in *Goblet of Fire*. On pages 149-150, for instance, Harry explains to Hermione that Trelawney's last prediction about Pettigrew came to pass:

> "You weren't there," said Harry. "You didn't hear her. This time it was different. I told you, she went into a trance—a real one. And she said the Dark Lord would rise again . . . *greater and more terrible than ever before* . . . and he'd manage it because his servant was going to go back to him . . . and that night Wormtail [Pettigrew] escaped."[5]

Book IV gives additional credence to Trelawney's occult powers by having the second half of her prediction come true (i.e., Voldemort's pseudo-resurrection). Yet another accurate forecast by Trelawney is her prediction of a "death" she sees during a session of crystal gazing; a session she is urged into by some unseen force.[6] This vision comes to pass with the murder of Cedric.

Divination is used in Rowling's series as a means of accurately foretelling the future. What is the danger? The danger is that this positive portrayal might stir in some children an unhealthy curiosity about divination, fortune-tellers and related practices. As Robert Knight of the Family Research Council says, Harry Potter "gives children an appetite for the occult."[7]

A similar hazard exists with Rowling's depiction of astrology which, although hinted at in *Sorcerer's Stone* (see Chapter 1), is boldly set forth in *Goblet of Fire*. On pages 200-201, for example, Trelawney not only speaks in a manner that echoes modern-day astrologers, but also assigns Harry and his friends the task of mapping out their astrological birth charts: "[E]ach of them had been given a complicated circular chart, and was attempting to fill in the position of the planets at their moment of birth."[8] Later in Book IV, we see one student showing another student her "completed horoscope,"[9] and Trelawney teaching a class on "planetary divination."[10]

Rowling argues that such passages are mere literary devices, and that her books do not advocate "learning magic."[11] At the same time, however, she has taken great pains to ensure that the occult-related material in her volumes accurately reflects true occultism.[12] In fact, up to one-third of the occultism in her series parallels information Rowling uncovered during her personal studies of witchcraft/magick.[13]

Perhaps even more significant is a comment Rowling made during an April 1999 interview about the artwork on various editions of her books: "[T]he Scholastic cover looks the most like the way I had fantasized that the book would look," she remarked excitedly. "It looks like a spell book because of the colors and the style of illustrations."[14] Rowling is talking here about how marvelous it is that her "fantasy" volumes closely resemble something very common to real witchcraft: a "spellbook," also known as a Grimoire.

Grimoires, which take various forms, are any magical texts that contain instructions for divination, spiritism and working magick (e.g., casting spells).[15] Some examples of these spellbooks would be *The Wicca Spellbook* by Gerina Dunwich, *The Witch's Workbook* by Ann Grammary, *The Wiccan Guide to*

Witches' Ways by Claire Lorde and Simon Lorde, and *Witches, Potions and Spells* by Kathryn Paulsen. A more personalized Grimoire (i.e., one containing private spells, thoughts, poetry, diary-like entries, experiments with magick, dream descriptions, divination experiences, etc.) would be called a Book of Shadows. These are more like spiritual diaries, but because they also contain spells, they are often simply called "spellbooks."

Why would Rowling be overjoyed that her books so closely resemble spellbooks? It may be because she has nurtured a fascination for occultism, especially witchcraft and wizardry, since she was a little girl. According to Ian Potter—a childhood friend of Rowling (the one on whom her "Harry Potter" character is partly based)—Rowling used to dress up as a witch all the time. Ian's younger sister, Vikki, who also grew up with Rowling, remembers, "Our favorite thing to dress up as were witches. We used to dress up and play witch all the time. My brother would dress up as a wizard. Joanne [J.K. Rowling] was always reading to us.... [W]e would make secret potions for her. She would always send us off to get twigs for the potions."[16]

Children are often moved by powerful images and characters because they can put themselves in the shoes, so to speak, of those characters and envision themselves as doing what those characters are doing. This natural tendency in children is sometimes so strong that they can forget that what they are reading is unreal. Younger children are especially susceptible to powerful images and long to be part of a story in which they have immersed themselves. In an interview with *Newsweek*, Rowling confirms this inclination in her readers:

> I get letters from children addressed to Professor Dumbledore, and it's not a joke, begging to be let into Hogwarts, and some of

them are really sad. Because they want it to be true so badly
they've convinced themselves it's true.[17]

What will children do when they discover that there is no real
Hogwarts? Where will they go satisfy their desire to engage in
activities similar to those in the Harry Potter books? Sadly, occult involvement is a possible direction that some children may
choose. There already exists a growing number of Internet sites
serving as a kind of cyberworld extension of the Harry Potter
novels. It is attracting young people by the thousands. At the
"Unofficial Harry Potter Website," for instance, a child can join
one of four Hogwarts Houses (Gryffindor, Slytherin,
Ravenclaw, or Hufflepuff), shop at Diagon Alley for magic supplies or take classes in potions and charms. This web site was
created by a thirteen-year-old London girl.[18]

Potter-related fantasy Role Playing Games (RPGs) also are
cropping up everywhere in cyberspace. At "Professor
Dumbledore's Hogwarts School of Witchcraft and Wizardry"
(http://hogwarts.homepad.com), which is run by fifteen-year-old
Tamsen Foote, players can take on a character and participate in
various activities associated with the Potter series (e.g., take
classes, shop at Diagon Alley, etc.). As of August 1, 2000, more
than 400 children were participating in the online RPG. When I
accessed the site, its visitor log read: "34,773 Witches and Wizards
have visited this site since . . . 5/08/2000."[19]

Adults, too, are making it easy for children to immerse themselves
not only in Harry Potter's world, but also in occultism. For example,
many children are using the Internet to reach mikids.com, a web site
run by Carolyn Gundrum (Technology-Teacher/Librarian at
Waukazoo Elementary School in Holland, Michigan). This popular
"domain"—i.e., Gundrum's "Harry Potter-Excellent Adventure"
web page—actually includes the photo-image of a *real* astrological

birth chart for Harry Potter.[20] This chart was plotted by professional astrologer Barbara Schermer, a published occultist (*Astrology Alive*, HarperCollins, 1989) who has her own Internet site called "Astrology Alive."[21]

In addition to Harry's chart, the "Excellent Adventure" web page contains a link to an astrological interpretation of it by Schermer! Children can even take themselves to Schermer's occult "Astrology Alive" site via another highlighted link reading: *"Click here for your own Horoscope!"*[22] The "Astrology Alive" site contains links to Scholastic and Bloomsbury (Rowling's American and British publishers), other fan sites (e.g., "Harry Potter's Realm of Wizardry," created by another fourteen-year-old) and astrology books available from amazon.com (e.g., *Mythic Astrology*, *The Inner Dimensions of the Birth Chart* and *Astrology, Karma & Transformation*).

Children also are enjoying the opportunity to dress up like Harry and other characters at bookstore-hosted Harry Potter parties. Many retail outlets have even held look-alike contests for the various Harry Potter characters. Some stores have gone so far as to hold "wizard breakfasts." This may all seem very fun and innocent. But where will this fascination with Harry Potter end? As Harry Potter fans mature, will they feel an increasing desire to dabble in occultism?

The whole attraction of the occult is power, excitement and entertainment, each of which is represented in the Potter series. Rowling's books, at the very least, will desensitize children to the dangers of occultism, which in turn may create in them a general sympathy toward a spiritually detrimental set of beliefs. For some children, the Potter series may even spark a desire for genuine occult materials and paraphernalia.

A young teen who reads Rowling's books, for example, might seek a Potteresque type of excitement by joining the London-based *Ordo Anno Mundi* (OAM), a sect of occultists who practice

Ophidian Witchcraft (i.e., serpent-venerating). Like Hogwarts, which takes its wizards through seven years of training, the OAM has seven degrees of "Magical Training" that include classes strikingly similar to those offered at Hogwarts:

Ordo Anno Mundi	Hogwarts School
"Ancient Runes" (General Education)	"Those are my books for . . . Divination, the Study of Ancient Runes" (*Prisoner of Azkaban*, p. 57).
"Divination" (1st Degree)	"We will be covering the basic methods of Divination this year" (*Prisoner of Azkaban*, p. 103).
"Spellcasting" (1st Degree)	"All students should have a copy of each of the following: *The Standard Book of Spells (Grade 1)*" (*Sorcerer's Stone*, p. 66).
"Werewolf" "Animal Transformation" [Transfiguration] (4th Degree)	"Transfiguration is some of the most complex and dangerous magic you will learn at Hogwarts" (*Sorcerer's Stone*, p. 134). "My transformations in those days were—were terrible. It is very painful to turn into a werewolf. . . . [My friends] could each turn into a different animal" (*Prisoner of Azkaban*, pp. 353-354).
"Magical Lore" [History of Magic] (5th Degree)	"Their very last exam was History of Magic" (*Sorcerer's Stone*, p. 263).

The connection between Rowling's books and actual occultism is so unmistakable that even occultists themselves see it. For instance, at "ParanormalAtoZ.com," a web site specializing in literature and information on occult subjects and personalities, J.K. Rowling is included in "A Compendium of the Paranormal, Occult, Unusual, Supernatural, and Unexplained Phenomenon." She is listed along with: Demons, ESP, Ghosts, Magic Spells, Ouija Boards, Tarot Cards, Wicca, Witchcraft, Zodiac and more. The only other authors on this lengthy inventory are horror novelists Stephen King and Anne Rice.

Despite the dangerous link between the Potter series and occultism, J.K. Rowling has consistently made dismissive statements such as:

- "I have yet to meet a single child who's told me that they want to be a Satanist, or are particularly interested in the occult because of the book;"[23]
- "I've never met a single child who asked me about the occult"[24]; and
- "[N]ot even one time has a child come up to me and said, 'Ms. Rowling, I'm so glad I've read these books because now I want to be a witch.' "[25]

Ironically, it is on the web site of Rowling's own publisher that there appears a message from a fourteen-year-old girl, Rachel G., which reads: "I like Ron, Hermione, and Harry a lot. Professor Dumbledore is great too. . . . I would love to be a witch or a wizard."[26] The following is a but a small sampling of many statements that Rowling either has not seen, or chosen to ignore; statements made by children who, because of the Harry Potter series, wish they could learn magick and/or be a witch/wizard:

- "I like what they learned there [at Hogwarts] and I want to be a witch." (Gioia Bishop, ten years old)[27]
- "I thought the story really made you feel like you could be a witch or a wizard." (Lily, eleven years old)[28]

- "This book is amazing and contains magic spells I wish I can do in the real world." (Wang Wen, twelve years old)[29]
- "I think Harry Potter books are absolutely fine! ... I like how they [Harry and friends] can use witchcraft for fun/good purposes." (Devon, eleven years old)[30]
- "I wish Hogwarts were real because then I could go and learn magic instead of quadratic equations." (Mairead, thirteen years old)[31]
- "The book made me want to go to Hogwarts. Hogwarts is a school for teaching magic. I would like to learn magic, but I haven't gotten my letter of invitation yet." (amazon.co.uk post, age unknown)[32]

It would be unrealistic to say that all of these youths, and the many children who share their feelings, will get involved with the occult. But it is equally improbable to say that none of them will do so.

POTTERETHICS

In reference to her series, Rowling has remarked, "I think they're very moral books."[33] Many other people feel the same way, including librarian and psychoanalyst Linda Goettina, who during an interview with *Nightline*, stated: "[E]ach book takes a theme ... with the idea of making choices in your life, and builds on them to give the child a sense of what it is to be a good human being."[34] And then there is the Very Reverend Nick Bury, Dean of Gloucester, who has granted Warner Brothers permission to film scenes involving Hogwarts School of Witchcraft and Wizardry at the historic Gloucester Cathedral (completed in 1350). Bury says Rowling has authored "splendid books," which emphasize that "truth is better than lies."[35]

But contrary to such pronouncements, Rowling's characters (the "good" ones) consistently make "choices" that have very little to do with living as a "good human being." As I have already demonstrated in previous chapters, Harry and his friends routinely steal, lie, cheat and seek revenge with clear consciences. While it is true that unrighteous acts play a part in many fairy tales and fantasy adventures, there is usually at least an implied understanding that the characters involved are either: a) "evil" characters; or b) "good" characters undergoing a deep internal struggle over their actions. In some cases, these "good" characters are behaving "badly" only because they are somehow being deceived/bewitched.

Throughout Rowling's works, however, "good" characters show no remorse over their "evil" actions. In fact, they are often rather proud of themselves and their misdeeds. Book IV, like Books I-III, contains countless examples of behavior (by children *and* adults) that Christian parents would deem less than admirable, not to mention unbiblical. The most frequent form of undesirable behavior that Rowling's "good" characters yield to is disobedience. They not only disregard rules, but also usually end up either not getting caught when they actually break a rule, or not suffering any penalties if they are caught.

Consider the characters of Fred and George Weasley, fifteen-year-old twins who throughout Rowling's first four volumes are intractably mischievous. Although they are depicted as "good" kids, they habitually disobey their parents, violate school ordinances and lie, while expressing gleeful satisfaction over their antics. In Book IV, for instance, it is revealed that for years the twins have been inventing dangerous magical gag-gifts in hopes of one day opening a joke shop.[36] They continue to do so even after their mother's instructs to stop making such products.[37]

Fred and George also ignore their father's request to abstain from gambling on the Quidditch World Cup game. Ultimately, a defeated Mr. Weasley capitulates to his sons, pleading: "*Don't* tell your mother you've been gambling."[38] Fred gleefully responds, "Don't worry Dad . . . we've got big plans for this money. We don't want it confiscated."[39]

Actually, Mr. Weasley seems to be the source of his sons' tendency toward rule-breaking and lying. Although an employee for the Ministry of Magic, he regularly circumvents wizard laws and regulations (cf. Book III). On page 45 of Book IV, he admits to having illegally connected the Dursley's fireplace to the wizard's network of fireplaces (a sort of magical conduit of travel for wizards). "Muggle fireplaces aren't supposed to be connected, strictly speaking," he confesses. "[B]ut I've got a useful contact at the Floo Regulation Panel and he fixed it for me."[40] Weasley also breaks rules for others. For instance, when the son of a friend "got into a spot of trouble" for illegally bewitching a Muggle object (a lawn mower), he "smoothed the whole thing over," effectively freeing the boy from any punishment.[41]

What messages might a child pick up from the actions of Mr. Weasley and his sons? Here are a some obvious ones: 1) disobedience is not a very serious offense; 2) when rules/laws are broken, it is possible to find a way to get around punishment, either by lying or by using "connections"; 3) obedience should be forsaken in favor of one's own desires; 4) sometimes it is appropriate to deceive one's spouse or conceal information from them.

A perfect summation of these lessons can be found in Dumbledore's announcement at the end of Book IV, "It is my belief . . . that truth is *generally* preferable to lies [emphasis added]."[42] Indeed, "generally preferable," rather than simply preferable, seems to be the overall position held by most of the characters in Rowling's series. Is this a "good" lesson for children?

Additionally, *Goblet of Fire* glamorizes dishonesty by having nearly everyone cheating throughout the Triwizard Tournament (including "good" characters). The rules are made clear on page 281 of Book IV: "The champions are not permitted to ask for or accept help of any kind from their teachers to complete the tasks in the tournament." Nevertheless, Hagrid reveals to Harry ahead of time that his first magical task will involve dragons,[43] and Sirius Black tries to tell Harry which spell to use to succeed in the task (see *Prisoner of Azkaban*).[44] Next, Harry, who has already cheated by listening to Hagrid and Sirius, cheats once again by telling Cedric what the task will be.[45] By listening to this information and not reporting it, Cedric becomes a cheater.

The web of dishonesty grows as Ludo Bagman, a member of the Ministry of Magic, attempts to help Harry, saying, "I don't mind sharing a few pointers, if you'd like them, you know, I mean . . . . you're the underdog here, Harry. . . . Anything I can do to help."[46] As well, Hermione is pulled into cheating when she begins helping Harry in response to him telling her about the dragons.[47] At the risk of overstressing this point, more cheating occurs in Book IV on pages 465, 485, 490-491.

The words of Professor Moody might best sum up the prevailing attitude demonstrated by Rowling's characters with regarding to good sportsmanship: "Cheating's a traditional part of the Triwizard Tournament and always has been."[48]

Book IV has Hagrid continuing to break rules and commit crimes, like breeding "skrewts," an illegal and highly dangerous hybrid of two different creatures.[49] Harry, Ron and Hermione see Hagrid's unending infractions of wizard law as amusing. Page 371 reads,

> "Just as long as he didn't import those skrewts illegally or anything." . . . They looked at one another—it was exactly the sort of thing Hagrid might do. . . . "Hagrid's been in loads of trouble before, and Dumbledore's never sacked him," said Ron consolingly.[50]

It appears that the only individuals troubled by "rules" are those whom Rowling paints as evil, prudish or obnoxious. For example, in reference to Hagrid's blatant disregard for long-standing wizard regulations pertaining to hybrid creatures, an annoying gossip columnist named Rita Skeeter writes in the *Daily Prophet*, "Hagrid . . . considers himself to be above such petty restrictions."[51] Rita, a thoroughly unlikable character in the story, is nonetheless correct. But the accurate viewpoint is devalued and tainted because it is presented by such a nasty character.

Also, there is the ill-tempered and unjust Professor Snape, who seems to be the only authority figure ever concerned with rebuking Harry. On page 516, he scolds Harry by telling him he is nothing but a boy "who considers rules to be beneath him." Like Skeeter, Snape is speaking the truth. Rules do indeed mean very little to Harry. But because Snape is an offensive character, his perception about Harry appears unjust. In contrast to Snape, there is lovable Hagrid, who responds quite differently to Harry's disobedience, stating, "Well, yeh might've bent a few rules, Harry, bu' yeh're all righ' really, aren' you?"[52]

And then there is Percy Weasley, who is Ron's older brother. He is indeed a "good" character, but because of his faithful adherence over the years to school regulations and community standards, he is painted by Rowling as a dreadful stick-in-the-mud who is "a great believer in rigidly following rules."[53]

Rowling employs this kind of "good" character vs. "evil" character device to subtly excuse Harry's total disregard for following rules and his penchant for lying, which is yet another habit of his that goes unchallenged in Book IV. Harry lies to Hermione (p. 443), a house-elf (p. 408), Hagrid (p. 456), Professor Snape (p. 516), Professor Trelawney (p. 577) and Cornelius Fudge, the Minister of Magic (p. 581)—all without negative consequence.

Additionally, Book IV contains a fair amount of profanity—more so, in fact, than in previous volumes. Again, this unbiblical behavior is presented as wholly acceptable from "good" characters as well as bad ones. As in the other books, there are the ubiquitous "gits" scattered throughout the text (pp. 53, 102, 731). But we also find the following:

Good Characters	Evil/Bad Characters
Mr. Weasley, Ron's father: "Damn" (p. 43). *Bill Weasley, Ron's brother*: "[N]o one at the bank gives a damn how I dress" (p. 62). *Ludo Bagman, Ministry of Magic*: "Damn them!" (p. 127). *Cedric Diggory, Hogwarts champion*: "What the hell d'you think you're doing?" (p. 626).	*Professor Moody, impostor*: "[H]e damn near beat it!" (p. 232); "You're a damn good flier" (p. 344); "Damn leg!" (p. 561). *Professor Snape, Hogwarts' professor*: "I don't give a damn" (p. 470).

There are other places in Book IV where Rowling pulls back on the language, choosing instead to use suggestive sentence structures, effectively leaving the reader to fill in the blank. Page 121 reads: "Ron told Malfoy to do something that Harry knew he would never have dared say in front of Mrs. Weasley." And on page 290, we have Harry saying: "Yeah, give Ron a good kick up the—"

An even more child-inappropriate obscenity appears on page 111 in the form of a vulgar hand gesture that Rowling couches in humor. It occurs during the Quidditch World Cup between Ireland and Bulgaria. After a foul by Bulgaria, the mascots for Ireland—an unruly throng of leprechauns—float into the air to form "a giant hand, which was making a very rude sign indeed."[54]

Why do such gross misrepresentations of what has been portrayed as "good" go virtually unnoticed by millions of readers? Why do the lies, the disobedience and the self-serving nature of Harry and other "good" characters remain relatively unchallenged by parents, educators and Christian leaders? The reason may lie in the fact that Rowling skillfully obscures the *mildly* evil deeds of her "good" characters behind the *horrendously* evil deeds of her "bad" characters. In other words, Rowling has made Voldemort, Pettigrew and the Death Eaters so repulsive that the immoral deeds of Harry and other "good" characters have an appearance of benevolence, fun and virtue. The result is a tacit acceptance of less evil characters as simply "good" ones.[55]

In fact, Book IV goes so far as to include a scene wherein Harry is commended for demonstrating exceptional "moral fiber" during Task Three. How so? By attempting to save three "good" students from their underwater captivity, although he only needed to save his friend, Ron Weasley. But is this feat truly extraordinary? And would he have made the extra effort for Malfoy or Professor Snape? That is doubtful because not once in all four books does Harry display any concern for characters other than those that show concern for him.

To paraphrase Jesus' words: "If you only love those who love you, what special credit is that to you? Even evil people love those who love them. And if you only do good to those who do good to you, so what? Evil people do the same thing" (Luke 6:32-33). Jesus' teaching is simple: To risk one's life for, or show kindness to, a friend is something anyone would do. But extraordinary "moral fiber" belongs to the one who will make a sacrifice and risk everything for someone of no particular value to them, even an enemy (cf. Romans 5:7-8).

So why is Harry honored for doing what is, at the most, a natural response, especially when the rest of his behavior includes an inclination toward disobedience, an affinity for lies and a selfish agenda? Because the scene strengthens Harry's image as a "good" character. Rowling downplays Harry's other moral issues by elevating two virtuous characteristics above all others: bravery and courage. As she herself has stated, "If the characters are brave and courageous, that is rewarded."[56]

What Rowling seemingly fails to recognize, however, is that even in her own books "evil" characters are brave and courageous, too. In the Potter series, we see some evil characters save each other's lives, magically heal each other's wounds, remain loyal to their side in the face of enemy persecution and sacrifice themselves for each other. At the end of Book IV we actually see Voldemort, in his own perverted way, *rewarding* Pettigrew for helping him rise again. In Voldemort's eyes, he is being "good" to Pettigrew, the only servant who helps him return to power. Voldemort also expresses gratitude to those who have remained faithful to him and speaks of how he will someday greatly honor them for the suffering they have endured as a result of their faithfulness.

Of course, Voldemort's method of operation may be drastically unlike Harry's, but the two characters share the same motivation: self-interest. Voldemort wants what he wants, as does Harry. The only difference between them rests in the rules they choose to break, the lies they choose to tell and the goals they choose to pursue.

This is why the whole "Harry-Potter-is-a-great-series-because-it-shows-a-battle-between-good-and-evil" argument is, in truth, without merit. This oft-quoted defense of Rowling's works is irrelevant, because the books do not contain a "battle between good and evil."[57] The war in Rowling's novels is a conflict between a *horrific* evil (Voldemort and his Death Eaters) and a *lesser* evil (Harry and the "good" characters) that only appears virtuous because it is so much less offensive and frightening than the greater evil.

Biblically speaking, Harry and all the other "good" characters are simply using one set of sinful behaviors to defeat another set of sinful behaviors. Drawing concepts of morality from either side is problematic, especially for children. Indeed, the Harry Potter series is not morally compatible with Christianity, which stands in direct opposition to using evil actions to conquer evil. Christians are instructed to overcome evil with good (Romans 12:21).

The Bible also states that it is best to avoid seeking revenge (Leviticus 19:18; Romans 12:17, 19; 1 Peter 3:9), pray for our enemies (Luke 6:27), consider others more important than ourselves (Philippians 2:3), view all people as inherently equal (Acts 17:26; Galatians 3:28), reject lying (Proverbs 12:22; Ephesians 4:25; Colossians 3:9), turn from drunkenness (Ephesians 5:18), live honestly (Hebrews 13:18), walk with integrity (Psalms 15:2, 26:1; Proverbs 11:3), flee hypocrisy (Luke 6:42; Romans 12:9; James 3:17), refrain from using corrupt and vulgar communication (Colossians 3:8, 4:6; Titus 2:8), accept the rule of higher authorities (Romans 13:1-5), remain at peace with everyone if at all possible (Romans 12:18), forgive those who have hurt us (Matthew 6:14-15; Ephesians 4:32) and avoid activities like occultism that lead away from God (Isaiah 44:25; Galatians 5:20; Revelation 21:8). In summation, Scripture tells us to behave in a way that is diametrically opposed to how Harry Potter and other "good" characters live.

Oddly, it is Rowling's series that many public schools are now using to teach morality to students. Scholastic actually has published a guide based on Rowling's books, which includes summaries of plot, theme, conflict, setting and characterization. It also contains questions designed to encourage discussion. Several of these deal with morality and ethics.

One question begins with the following quote from *Sorcerer's Stone*: "There is no good and evil, there is only power, and those too weak to seek it" (p. 291). The guide then asks, "Do you agree with this? Is this the reality of the world? Or if good and evil do exist, what makes them so? Which is more important in the world, power, or good and evil?"[58] Another question reads, "Lupin tells Harry that 'James [Potter] would have been highly disappointed if his son had never found any of the secret passages out of the castle' (pp. 424-425). Why would James want Harry to do anything other than follow all the rules? Is this a fun side of James coming out, or something else?"[59]

These questions not only raise ethical-moral problems, but could easily stimulate a crossover conversation that draws out religious beliefs. Are public school teachers qualified to handle these moral and theological questions in a non-biased manner? What slant will a Buddhist teacher bring to the discussion? How about a Muslim? An atheist? A New Ager? A Scientologist? In my opinion, the difficulties that could arise from the discussions pose a legitimate and serious problem. This unwise practice, however, has already become widespread.

"I truly didn't set out to teach morals," Rowling has claimed.[60] But teaching morals is exactly what she has ended up doing. Tragically, most of them are far from the biblical standard of "good."

AGES 6 & UP?

When J.K. Rowling began writing *Sorcerer's Stone*, she never imagined that it would be marketed to children. Consequently, she did not author the book with them in mind. She remembers, "I was very interested to see what age group the publishers would decide that they were for."[61] This may explain the mature themes permeating her work. Of course, plenty of juvenile material has now been thrown in the books to appeal to kids (see Chapter 5). But the overall substance of the series remains adult in nature. The result is a bizarre mishmash of whimsical characters, macabre humor, adult-level violence, silliness and frightful imagery. Is it appropriate for children?

Consider the contents of Book IV, which begins the discovery of Voldemort's murdered father and grandparents (pp. 2-3). Next comes a discussion about the murder of a witch named Bertha Jorkins (p. 11), who was "tortured" before being killed (pp. 655, 687). Then, Voldemort kills Frank Bryce, the Riddles' gardener (p. 15). At the Quidditch World Cup, evil wizards torment a family of four Muggles (including a woman and two children) by contorting their bodies "into grotesque shapes" and levitating them high into the sky (pp. 119-120).

On page 465, readers again encounter the ghost of Moaning Myrtle (see *Chamber of Secrets*), who laments the day she was murdered in a Hogwarts bathroom: "Nobody missed me even when I was alive. Took them hours and hours to find my body. . . . Olive Hornby came into the bathroom. . . . And then she saw my body . . . ooooh, she didn't forget it until her dying day, I made sure of that . . . followed her around and reminded her, I did."[62] Book IV also mentions:

- Muggle killings "done for fun" by Voldemort's followers (p. 143)
- the killing of two evil wizards (p. 531)
- the killing of another Death Eater (p. 589)
- the "torture" of countless Muggles (p. 589)
- a good wizard and his witch wife being tortured to the point of insanity (pp. 595, 603)

- Cedric's murder in front of Harry (p. 638)
- Pettigrew severing off his own hand to put in a boiling cauldron (pp. 641-642)
- Harry having blood drained into a vial after being slashed in the arm by Pettigrew (p. 642)
- Voldemort's statement that his survival depends on drinking a mixture of snake venom and unicorn blood (p. 656)
- a child killing his father, turning the body into a bone, and burying it (p. 690)

Rowling herself has repeatedly stated that this is only the tip of a very sinister iceberg of evil that will gradually be revealed in successive books. "I can tell you that the books are getting darker," Rowling has warned. "Harry's going to have quite a bit to deal with as he gets older."[63]

And sure enough, each volume has been markedly harsher than the last. Steve Bonta, in *The New American*, observes, "[E]ach new book seems a bit darker and more morbidly tragic than the one preceding."[64] In agreement, Rowling has said, "[D]eath and bereavement and what death means, I would say, are one of the central themes in all seven books."[65]

Goblet of Fire is already being compared to Stephen King horror novels by some reviewers.[66] And several published critiques of Book IV have included warnings such as these:

- "Parents should be aware that there are some really dark and spooky scenes in this novel; more so than the first three. Some of the scenes involving this character [Voldemort] could really have the kids checking under the bed for monsters."[67]
- "[T]his is a different, darker story from the first page of J.K. Rowling's new novel. It just might be time to rethink

that whole *"Harry Potter* is a children's book" theory. Letting an eight- or nine-year-old read this right before bedtime might not be the best way to ensure untroubled sleep."[68]

- "Images of death and violence, however, do haunt the story, and it is here that the rising idea that the Potter books are some sort of universal literature [for adults and kids] needs to be questioned. My five-year-old assistant critic had a troubled Saturday night after hearing the first one hundred pages."[69]

How much darker can Rowling's books get? The conclusion of Book IV suggests that Books V to VII will revolve around a kind of full-scale war pitting Voldemort and his Death Eaters against Harry and the rest of the wizarding world. This will no doubt lead to more murders, heightened violence, bloodier scenes and an expansion of occultism to accommodate the increased "power" that will inevitably be released by the combative forces in Rowling's so-called "good" vs. "evil" battle. These future volumes will no doubt cause more debates, some of which may raise issues that have yet to be considered.

A word must be said at this point about the hints of sexuality that Rowling's fourth book incorporates into the series. She has stated that her young characters will be "discovering their hormones" as they grow up, and *Goblet of Fire* seems to include their first steps in that direction. Indications of this theme first appear in Book IV during the Quidditch World Cup. As it turns out, the Bulgarian mascots are about one hundred *Veelas*—i.e., extremely sensual, highly erotic and indescribably attractive pseudo-human females. They are "the most beautiful women Harry had ever seen."[70]

Both Harry and Ron are utterly captivated by these females, who make their presence known to the crowd by running out on the playing field (somewhat like a cheerleading squad) for a pregame dance-show. Their intensely erotic movements cause "wild, half-formed thoughts" to race through Harry's "dazed mind."[71] He is so affected that he almost leaps onto the field from the stands. Ron is similarly overwhelmed. Later in the book, Ron meets a half-Veela and instantly falls into puppy-lust.[72]

A final dip into the well of sexuality occurs on the night of the Yule Ball, when numerous teen couples are caught necking in the shrubbery and are subsequently shooed back indoors by Professor Snape.[73] How far might Rowling take this particular subject in future volumes?

CONCLUSION

However one judges the literary caliber of Rowling's books, it cannot be legitimately denied that she is meeting some widespread need shared by adults and children alike. It may be as straightforward as a need for "fun." Then again, it may be something deeper, especially since the overall thrust of the Harry Potter series seems, at first glance, to depict an age-old source of concern for all humanity: the need for good to triumph over evil.

As we have already discovered, however, Rowling does not cleanly present this conflict. Her fantasy tales, in fact, only make the perennial "good vs. evil" struggle more confusing, as Steve Bonta observes in *The New American*:

> [Like] European witch cults of the Middle Ages, Voldemort sets a mark on the members of his secret circle of followers. . . . the "dark mark" is placed on the arm, and causes the bearer pain whenever he is summoned by Voldemort. Yet Harry has been marked as well; his fore-

head scar erupts into agonizing pain whenever Voldemort is nearby, or his power is manifest. . . .

The fact that occult symbols like the above-mentioned fill the pages of the Potter books and are associated with both the hero and the villain creates a cloud of ambiguity around their motives and those of their creator. Good and evil are never clear-cut, it seems: Harry is part Voldemort and Voldemort part Harry. Likewise, many of the supporting characters are confusingly two-sided. The "lovable" groundskeeper Hagrid, for example, is one of Harry's staunchest friends, but has a penchant for keeping deadly animals in his house as pets, animals which frequently endanger Harry and the other students. Professor Lupin, Harry's friend and ally in Book Three, is a werewolf. Severus Snape, who seems to detest Harry and opposes him at every opportunity, turns out at the end of Book One [and Book IV] to be a good guy—sort of. In Book Four, we learn that Severus has a secret: He was once one of Voldemort's Death Eaters, and bears the dark mark on his arm, but now he wishes to fight his old master. Sirius Black, the eponymous "prisoner of Azkaban" . . . turns out not to be the dangerous psychopathic murderer he was thought to be, but a friend and godfather of Harry. Endearing little Ginny Weasley, who has a crush on Harry, turns out to be the student responsible for the basilisk's rampage in Book Two. And on and on.[74]

So, how much will Harry Potter and his morally confusing world continue to influence children? What will be the ramifications of having Rowling's works used in public schools as teaching guides for ethics? Is the world of occultism going to reap a harvest of souls from the Harry Potter books? Does a Hollywood-Potter alliance foreshadow even darker and more powerful images? Unfortunately, these questions cannot now be answered. The best any of us can do is wait, watch, hope and pray for God's perfect will to be accomplished.

As Hagrid says toward the end of Book IV, "No good sittin' worryin' abou' it. . . . What's comin' will come, an' we'll meet it when it does."[75]

ENDNOTES

1. Lee Siegel, "Fear of Not Flying," *The New Republic*, November 4, 1999, available online at www.tnr.com/112299/siegel112299.html.

2. J.K. Rowling, interview with Barnes and Noble, September 8, 1999, available online at www.barnesandnoble.com.

3. Leslie A. Shepard, ed., *Encyclopedia of Occultism and Parapsychology* (Detroit: Gale Research, 1991), 1:292.

4. J.K. Rowling, *Harry Potter and the Goblet of Fire* (New York: Scholastic, 2000), 578.

5. Rowling, *Goblet of Fire*, 149-150.

6. Rowling, *Goblet of Fire*, 372.

7. Robert Knight, quoted in Deidre Donahue, "Are Parents Pushing 'Potter' On the Young," *Tulsa World*, June 20, 2000; cf. *USA Today* article of same title, available online at www.northernlight.com.

8. Rowling, *Goblet of Fire*, 201.

9. Rowling, *Goblet of Fire*, 212.

10. Rowling, *Goblet of Fire*, 221, 371, 575.

11. J.K. Rowling, quoted in Judy O'Malley, "Talking With J.K. Rowling," *Book Links* (Vol. 8, No. 6, pp. 32-36: Online Version), available online at www.northernlight.com.

12. J.K. Rowling, interview on *The Diane Rehm Show*, WAMU, National Public Radio, October 20, 1999, available online at www.wamu.org.

13. Rowling, interview on *The Diane Rehm Show*..

14. J.K. Rowling, quoted in O'Malley, available online at www.northernlight.com.

15. Craig Hawkins, *Witchcraft: Exploring the World of Wicca* (Grand Rapids: Baker, 1996), 74.

16. Ian Potter and Vikki Potter, quoted in Danielle Demetriou, "Harry Potter and the Source of Inspiration," *Electronic Telegraph*, July 1, 2000, available online at www.telegraph.co.uk; cf. "Potter Novelist Reveals Characters' Inspiration Ian 'Harry' Potter 'Had a Thing About Slugs'," available online at www.nationalpost.com.

17. Malcolm Jones, "The Return of Harry Potter!," *Newsweek* (Online), July 1, 2000, 4.

18. Statements available online at http://members.tripod.com/k.killy/home.html.

19. Statements available online at http://hogwarts.homepad.com.

20. Statements available online at www.mikids.com. Interestingly, Schermer's date for Potter's birth (July 31, 1979) is incorrect. According to various time-related passages, Harry was born in July 1980.

21. Statements available online at www.astrologyalive.com.

22. Statements available online at http://www.mikids.com/harrypotter/Astrology.htm.

23. J.K. Rowling, quoted in Nicole Martin, "Children Are Safe With Harry Potter, Author Tells Critics," *Electronic Telegraph*, 18 October 1999, available online at www.northernlight.com.

24. J.K. Rowling, quoted in Linton Weeks, *The Washington Post*, October 20, 1999, available online at www.northernlight.com.

25. J.K. Rowling, quoted in Kathleen Koch, "Success of Harry Potter Bowls Author Over," *CNN Online*, October 21, 1999, available online at www.cnn.com.

26. Rachel G., message posted at http://apps.scholastic.com/tabteens/reading.asp.

27. Letters to the Editor, "What Readers Think About 'Goblet,' " *San Francisco Chronicle*, July 26, 2000, available online at www.sfgate.com.

28. Lily, "Reader Comments," http://hosted.ukoln.ac.uk/stories/gallery/reviews/rowling/rowling-stone.htm.

29. Wang Wen, "Readers Comments," http://hosted.ukoln.ac.uk/stories/gallery/reviews/rowling/rowling-stone.htm.

30. Devon, "Readers Comments," http://yabooks.about.com/teens/yabooks/bl_potter2_more1.htm?terms=occultism+Potter.

31. Mairead, "Readers Comments," http://yabooks.about.com/teens/yabooks/bl_potter2_more7.htm.

32. Customer Reviews, statement available online at amazon.co.uk.

33. J.K. Rowling, "Harry Potter Fights Back," BBC interview, available online at www.bbc.co.uk, Oct. 17, 1999.

34. Linda Goettina, *Nightline* (ABC), July 7, 2000, transcript available online at www.abcnews.go.com.

35. Reverend Nick Bury, quoted in Ruth Gledhill, "Protest Threat to Potter Cathedral," *The Times* (London), August 16, 2000, www.Sunday-times.co.uk.

36. Rowling, *Goblet of Fire*, 55.

37. Rowling, *Goblet of Fire*, 88, 367.

38. Rowling, *Goblet of Fire*, 88-89, 117.

39. Rowling, *Goblet of Fire*, 117.

40. Rowling, *Goblet of Fire*, 45.

41. Rowling, *Goblet of Fire*, 61.

42. Rowling, *Goblet of Fire*, 722.

43. Rowling, *Goblet of Fire*, 329.

44. Rowling, *Goblet of Fire*, 334.

45. Rowling, *Goblet of Fire*, 341.

46. Rowling, *Goblet of Fire*, 351.

47. Rowling, *Goblet of Fire*, 338-339.

48. Rowling, *Goblet of Fire*, 343.

49. Rowling, *Goblet of Fire*, 438.

50. Rowling, *Goblet of Fire*, 371.

51. Rowling, *Goblet of Fire*, 438.

52. Rowling, *Goblet of Fire*, 391.

53. Rowling, *Goblet of Fire*, 90.

54. Rowling, *Goblet of Fire*, 111.

55. This insightful observation was first raised by Michael O'Brien in his important work, *A Landscape with Dragons* (San Francisco: Ignatius Press, 1998), 68.

56. J.K. Rowling, quoted in Deirdre Donahue, "Harry Potter's Kid Appeal: Proof Positive," *USA Today*, December 2, 1999, available online at www.usatoday.com.

57. Jennifer G., "Harry Potter: Magical or Harmful?: The Beloved Wizard—Revisited!," available online at www.momsonline.oxygen.com/agesandstages/schoolage/activities/articles.asp?key=mk110299.

58. Statements available online at www.scholastic.com/harrypotter/books/guides/index.htm.

59. www.scholastic.com/harrypotter/books/guides/index.htm.

60. J.K. Rowling, Barnes and Noble interview, March 19, 1999, available online at www.barnesandnoble.com/community/archive/transcript.asp?userid=54CE6SM CB8&evenltd=1517.

61. Nigel Reynolds, "Children's Book of Magic Tops Best-seller Charts," *Electronic Telegraph*, July 8, 1998, available online at www.telegraph.co.uk.

62. Rowling, 465.

63. J.K. Rowling, Stories from the Web interview, http://hosted.ukoln.ac.uk/stories/stories/rowling/interview1.htm; cf. Emily Farache, "Darker and Scarier Harry Potter Going Hollywood?," September 25, 1999, available online at www.eonline.com.

64. Steve Bonta, "Harry Potter's Hocus Pocus," *The New American*, August 28, 2000, available online at www.thenewamerican.com/tna/2000/08-28-2000/vo16no18_potter.htm.

65. J.K. Rowling, quoted in Bonta, available online at www.thenewamerican.com.

66. Mary Ann Grossman, "Newest Harry Potter Adventure a Bit Thick with Wizard History," *St. Paul (MN) Pioneer Press*, July 9, 2000, 1A, available online at www.pioneerplanet.com/columnists/docs/GROSSMAN/docs/031617.htm; cf. Connie Fletcher, "Longer and Darker, But More Riveting," *MSNBC*, July 26, 2000, available online at www.msnbc.com.

67. Pam Ciepichal, "Goblet of Fire Delivers Twists, Turns," *Pencil News* (MSNBC), available online at www.msnbc.com.

68. Deepti Hajela, "Potter In Fine Form," July 8, 2000, *ABC News*, available online at abcnews.com.

69. Mark Lawson, "Hype At Its Hottest, but Rowling May Survive It," *The Guardian*, July 10, 2000, www.guardianunlimited.co.uk/Archive/Article/0,4273,4038672,00.html.

70. Rowling, *Goblet of Fire*, 103.

71. Rowling, *Goblet of Fire*.

72. Rowling, *Goblet of Fire*, 252-253.

73. Rowling, *Goblet of Fire*, 426, 429.

74. Bonta, available online at www.thenewamerican.com/tna/2000/08-28-2000/vo16no18_potter.htm.
75. Rowling, *Goblet of Fire*, 719.

PART
TWO

OUT OF THE
DARKNESS

NINE

THE ENDURING BATTLE: GOOD VERSUS EVIL

[J.K. Rowling's] books have a strong moral message and clearly portray good and evil.

Bloomsbury Publishing[1]
publisher, Harry Potter series

[T]he theme running through all of these books is the fight between good and evil.

J.K. Rowling[2]

Nearly every civilization and culture throughout history has accepted the belief that there exists an ongoing cosmic struggle between the forces of good and the forces of evil. The Vikings (c. 800-1000 A.D.) believed that the gods they worshiped were in continual strife with evil creatures known as *Jotnene*. Prior to the Norsemen, Persians in Mesopotamia (c. 650 B.C.) held that the universe was controlled by two warring gods—*Ahura-Mazda*, the creating god, full of light and good; and *Ahriman*, the god of dark and evil. And before the Persians, the ancient Hebrews had taught about the perennial conflict between Lucifer (a fallen angel) and Yahweh (the one true God).

This universal knowledge explaining the presence of sin in the world dates back to the very beginning of time, to a place called the Garden of Eden. There, the Bible tells us, God created the first humans; namely, Adam, who was made from the dust of the earth (Genesis 2:7), and Eve, who was fashioned by God from a portion of bone taken from Adam's side (2:21-22). Both of them were perfect and received their life directly from God Himself (1:27). Moreover, Adam and Eve were provided with great blessings: a beautiful world in which to live (1:29), plentiful food (1:29-31), the loving companionship of one another (2:21-25) and unimpeded access to God (1:29-31). Adam and Eve also were given free will, a necessary component of any loving relationship among individuals.

For a time, the couple enjoyed an unhindered rapport with each other and with God through their free will. But to test their hearts, God gave them one command to follow as a sign of their obedience and subjection to Him: "And the LORD God commanded the man, saying, Of every tree of the garden thou mayest freely eat: But of the tree of the knowledge of good and evil, thou shalt not eat of it" (2:16-17). This test was designed to give Adam and Eve a knowledge of good and evil through obedience. But God's enemy, Lucifer (a fallen angel), wanted to destroy the relationship between God and His creations, so he deceived Eve into transgressing God's command.

Ultimately, both Adam and Eve decided to disobey God's directive, thereby learning the difference between good and evil in a reverse manner, i.e., through disobedience (3:6-7). Through these first sins ever committed on Earth came God's judgment on the whole human race (3:16-19). Thus humanity entered into the great war between good (God) and evil (Lucifer).

The consequences of Adam and Eve's disobedience were disastrous. Earth was cursed and rendered incapable of spontaneously bringing forth adequate amounts of food (3:17-19), and human beings could no longer live forever as they were originally designed to do (2:16-17). As theologian Louis Berkhoff pointed out in his *Systematic Theology*, physical, emotional and psychological suffering also began to affect humanity:

> Sin brought disturbance in the entire life of man. His physical life fell prey to weaknesses and diseases, which result in discomforts and often in agonizing pains; and his mental life became subject to distressing disturbances, which often rob him of the joy of life, disqualify him for his daily task, and sometimes entirely destroy his mental equilibrium. His very soul has become a battlefield of conflicting thoughts, passions, and desires. The will refuses to follow the judgment of the intellect, and the passions run riot without the control of an intelligent will.[3]

As the human race continued on its course of development, the tendency to disobey God increased exponentially to include murder (4:8), drunkenness (9:21), lying (12:13), adultery (16:4), homosexuality (19:5) and incest (19:32-36). In the *Moody Handbook of Theology*, Dr. Paul Enns insightfully explains that these and other sins basically fall into two distinct categories—wrongful acts toward God and wrongful acts toward other human beings:

> Romans 1:18 refers to "ungodliness and unrighteousness of men." Ungodliness refers to man's failure to obey God and keep commandments related to Him (Exodus 20:1-11); unrighteousness is seen in man's failure to live righteously toward his fellow man (Exodus 20:12-17).[4]

According to renowned Christian scholar J.I. Packer, sin "may be comprehensively defined as lack of conformity to the law of God in act, habit, attitude, outlook, disposition, motivation and mode of existence."[5] More specifically, sin may be defined in four distinct, yet related, ways:[6]

1. Breaking God's law or standards of right conduct (Romans 4:15; cf. Romans 2:23; 5:14; Galatians 3:19)
2. Nonconformity to what one knows to be the right course of action (Romans 14:23; James 4:12)
3. A principle within man known as the sin nature, often called the flesh (Romans 7:14, 17-25)
4. A state of mind that not only tolerates but also actively pursues lawlessness (1 John 3:4)

The effects of Adam's choice to disobey God have traveled down through successive generations as a hideous moral cancer. Everyone is born with a sinful nature (Psalm 14:1-3; Romans 3:23); as Packer observes, "we are not sinners because we sin, but rather we sin because we are sinners, born with a nature enslaved to sin."[7] Today, the battle between good and evil still goes on in this world, with one side of combatants embracing darkness (i.e., sin) and the other side pursuing the light of God's truth, justice and morality as expressed in the person of Jesus Christ (John 1:1-2, 18; Hebrews 1:1-3).

But Lucifer is a cunning foe, who has for many millennia continued through deception to draw humans away from God and His righteousness. Perhaps Satan's cleverest tool has been false religions, especially those religious belief systems that make adherents feel as if they have control over the world around them. One such belief system, nearly as old as humanity itself, is occultism—which, as we have seen in previous chapters, is the foundation of J.K. Rowling's Harry Potter series.

ROWLING'S INSPIRATION

The occult is a vast system of religious studies, theories, practices and beliefs that allegedly enable participants to obtain supernatural knowledge, which can then be used to control or at least in some way influence their environment (e.g., change the future, bring harm to an enemy, make someone fall in love or secure sudden wealth). The word "occult" derives its meaning from the Latin word *occulere* ("to hide"), a term originally used in reference to the knowledge held by initiates of various "mystery religions" and secret societies. Modern occultism's link to this term can be seen in its ultimate goal, which is to gain "secret powers" of the mind and spirit.[8]

Occult practices can be traced back thousands of years to an era when people believed that "apparent deviations from natural law involved mysterious and miraculous 'supernatural' or occult laws, deriving from gods, invisible entities or the souls of the dead."[9] Hoping to access the power behind these forces, individuals and cultures developed magick rituals, which in turn gave rise to witch doctors and shamans, who claimed a heightened ability to perform magick. Thus began humanity's quest to control an uncontrollable world through the alteration, refocusing or suspension of various laws of nature.

Today, the occult label is applicable to numerous practices, including astrology, alchemy, automatic writing, channeling, crystal gazing, dowsing, dream interpretation, extrasensory perception (ESP), fortune-telling, necromancy (communication with the dead), numerology, Ouija boards, out-of-body travel (astral projection), palm-reading, psychic healing, psychokinesis, pyramidology, Satanism, shamanism, Tarot cards, telekinesis, voodoo and witchcraft.

Occultism additionally encompasses various abnormal or unusual phenomena such as UFO abductions, hauntings and reports of unexplained creatures (e.g., Bigfoot, the Loch Ness Monster and Mexico's Chupacabra [a vampire-like creature]). Paranormal events that seem to defy natural explanation (psychic visions, premonitions, etc.) also fall within occultism. The modern world of the occult basically involves "anything from the conjuror's [sic] hat-trick to the dark ceremonies of the witches' sabbat."[10] This, of course, has made discussion of the occult a daunting task, as Julien Tondriau's explains in *The Occult: Secrets of the Hidden World*:

> Occult belief comprises traditions both of immense antiquity and great complexity in which it is nearly impossible to find any degree of uniformity and consistency, and the followers of occultism are themselves notoriously given to mystification so that their own accounts of an [sic] subject are full of strange pseudo-scientific jargon and merely add to the confusion.[11]

In an attempt to understand the highly complex and multifaceted world of the occult better, sociologists have divided occultists into three separate categories:

> At the first level are people whose involvement in the occult is minimal who do not see themselves as occultists per se but as concerned individuals interested in explaining such strange occurrences as flying saucers, assorted land and sea monsters and various parapsychological phenomena. Typically their activities are characterized by an absence of mysticism, supernaturalism and anti-scientific thought; in fact, scientific support for their beliefs is highly valued. . . . [On the] second level of occultism are people who seek to understand mysterious causal relationships between events—who express an interest, for example, in numerology, sun-sign astrology and palmistry. Knowledge gained at this level is more likely to be a scientific or extra-scientific rather than anti-scientific. . . . [The] third level of occultism is concerned with those complex belief systems—witchcraft, Satanism, ritual magic and other mysti-

cal traditions—that combine elements from the first two levels. Third-level believers often question or contradict scientific validation of an event or relationship and thus may see themselves as competitors to science. . . . [A]lthough some occult believers exist in "pure form," most are a combination of all three types.[12]

Interestingly, some avowed scientists actually have spent a considerable amount of time trying to prove the existence of occult powers. This pseudoscientific field of study, dubbed parapsychology, originated in the 1930s with Duke University professor, Joseph Banks Rhine. He was the first individual to look scientifically "for evidence of a strange and remarkable capability that he called extrasensory perception, or simply ESP."[13] Rhine's search included at least four "senses" that science had supposedly missed:

- Telepathy, or mind reading ("direct mental communication between two persons").
- Clairvoyance, or second-sight ("specific perception of an event or object through means that do not involve the known senses").
- Precognition, or telling the future ("perceiving of future events without deducing their occurrence from existing knowledge").
- Psychokinesis, or use of one's mind power to "effect change in external matter."[14]

These four areas of investigation are commonly referred to as "psi," a word corresponding to the twenty-third letter of the Greek alphabet, which is sometimes used in scientific equations for an unknown quantity. Although emergence of parapsychology has opened up yet another avenue for occult involvement and obsession, the three segments of occultism that seem to be drawing the most adherents today are Paganism, Witchcraft and Satanism.

THE PAGAN PARADIGM

America's occult landscape is populated by a highly diverse collection of individuals espousing a variety of religious beliefs. Because most of them tend to be eclectic in their views, not every occultist can be easily categorized. But of those who do fall into some sort of classification, the largest segment of persons would have to be neopagans. *Neo*paganism basically is a modernization of ancient paganism, which took root in prehistoric times and continued in popularity until suppressed by the rise of Christianity.

The word paganism comes from the Latin word *paganus*, meaning "country dweller." This term refers back to the primitive people who developed "paganism" as a means of explaining the world around them. Their religious belief system was based on the worship of: 1) a Mother Goddess, who represented creation, birth, food-gathering, agricultural plenty and the summer; and 2) the Horned God, male consort of the Mother Goddess, who represented the hunt, death and the winter months. To these two prime deities, various cultures added other gods and goddesses until a pantheon of deities was available for worship: Isis, Cernunnos, Balder, Pan, Osiris, Odin, Diana, Astaroth, Brighid, Aphrodite, Athena, Cerridwen, Freya, Artemis, Ceres, Hecate, Kali, Cybele, Cerridwen and Gaia.

Now, all of these ancient deities are being revered by a whole new generation of pagans (i.e., neopagans). In fact, the Internet's "Book of Deities" web site lists more than 1,700 gods and goddesses invoked by modern pagans. But beyond recognizing an acceptance of multiple deities it is a daunting task to present any clearly defined set of pagan beliefs. Each person essentially defines his or her own brand of paganism based on what "feels" right. "Pagans pursue their own vision of the Divine as a direct and personal experience."[15] Nevertheless, a general outline of what *most* pagans believe can be deduced from pagan literature:

> Neopagans hold a reverence for the Earth and all its creatures, generally see all life as interconnected and tend to strive to attune one's self to the manifestation of this belief as seen in the cycles of nature. Pagans are usually polytheistic (believing in more than one god) and they usually believe in immanence, or the concept of divinity residing in all things. Many pagans, though polytheistic, see all things as being part of one Great Mystery. The apparent contradiction of being both polytheistic and monotheistic can be resolved by seeing the God/[Goddesses] as masks worn by the Great Mystery. Other pagans are simply monotheistic or polytheistic and still others are atheistic.[16]

In addition to these views, neopagans often identify with one of many pre-Christian religious traditions (e.g., Druidic, Greek, Egyptian, Norse, Roman, etc.). One of the most popular is Druidism, which focuses on interaction with the gods and goddesses of the Celtic past. According to The Pagan Federation, Druidism "stresses the mystery of poetic inspiration and explores healing, divination and sacred mythology."[17] Other highly favored branches of neopaganism include:

- Odinism, which draws upon Norse and Anglo-Saxon mythologies for its rituals and spirituality;
- Shamanism, an incredibly diverse form of neopaganism wherein adherents focus mainly on deepening one's spiritual life through communion with entities in the spirit world;

- the Dianic Movement, which is primarily a feminist spirituality movement that concentrates on worshiping the goddess Diana, thereby enabling women to reestablish their feminine powers and reclaim the deeper significance of what it means to be female.[18]

But out of all the many different traditions of paganism that exist, none is more popular or influential today than Wicca, also known as either Witchcraft or The Craft.

A WORD ABOUT WICCA[19]

Wicca is perhaps one of the most misunderstood religions in our society. The mere mention of the word "witch" conjures up images of old hags, boiling cauldrons and flying broomsticks at Satan's beck and call. Nothing could be further from the truth. Contemporary witches actually tend to be peace-loving, nature-honoring individuals who take somewhat of a "you-leave-me-alone-and-I'll-leave-you-alone-let's-just-do-our-own-thing" approach to life. Craig Hawkins, a Christian expert on Witchcraft, explains the basics of Wiccan beliefs in his excellent book *Witchcraft: Exploring the World of Wicca*:

> *Witchcraft*: (Also known as wicca, the craft, or the craft of the wise.) An antidogmatic, antiauthoritarian, diverse, decentralized, eclectic, experience-based, nature-oriented religious movement whose followers are polytheists and/or pantheists and in some sense believe in or experience and/or invoke and/or worship the Mother Goddess and generally her consort the Horned God as well. It is a generic term covering numerous perspectives on the subject. *Witches*: Individuals who practice or concur with the views or experiences of witchcraft. Most view divinity as immanent in nature, seeing all life as sacred, thus denying any sacred/secular distinction. They

are nature-oriented and also see no ultimate distinction between matter and spirit—the material and the spiritual. They may believe in or invoke a pantheon of gods and goddesses, but they primarily experience, and/or invoke, and/or worship the Mother or Triple Goddess and her male consort, the Horned God. Witches generally practice multiple forms of divination, participate in trance and other altered states of consciousness and perform magical spells and incantations. Most observe seasonal holidays and festivals (e.g., the summer and winter solstices). Most believe in some form of reincarnation. The widely believed notion that a female is a witch whereas a male practitioner is a warlock or wizard is a misnomer. The terms witch or wiccan apply to both genders.[20]

Because Wicca fits under the umbrella category of paganism, the two religious systems have many similarities. Both paganism and witchcraft are antidogmatic, antiauthoritarian, polytheistic, find divinity in nature, love/worship nature to some extent, believe in humanity's inherent divinity, cultivate psychic abilities and practice magick.[21] And as with paganism, Wicca-witchcraft has many strains: Gardnerian, Algard, Alexandrian, Cymry, Dianic, Corelliam and Guyddon, to name a few. The most common elements binding together these and other forms of witchcraft are as follows:

1. Exaltation of experience over any set of dogmatic beliefs.
2. Acceptance of diversity of beliefs as healthy and essential to humanity's well-being.
3. Denial of absolute truth. No single religion or morality is objectively right. "True is what is true for you; right is what is right for you.... Your path may not be my own,

but both are equally viable trails of truth and spiritual-ity."[22]

4. Adherence to the Wiccan ethical code: "If ye harm none, do what ye will."

5. Working of magick and various divination techniques.

6. Development of personal psychic abilities.

Witchcraft is particularly attractive today for various reasons, as Ronald Hutton observes in his 1991 book *The Pagan Religions of the Ancient British Isles*:

> The advantage of the label "witch" is that it has all the exciting connotations of a figure who flouts conventions of normal society and is possessed of powers unavailable to it, at once feared and persecuted. It is a marvelous rallying-point for a counter-culture and also one of the few images of independent female power in early modern European civilization.[23]

It is important to remember that although pagans and witches share many values and views, there are many distinctions between them. All witches may be pagans, but not all pagans are witches. Even more important is to remember that witchcraft and paganism are not synonymous with Satanism, which is an altogether different form of occultism.

SATAN'S LAIR

The developmental history of Satanism is a long and twisted path that winds back through centuries of witchcraft, superstition, religious folklore and ancient paganism. It emerged when various aspects of all these traditions were blended together by persons seeking to fight Christianity's growing theological and moral influence (c. 400s-1600s A.D.). Consequently, Satanism has come to represent the ultimate expression of rebellion against

God. Although this system of religious beliefs technically falls into the world of occultism, it is unique for several reasons.

First, Satanism "is not a monolithic, unified whole in its organizational structure, beliefs and practices."[24] The components of Satanism are as diverse as the personalities of those involved. According to Satanism experts Bob and Gretchen Passantino, this is because all Satanists are characterized by a self-serving attitude. Consequently, "it is to be expected that Satanism could have almost as many definitions as practitioners."[25]

Second, Satanists have no universal definition for their object of worship and service (i.e., Satan). Journalist Arthur Lyons, in his investigation of contemporary American Satanism, found that a Satanist is anyone who sincerely describes himself as a worshiper of "the devil," whatever he perceives that to mean.[26] Satan is variously identified as "a supernatural person, a deity, a devil, a supernatural force, a natural force, an innate human force, or, most commonly, the self."[27]

Third, Satanism is a deliberate reversal, or inversion, of an established world religion: Christianity. It is literally anti-Christian in all that it teaches. For example, Christian vices such as pride, greed and lust are viewed by Satanists as virtues. Christian virtues such as humility, self-control and sacrificial love are seen by Satanists as utterly abhorrent and worthy of destruction. Even satanic rituals, when initially formulated, were designed to mirror Christian rituals, but in a mocking fashion. This is extremely unlike witchcraft or paganism, neither of which came into existence in response to the rise of Christianity in Europe. The only animosity pagans/witches feel toward Christianity (or any religion) is "to the extent that its institutions have claimed to be 'the only way' and have sought to deny freedom to others and to suppress other ways of religious practice and belief."[28]

Religion scholar J. Gordon Melton categorizes all Satanists into two main groups. On the one hand are the "public groups which take Satanism as a religion seriously and have developed articulate theologies which do not resemble in many ways what one might expect."[29] Individuals involved in such groups—sometimes called "religious" Satanists—rarely commit occult-related criminal acts and frown upon those who do. Church of Satan founder Anton LaVey (1930-1997), for instance, has stated: "Satanism has nothing to do with kidnaping, drug abuse, child molestation, animal or child sacrifice, or any number of their acts that idiots, hysterics or opportunists would like to credit us with."[30]

On the other hand, Melton recognizes that there are Satanists who constitute many

> disconnected groups of occultists who employ Satan worship to cover a variety of sexual, sad-masochistic, clandestine, psychopathetic and illegal activities. These groups typically engage in grave-robberies, sexual assaults and bloodletting (both animal and human) . . . [and] are characterized by a lack of theology, an informality of gatherings, ephemeral life and disconnectedness from other similar groups.[31]

Participants in this latter group are commonly referred to as "self-styled" Satanists. They invent their own brand of Satanism based on an eclectic collection of beliefs/rituals that they have been exposed to through satanic literature, sensationalized accounts of Satanism, occult movies, rumors about Satanism and occult music.

In his book *Satan Wants You*, journalist Arthur Lyons takes a different approach by dividing Satan-worshipers into three separate groups: 1) solitary Satanists; 2) "outlaw" cults; and 3) neo-Satanic churches. He describes these in the following manner:

"Solitary" Satanists belong to no cult and employ their own made-up brand, which they usually procure from books on the subject. . . . [T]hese Satanists are alienated teenagers who have a difficult time socializing, and the rituals they perform usually involve some sort of wish fulfillment, such as the acquisition of money, popularity, romance, or sex. Often the practices of these individuals are tied to drug use and a fanatical devotion to rock music—particularly heavy metal rock—and their Satanic "rituals" consist of little more than getting stoned, lighting candles, and reading a passage aloud from Anton LaVey's *The Satanic Bible*, to the accompaniment of an Ozzy Osbourne tape. "Outlaw" groups worship Satan as the Evil One of the New Testament, and their practices reflect that orientation. . . . [T]he focus of such groups has tended to be more on drugs, music, and vandalism than sex. The members are usually young (fifteen to twenty-five), socially alienated, and held together by a charismatic leader. Meetings are generally sporadic and lack any coherent theology; the rituals, like those of solitary Satanists, tend to be slapped together from movies and books on black magic. . . . [T]he rituals often include socially deviant, and sometimes violent, acts. . . . [Then there] are the "neo-Satanic" churches. . . . These groups—which constitute the overwhelming bulk of the current Satanic membership—strictly prohibit the ritualistic harming of any living thing, and enjoin members from participating in illegal activities. . . . They advocate egotism, indulgence and the acquisition and use of personal and political power, have well-defined theologies and authority structures, and recruit members openly. . . . [T]wo such groups, the Church of Satan and the Temple of Set, maintain listings in the San Francisco yellow pages.[32]

The two underlying beliefs that seem to connect all forms of Satanism are selfish hedonism and nonconformity. A Satanist's personal needs are of primary importance and the more a Satanist can get those needs met by going against the grain of society, the better off he or she will be. In fact, nonconformity is "Satanism's strength."[33] According to Anton LaVey, a Satanist "should not allow himself to be programmed by others.... [T]hat is the greatest enemy to his freedom of spirit. It is the very denial of life itself, which was given to him for a wondrous unique experience—not for imitation of the colorless existence of others."[34]

The term Satanism could just as easily be replaced by the term hedonism. Why, then, did LaVey bother calling his belief system Satanism? One reason, he stated, is "because it's fun." Another reason stemmed from the emotional punch held by the word Satan, as well as its inherent link to rebellion, as LaVey explains: "I have termed my thought 'Satanism' because it is most stimulating. . . . Self-discipline and motivation are effected more easily under stimulating conditions. Satanism means 'the opposition' and epitomizes all symbols of nonconformity."[35] LaVey additionally felt that using the term Satanism better identified his worldview as a legitimate religion complete with ceremonies and rituals, which he felt could meet the emotional needs of his unholy flock.[36]

Satanists view their approach to life as the fullest expression of living, even though others might perceive their actions as evil. A Satanist's obsession with the self is epitomized in "The Nine Satanic Statements" of LaVey's Church of Satan, as listed in *The Satanic Bible*:

1. Satan represents indulgence, instead of abstinence!
2. Satan represents vital existence, instead of spiritual pipe dreams!

3. Satan represents undefiled wisdom, instead of hypocritical self-deceit!
4. Satan represents kindness to those who deserve it, instead of love wasted on ingrates!
5. Satan represents vengeance, instead of turning the other cheek!
6. Satan represents responsibility to the responsible, instead of concern for psychic vampires!
7. Satan represents man as just another animal, sometimes better, more often worse than those that walk on all-fours, who, because of his "divine spiritual and intellectual development," has become the most vicious animal of all!
8. Satan represents all of the so-called sins, as they all lead to physical, mental, or emotional gratification!
9. Satan has been the best friend the church has ever had, as he has kept it in business all these years![37]

This list reveals yet another hallmark of Satanism: a hatred of Christianity. Satanists hold that Christian morality "is based on guilt and self denial, is a load of hogwash."[38] They see followers of Jesus as hypocritical, narrow-minded, ignorant fools. LaVey writes: "Christian doctrine has become outmoded and unbelievable, even to the most feebleminded. One wonders, 'How is it possible for people to be so stupid as to believe the lies they are taught by ministers and priests?' "[39] One reason Satanists find Christianity so detestable is that they feel the Christian church has historically been concerned with nothing but controlling the populace through dreary "lists of don'ts":

> The squealing Christian creep is correct in assuming Satanism is dangerous. . . . Satanism is dangerous because it encourages originality over herd mentality. Large masses of

people who all act and think within a prescribed set of op-
tions are much easier to control. And exploit.[40]

Given the stress placed on self-indulgence by Satanists, it is
only natural that they would view Christianity—a religion marked
by self-control and love of others—as a loathsome belief system.
In response, they do all they can to practice a reversal of Christianity. For example, Satanists have been known to recite the
Lord's Prayer backward during their ceremonies and to use an in-
verted cross to mock Christ's crucifixion.

It must be stressed that in rejecting Christianity, most Satanists
are not necessarily pledging allegiance to the personal spirit-being
whom Christians identify as Satan. The majority of Satanists de-
nounce all forms of spirituality and hold to a philosophy that is
basically materialistic and atheistic. Satan, whom they "worship,"
is merely a symbol for the self. In LaVey's words, "We don't worship Satan, we worship ourselves using the metaphorical represen-
tation of the qualities of Satan."[41]

Obviously, Satanism, Witchcraft-Wicca and paganism are
distinct belief systems in the overarching structure termed occultism. Although disparate in their approach to life, there is
one thing common to all of them: magick.

Magickal Mysteries

A key component of witchcraft, paganism and Satanism is occult magick, which basically is "the attempt to control, manipulate, bend, shape, twist, turn, or direct reality for one's own ends
or goals. This is supposedly accomplished by invoking or employ-
ing spirits or extradimensional entities or beings, or mysteries, unknown or seldom used powers, forces, rules, guidelines and/or
laws [of nature]."[42] Magick normally is accomplished through
spells or incantations. These often consist of highly evocative im-

agery such as repetitive phrases and/or power words designed to bring forth natural external forces or the inner powers of the self.

The Encyclopedia of Occultism and Parapsychology defines a spell as a "written or spoken formula of words supposed to be capable of magical effects."[43] The theory behind spells comes from the idea that there is a natural and intimate connection between words and whatever objects or persons they signify. It is believed that under the right circumstances a magician can cause an event to occur by either chanting about or describing the event desired, while at the same time describing the actions of the objects/people/spirits involved in the event.[44]

Although the essence of magick has yet to be precisely defined, many occultists (especially witches) view magick as something that actually is quite natural, rather than supernatural. In *Witchcraft: The Old Religion*, Leo Martello remarks, "I make no claims as a Witch to 'supernatural powers,' but I totally believe in the *super* powers that reside in the *natural*."[45] Witch spokesperson Scott Cunningham agrees: "Folk magic cannot and could not be construed as a supernatural, otherworldly process. . . . It's a perfectly natural process that most of us simply haven't used."[46] Cunningham writes, "Folk magicians don't use supernatural powers. . . . They simply sense and utilize natural energies which have not yet been quantified, codified and accepted into the hallowed halls of science."[47] In other words, magick is merely a way of harnessing natural forces yet to be discovered by science.

Herein lies what seems to be another interesting and significant link between witchcraft/magick and J.K. Rowling, the creator of Harry Potter. While Rowling has consistently maintained through carefully worded statements that she does not believe in the supernatural "wand waving sort of magic" found in her books, she has never disowned other types of magick (see Chapter 2)—e.g., "natural" magick accepted by occultists. In fact, Rowling has made various comments that sound strikingly similar to opinions voiced by witches and pagans about magick and its relation to science, individuals and the world in general. Consider the following:

Witchcraft-Paganism	J.K. Rowling Interview
"Magic . . . is obeying laws that the observer has not yet understood. A sixteenth-century scientist, for example . . . if he could have seen television might well have branded it as supernatural."[48]	*Q:* "Did you do any research on wizard customs [and believe in magick]?" *J.K.:* "I don't believe in it myself, [but] we shouldn't be too arrogant. Some stuff we believe today will be considered rubbish in years to come, and things we think of as rubbish now will be considered true."[49]

Additionally, remarks have been made by Rowling about her belief in the magickal properties of the number seven, which in part has determined the final number of volumes in her fantasy series (see Chapter 2). Interestingly, the number seven was discussed in great detail by occultist Helena Petrovna Blavatsky (1831-1891), whose name seems to appear in the form of an anagram in *Harry Potter and the Prisoner of Azkaban* (i.e., Vablatsky, see Chapter 2). Blavatsky's article titled "The Number Seven" reads as follows:

> The number *seven* was considered sacred not only by all the cultured nations of antiquity and the East, but was held in the greatest reverence even by the later nations of the West. The astronomical origin of this number is established beyond any doubt. . . . [and is related to] the planets which the whole antiquity numbered as *seven*. In course of time

these [planets] were transformed into *seven* deities. The Egyptians had *seven* original and higher gods; the Phoenicians *seven* kabiris; the Persians, *seven* sacred horses of Mithra; the Parsees, *seven* angels opposed by *seven* demons, and *seven* celestial abodes paralleled by *seven* lower regions. To represent the more clearly this idea in its concrete form, the *seven gods* were often represented as one *seven-headed* deity. The whole heaven was subjected to the *seven* planets; hence, in nearly all the religious systems we find *seven* heavens.[50]

Blavatsky also pointed out these magical aspects to the number seven:

- Ancient Egyptians believed seven states of soul purification.
- Buddhists teach seven stages of progressive development of the disembodied soul.
- In Mithraism, an ancient mystery religion, there were seven gates, seven altars, seven mysteries.
- Priests of many Oriental nations were subdivided into seven degrees; seven steps led to the altars and in the temples burnt seven candles in seven-branched candlesticks.
- Arabian legends assert that "seven angels cool the sun with ice and snow, lest it should burn the earth to cinders; and seven thousand angels set the sun in motion every morning."
- Eastern antiquity valued seven principal rivers (Nile, Tigris, Euphrates, Oxus, Yaksart, Arax and Indus), seven famous treasures, seven cities full of gold and seven marvels of the world.[51]

Obviously, not everything connected to the number seven is occult in origin. The Bible, for example, uses the number seven as a symbol of completion, since God completed the world in seven days. But Blavatsky does not consider the number seven to be a mere symbol, but to possess magical power—a far cry from biblical teaching. This magicality of the number seven is not the only occult concept Rowling has mentioned in passing. In a promotional video produced by Scholastic, she stresses: "It's important to remember that we all have magic inside us."[52] Compare this idea to the words of renowned witch, Doreen Valiente: [T]he powers of witchcraft, magic, shamanism, or whatever one likes to call it, are latent in everyone."[53] Valiente goes on to say that the only thing any of us have to do is properly train our abilities via "techniques which will bring them out and develop them."[54]

Such a belief finds clear literary expression in the foundational plot of the Harry Potter series: that young witches and wizards must learn how to control their magical potential. The Hogwarts philosophy mirrors with surprising accuracy the *General Practices* of The Covenant of Goddess organization, which states: "We see psychic abilities as a natural human potential, and are dedicated to developing this as well as all of our positive human potentials."[55]

And so it seems that Rowling may accept various scattered principles of magick and occultism. At the very least, she clearly is sympathetic to the world of occultism/witchcraft and the possibility that some kinds of magick—other than the "wand waving" magic that appears in her books—may indeed exist. Exactly how much occultism Rowling has embraced due to her studies of witchcraft and wizardry is uncertain because she has consistently refused to reveal her spiritual beliefs. As one highly observant witch noted, the published material about Rowling "says surprisingly little about her religious persuasion."[56]

In a CNN interview, Rowling stated, "I absolutely did not start writing these books to encourage any child into witchcraft." She continued, "I'm laughing slightly because to me, the idea is absurd."[57] But it is neither absurd, nor laughable, to suppose that the Harry Potter books might lead some children into the world of occultism since the series contains actual beliefs and practices associated with witchcraft and paganism, including: divination, astrology, numerology, familiars, pagan gods/goddesses, spellcasting, potions, necromancy (i.e., communication with the dead/ghosts), mediumship/channeling, crystal gazing, palmistry, charms, arithmancy and magick (spelled with a "k," see Chapter 6).

In Britain, Rowling's imaginary tales have already prompted youths to seek information about occultism from the Pagan Federation (see Chapter 4). This demonstrates that Rowling's "fantasy" is potentially harmful because it brings children so close to actual occultism. Ultimately, only a short distance needs to be covered in order to cross over from Harry Potter's world into the realm of occultism. And the effects of occultism, especially with regard to using magick, can have devastating results, as we shall see in the next chapter.

ENDNOTES

1. Public Statement, quoted in Patrick Goodenough, "Harry Potter Books Alarm UK Christian Educators," *Cybercast News Service*, March 30, 2000, online report republished by *Free Daily*, ServeHim.com, available online at www.freedaily.com. Also available at www.religioustolerance.org/potter.htm.
2. J.K. Rowling, quoted in Chuck Colson, "Witches and Wizards: The Harry Potter Phenomenon," *BreakPoint Commentary*, #91102, November 2, 1999, available online at www.breakpoint.org.
3. Louis Berkhoff, *Systematic Theology* (Grand Rapids: Eerdmans, 1939 reprint), 259.
4. Paul Enns, *Moody Handbook of Theology* (Chicago: Moody, 1989), 310.
5. J.I. Packer, *Concise Theology* (Wheaton, IL: Tyndale House, 1993), 82.
6. Enns, 310.

7. Packer, 83.

8. *The Steinerbooks Dictionary of the Psychic, Mystic, Occult* (Blauvelt, NY: Rudolf Steiner Publications, 1973), 148.

9. Leslie A. Shepard, ed., *Encyclopedia of Occultism & Parapsychology* (Detroit: Gale Research, 1991), 2:1207.

10. Julien Tondriau, *The Occult: Secrets of the Hidden World* (New York: Pyramid Communications, 1972), 5.

11. Tondriau.

12. Arthur C. Lehmann and James E. Meyers, *Magic, Witchcraft, and Religion* (Mountain View, CA: Mayfield Publishing, 1993), 369-370.

13. Will Bradbury, ed., *Into the Unknown* (Pleasantville, NY: Reader's Digest, 1981), 203.

14. Bradbury.

15. "Traditions of the Pagan Religion," The Pagan Federation Online, available online at www.paganfed.demon.co.uk/infopacks/pf/pf_trad.html.

16. Susan Harwood Kaczmarczik, et al., "Alt.Pagan Frequently Asked Questions," January 25, 1993, accessible from Beverly's Homepage at http://homepage.mac.com/paganrain/altpagfaq.html.

17. The Pagan Federation Online, available online at www.paganfed.demon.co.uk/infopacks/pf/pf_druid.htm.

18. Information available online at www.paganfed.demon.co.uk.

19. The word "wicca" is the original Anglo-Saxon spelling for the modern English word "witch" (Margot Adler, *Drawing Down the Moon: Witches, Druids, Goddess-Worshippers and Other Pagans in America Today* [Boston: Beacon Press, 1979], 11).

20. Craig Hawkins, *Witchcraft: Exploring the World of Wicca* (Grand Rapids: Baker, 1996), 21.

21. Hawkins, 28

22. Hawkins, 32.

23. Ronald Hutton, *The Pagan Religions of the Ancient British Isles* (Oxford: Blackwell, 1991), 335.

24. Craig Hawkins, "The Many Faces of Satanism," *Forward*, Fall 1986, 17.

25. Bob and Gretchen Passantino, *Satanism* (Grand Rapids: Zondervan, 1995), 7.

26. Arthur Lyons, *Satan Wants You* (New York: Mysterious Press, 1988), 9.

27. Bob and Gretchen Passantino, *When the Devil Dares Your Kids* (Ann Arbor, MI: Servant, 1991), 159.

28. Council of American Witches, "Principles of Wiccan Belief," as quoted in Hawkins, *Witchcraft*, 31.

29. J. Gordon Melton, *Encyclopedia of American Religions* (Detroit: Gale Research, 1996), 165.

30. Anton LaVey, *The Devil's Notebook* (Portland, OR: Feral House, 1992), 93.

31. Melton, 165.

32. Lyons, 9-11. Another common term, "dabblers" (which Lyons includes among "solitary" Satanists), would include people who only have a light association with

Satanism. Their involvement usually goes no further than the most superficial traits held in common by Satanists: fascination with satanic literature (e.g., *The Satanic Bible*), love of horror/satanic movies, fantasy role-playing games containing satanic elements, and "heavy-metal" music that relies on satanic lyrics and symbols. Most dabblers are teenagers going through that difficult period of transition from childhood to adulthood. During this time many teens try to assert their own independence by breaking connections with family and parents through deliberate use of anything that marks them as unique, such as odd hairstyles or strange clothes. Some young people gravitate toward satanic symbols, music, movies and games because such elements reek of nonconformity.

33. LaVey, 64.
34. LaVey, 63.
35. LaVey, 10, 9.
36. Anton LaVey, *The Satanic Bible* (New York: Avon Books, 1969), 52-54.
37. LaVey, p. 25.
38. Simon Dwyer, "The Plague Yard," *Rapid Eye*, vol. 2 (London: Creation Books, 1992; 1995 edition), 170.
39. LaVey, *The Devil's Notebook*, 22.
40. La Vey, 27.
41. Anton LaVey, quoted in Blanche Barton, *The Secret Life of a Satanist* (Los Angeles: Feral House, 1990), 205.
42. Hawkins, *Witchcraft*, 52-53.
43. Shepard, 2:1569.
44. Shepard.
45. Leo Martello, *Witchcraft: The Old Religion* (Secaucus, NJ: Citadel Press, 1973), 12.
46. Scott Cunningham, *The Truth About Witchcraft Today* (St. Paul: Llewellyn Publications, 1988), 23.
47. Cunningham, 3.
48. Janet Farrar and Stewart Farrar, *A Witch's Bible Compleat* (New York: Magickal Childe Publishing, 1984), 2:110.
49. J.K. Rowling, quoted in Mark McGarrity, "Harry Potter's Creator Meets Her Public," *The Record Online*, October 16, 1999, available online at www.montclairkimberley.org.
50. "Culture-Historical Essay," *Die Gegenwart*, quoted in Helena Petrovna Blavatsky, "The Number Seven," *Theosophist*, June, 1880, available online at www.blavatsky.net/blavatsky/arts/NumberSeven.htm.
51. www.blavatsky.net/blavatsky/arts/NumberSeven.htm.
52. J.K. Rowling, video interview for Scholastic Press, available online at www.scholastic.com.
53. Doreen Valiente, *The Rebirth of Witchcraft* (Custer, WA: Phoenix Publishing, 1989), 92.
54. Valiente, 92.
55. Statement available at www.cog.org/general/iabout.html#PHIL.
56. Okelle, "Harry Potter and the Witch Conspiracy," available online at www.paganwiccan.about.com/religion/paganwiccan/library/weekly/aa0080800a.htm.

57. J.K. Rowling, quoted in "Success of Harry Potter Bowls Author Over," October 21, 1999, available online at www.cnn.com/books/news/9910/21/rowling.intvu/.

TEN

THE ENDURING BATTLE: CHOOSING SIDES

Humanity's most lofty power,
  Reason and knowledge pray despise!
But let the Spirit of all lies
  With works of dazzling magic blind you,
Then absolutely mine, I'll have and bind you!

The Devil
Faust, Goethe (1749-1832)

Death by lethal injection. This decision ended the 1986 trial of seventeen-year-old Sean Sellers, the youngest person ever to be placed on death row at the Oklahoma State Penitentiary. It seemed a predictable ending to a life marked by nothing but anger, bitterness, frustration and hatred.

Sean's childhood of misery began when he was born to a sixteen-year-old girl, who abandoned him to be raised by her parents when she turned twenty-one. She returned every few weeks, but would inevitably leave her small boy again. Sean would later reveal, "Every time she and Dad left, I smiled, waived [sic] good-bye, and went to the bathroom, closed the door, and cried. Every time. And I never once let anyone see me do it."[1]

After Sean turned eight, his mother and new stepfather, Lee, began moving him around with them while they pursued their jobs as cross-country truckers. Sean never stayed in one house for more than a few months, or in the same town for more than a year, and during that time he usually was left with relatives. Throughout this period, he was both sexually abused and physically beaten, which greatly contributed to the high level of anger and resentment that eventually filled his life.

The emotional void Sean felt gradually led him to where many of today's youths find themselves: the world of occultism. It began indirectly with his involvement at the age of fifteen in a local Dungeons & Dragons (D&D) fantasy role-playing group. This provided an ideal distraction from the pain of the real world. He excelled at the game and soon became Dungeonmaster. Now that he was elevated to a position of honor—probably for the first time in his life—he began to scrutinize any and all material that might help him become the best Dungeonmaster possible.

In a 1990 letter to a Michael Stackpole, Sellers explained: "When I was playing D&D I was not a Satanist. . . . I was interested in witchcraft and Zen, however. In doing some research at the library for a D&D adventure I was leading, I happened upon other books that led to my study of occultism."[2] Unfortunately, Sean found his way into a satanic coven, complete with animal sacrifices, worship rituals and baptismal ceremonies:

> The leaders would be in black robes, but the new person would be in a white robe. They would stand in front of an altar that had black candles and a silver chalice on it. They made the new person strip, kneel before the altar; then we'd cut his hand and let the blood drip into the chalice. Then we would pass the cup around, drinking the blood and dedicating ourselves to Satan.[3]

Sean read as much as he could on witchcraft, Satanism, wizards and black magic. He also started casting spells such as the following, which was found in his personal diary:

> O great desolate one, spawn of the abyss, enemy to the weak, send forth your most glorious blessing and heal the wounds of one of your children. Send forth the dire powers of darkness so that we may do your will. Send to us a burning flare of change so that we may place ourselves to help you. Cast down the cowardly lies of suppression with a clap of earth-shattering thunder! Let your presence be known, for you are among your most talented. Upon this night, send the soul of mortality to your newfound child and grasp him/her as you would a lover. We unite to strengthen through the true power of darkness an abandoned god, in all the black glory and richness of truth. Unite among us the powerful force of freedom, and through our power rise, to someday be free. Allegiance to your power shall be sworn, as eternity revolves without end.[4]

Sean's D&D knowledge soon came into play: "After I became a Satanist, I used D&D manuals for their magical symbols and character references for my initial studies. I also used my experience as a Dungeonmaster to introduce people to Satanic behavior concepts and recruit them into the occult."[5] Interestingly, his involvement with D&D, the occult and Satanism might never have happened if it was not for a fifteen-year-old witch he met during his sophomore year in high school. She gave him his own incantation, claiming that it was a powerful prayer to the devil. When Sean recited it during a ceremony at his homemade altar, he was not disappointed:

> I felt a power there. The temperature in the room dropped about ten degrees. I got a shot of adrenaline and I felt my

blood pressure go up. There was an erotic sensation, a lifting sensation in my whole body. And sharp claws—fingers—touched me. I opened my eyes and saw bright spots dancing around the room. There was this mist, and I saw demons flying. And then there was this voice. A whisper. It said, "I love you." I knew that God didn't love me; but Satan did.[6]

Satanism seemed to be a golden key of opportunity and healing, as Sean would later recount:

[T]he stuff I read on Satanism said two things that appealed to me. #1—it offered freedom, and #2—it promised power to control my life, and others. I'd been carted all around the state[s] and Colorado all my life, slapped, smacked, hit, and had whatever I wanted ignored. I was mad and the idea of controlling my life to get what I wanted was like candy to me. Plus I looked at the way everyone around me lived and the stuff I read in *The Satanic Bible* in principle was lived out in lifestyle by Mom and Dad and everyone else I knew. No one was a real Christian. We didn't go to church. We didn't talk about God. Mom and Dad cussed like the truck drivers they had been for so many years . . . we'd stolen stuff out of the trucks Dad drove, I'd seen Mom lie to people's faces to get a deal or sell something, my aunt and uncle, and mom and dad smoked pot, and bought speed, so what was the point of pretending to serve God when we lived like Satanists? Satanism taught me that I should make my own rules to live by in life, and that's just what everyone I'd grown up around did, so I got very involved in Satanism. I truly thought it was an honest way to live, and the rituals of it would enable me to control my life. Even then I didn't want to kill anyone. That desire didn't start until later.[7]

Sean soon formed his own coven—"The Eliminators Club"—based on D&D's multilevel system of advancement. He was anything but secretive about its existence or his role as its leading devil-worshiper. In fact, Sean went out of his way to appear bizarre in front of classmates. He grew his left pinkie fingernail extremely long and painted it black. He carried vials of his own blood, which he would drink in front of horrified students in the school cafeteria. But the attention only made Sean more of an outcast. This in turn caused him to pursue with even greater fervor the one whom he considered the King of Outcasts, the one who would be his source of strength—Satan.[8]

Before reaching this point of no return, however, Sean tried to get help. He mentioned to several adults that he might be going insane and sought counseling from a priest, a teacher and various Christian ministries. He even tried to make friends with some born-again believers at school. The results were devastating to his already disturbed mind:

> Satan was really fouling things up. My mom was always crying, my dad was wanting to kill me. I'd open my eyes and think, "This is not what I want to be doing; this is not what I want to be like. I want out of this mess." And I called different Christian ministries and talked with them and they didn't tell me anything. I went to a priest; and he told my mom to give me back my satanic books. She'd taken them away and he says, "They're not your books; they're his books. Give them back to him." And so that didn't work. I went to a prayer group thing and they quoted a lot of Scripture to me but they didn't tell me what I now know I needed to hear, which was, "You don't have to be involved in the occult to be somebody. You don't have to be like that. . . ." The Christians at my school didn't say anything

about the way Jesus loves me; it was just: "That's the guy that drinks blood; that's the guy that ate a live frog over there. Don't mess with him." I'd go "Hi" and they'd go "Bye." My mom walked in on me one time while I was calling a counseling hotline from a Christian ministry and she didn't like the fact that I was doing it. . . . [P]arents feel threatened by the fact that their kids need help because it might suggest they're not doing a good job as parents. . . . I remember asking [my mom] a couple of times, hinting around that, "I think I'd really like to talk to someone. . . . I think I'm going crazy." But she'd say, "Well, if you think you're going crazy, that's a good sign you're not." . . . I think I was really reaching out but there just didn't seem to be anybody there. . . . So it felt like no one was ever there. And I got so mad, I got so frustrated with all these "good" people around me that I said, "Fine. Forget it. I can't get out." And that's what I was always told: Once you're involved in Satanism you can't get out. So that's when I really got into it. I dove into it with everything I had. Because I figured, "Well, if I can't get out of it, then I'm going to do the best I can in it." That's when I jumped in with both feet and got in over my head and started drowning.[9]

By the time Sean reached his junior year, he was fascinated with death and murder, especially the kind displayed in horror films. Moreover, the line between fantasy and reality was rapidly blurring. In a school essay he wrote: "I can kill without remorse and I feel no regret or sorrow."[10] Sean also had begun hearing demons talking in his head, started suffering prolonged periods of sleeplessness and experienced occasional blackouts where he couldn't remember what he'd been doing. Meanwhile, Sean's abuse of amphetamines, alcohol and marijuana continued taking its own toll.

Finally, just after beginning his junior year in 1985, Sean decided it was time for an "offering to Satan."[11] His first victim was Robert Bower, a convenience store clerk who had refused to sell beer to Sean's best friend, Richard Howard. Vengeance was taken when Sean took a .357 revolver, walked into the store and shot Bower at close range. The homicide went unsolved for six months as Sean spiraled downward into a living hell. He now believed he was actually possessed by a demon named Ezurate.

Things were already unbearably stressful at home. His mother was still physically abusing him and would verbally scream at him over his love for a fifteen-year-old girl named Angel. Sean's mother hated the girl, often calling her a "little tramp" and "a loser," and sought every way possible to keep the two teenagers apart. Sean's stepfather also continued the verbal abuse, incessantly harping on Sean about any number of things. Then something happened: Ezurate, the entity allegedly possessing Sean, prompted him to make the ultimate Satanic sacrifice: his mother, Vonda, and his stepfather, Paul Bellofatto.

On the night of March 4, 1986, sixteen-year-old Sean dressed in black underwear and a black cape, knelt down by the satanic altar in his bedroom and invoked demonic help for what he was about to do. He then grabbed the .44-caliber handgun belonging to his stepfather, walked into the room where his parents were sleeping and shot Paul in the head. Then he shot his mother. "When I killed my parents I stood over their bodies," Sean recalled. "I watched blood pour from the hole in my mother's face and I laughed. . . . It haunts me that I could have been the person that did that."[12]

Sean remembers, "There was some sense of 'Sean needs to be free and this will free him. This is the only way.' That was not a conscious thought, just a sensation. It's like that was the motivation behind it. I wasn't committing murder, I was removing an obstacle from my way. I was knocking down a door to a prison cage."[13] Sean spent the rest of the night with his friend, Richard. When he returned home the next day, he pretended to be a "shocked and innocent son, horrified by his parents' brutal deaths."[14] All of the evidence, however, pointed to Sean and he was arrested. Satan had betrayed him. His life was ruined.

Amazingly, Sean came to realize through reading the Bible in prison that even he could be forgiven by God through the life, death and resurrection of Jesus Christ. Subsequently, he became a Christian and started using the collect-calls-only phone in his cellblock to counsel troubled teens dabbling in Satanism, telling them, "If there's anything to say about getting involved in Satanism, it's: Don't! Don't get involved. Get out of it. It's not worth it 'cause it's going to destroy your life. That's all there is to it. It will destroy your life. And I'm living proof that it's true."[15] He also wrote a public "Confession of My Crimes"/Apology to the families of his victims, a portion of which reads:

> I've lived for 12 years now with the memories, knowledge, and grief of those 3 murders. . . . What I remember horrifies me. I see Robert Bowers' eyes, panic struck. I imagine the sheer terror of his last moments alive, and I wonder how long he laid there dying. Was he conscious? How could I have done that?
>
> I hear the words Dad said about rebuilding my pickup's engine. We would have done that together! We finally would have done something together. I see Christmas dinners that never happened. My mom with a grandchild on her lap.
>
> These are the ghosts I live with, and I hate myself for all I became and did. I am not just sorry, I am haunted. I think of all the people I hurt, of all the moments I stole from YOUR

lives, and I know I deserve to die. It's not right for me to go on living when these 3 people didn't. All I can offer you are the answers to why I did it, and to tell you it destroyed my soul when I did. No matter how long I live, or where I live, I destroyed myself when I killed Robert, and Dad, and Mom.

I beg for your forgiveness. I know I do not deserve it, and I know you hate me and always will, but I beg you, please, know that I am so sorry for it. Forgive me for the pain I caused you. . . .

I am the one responsible for my actions, and I take full blame upon myself alone. . . .

Please know that for as long as I live I will be haunted with the sorrow for what I did, and when I die I will have counted it more mercy than I deserved to have lived the life I did. Until that day, I want you to also know, I will spend my life trying to do things that will touch the world in a good way, to give back for all I took from you. That's the only thing I can offer with my hands and my heart. It's simply all I have.

Please forgive me.
—Sean Sellers.[16]

On Thursday, February 4, 1999, at seventeen minutes past midnight, twenty-nine-year-old Sean Sellers was executed by lethal injection. During his final days before being put to death, a number of people, including state officials, family members and self-professed Satanists, vilified Sellers, claiming that his thirteen-year-long Christian testimony had been nothing but a stunt to win a pardon. Some even predicted that he would renounce God upon realizing that he would not be saved from execution.

But Sean's final moments were quite different than from those predictions. "Here I come, Father. . . . I'm coming home," he said as he laid his head down on the table. Sean then turned to warden Gary Gibson and said, "Let's do it, Gary. Let's get it on." As the deadly chemicals from the injection coursed through his veins, Sean sang two verses from his own song, *Set My Spirit Free*: "Set my spirit free that I might praise Thee. Set my spirit free that I might worship Thee." Sean's last words were as follows:

> All the people who are hating me right now and are here waiting to see me die, when you wake up in the morning you aren't going to feel any different. You are going to hate me as much tomorrow as you do tonight. When you wake up and nothing has changed inside, reach out to God. . . . He will heal you. Let Him touch your hearts. Don't hate all your lives.[17]

❖   ❖   ❖   ❖

From a sociological perspective, not all forms of occultism are as destructive as the occultism practiced by Sean Sellers. And, of course, not everyone who indulges in occult activity will end up a murderer. Nevertheless, it cannot be denied that occultism often accompanies violent, criminal behavior in young people. Occult involvement actually has been identified as one of the warning signs of potential violence in a child, according to psychologist Reid Kimbrough of The Justice Center, a Nashville-based organization that conducts seminars nationwide for law enforcement personnel and educators relative to youth and school violence.

Kimbrough, who since 1997 has been teaching his "Children at High Risk for Violent Behavior" course, says occult involvement includes a student listening to music which has death or suicide in its lyrics, possessing paraphernalia such as skulls, black candles or a satanic bible, preoccupation with a Ouija board or tarot cards, drawing satanic symbols on themselves or property and wearing black clothing.[18] Kimbrough's assertions, far from being reactionary or sensationalistic, are a balanced assessment of how young people respond to various types of stimuli that they receive at a critical time in their emotional and psychological development.

Norvin Richard, chairman of the philosophy department at the University of Alabama, agrees. He believes youths who gravitate toward occultism could be looking for a value system that opposes the values of previous generations. "I think one could say those who dabble in the occult have lost faith in ordinary senses of good and evil," he stated. "They've lost faith in the principles and the sources of those principles that are more conventional and they're looking for direction elsewhere."[19]

Even in the absence of such emotional and psychological dangers (e.g., when an emotionally well-adjusted, mature adult chooses to become a pagan or a Wiccan and practice divination), there still exists a spiritual peril. Consequently, the Bible strictly forbids tampering with occultism or condoning it as an acceptable option for spiritual growth. But what precisely are the dangers? And where does Scripture mention occult activity? Answering these questions will be the focus of this chapter's remaining pages.

HOGWARTS: FOUNDATION OF DIVINATION

As already discussed in previous chapters, J.K. Rowling's Harry Potter series contains several forms of divination (i.e., gaining information about the past, present or future by occult means): astrology, crystal gazing, palmistry, fire omens (pyromancy), runes, reading tea leaves and trance states. All of these are condemned in both the Old and New Testaments. The classic passage dealing with divination, along with several other forms of occultism, is Deuteronomy 18:10-12:

> There shall not be found among you any one that maketh
> his son or his daughter pass through the fire, or that useth
> divination, or an observer of times, or an enchanter, or a
> witch, or a charmer, or a consulter with familiar spirits, or a
> wizard, or a necromancer. For all that do these things are an
> abomination unto the LORD.

If this were the only passage dealing with occultism, it would be enough to forbid all of the practices found in the Harry Potter series. But there are numerous other verses to consider, such as Second Kings 17:17, which is God's denunciation of Israel for their abandonment of His ways in favor of using "divination and enchantments," thereby making themselves evil in His sight: "[T]hey caused their sons and their daughters to pass through the fire, and used divination and enchantments, and sold themselves to do evil in the sight of the LORD, to provoke him to anger."

In the Old Testament, the two Hebrew words usually rendered "divination" are the verbs *nahas* and *qasam*. *Nahas* means to practice divination/fortune-telling or to observe signs/omens in order to direct one's choices.[20] *Qasam*, like *nahas*, refers to using divination, but also seems to be a general descriptive term for a wide variety of occult practices. Both words appear in Deuteronomy 18:10 and Second Kings 17:17, as well as in many other verses (Leviticus 19:26; Joshua 13:22; 2 Chronicles 33:6; Isaiah 44:25; Jeremiah 27:9; 29:8; Ezekiel 13:9, 23; 21:29; 22:28; Zechariah 10:2). *Qesem*, the noun form of *qasam*, also can be found in several places, including the oft-quoted First Samuel 15:23, which reads: "For rebellion is as the sin of witchcraft [*qesem*]."[21]

In the New Testament, God's prohibition against divination is confirmed by Acts 16:16-18, which recounts the story of a young demon-possessed woman who brought her masters a great deal of wealth through fortune-telling. Verse 16 says that the girl had a "spirit of divination," which in the Greek text reads *pneuma pythona*. This phrase, which could easily be translated "a spirit, a python" or "a python spirit" is probably a thinly veiled reference to *Pytho* (the region in which Delphi, the famous Greek oracle was located) and *Python* (the name of the serpent that kept guard at Delphi). By linking this spirit to the girl, the writer of Acts is indicating that the girl's powers stemmed from the same spirit active at Delphi (i.e., a spirit of divination).

In the *Tyndale New Testament Commentaries*, Howard Marshall, Professor of New Testament Exegesis (University Aberdeen), rightly notes that this term phython "originally meant a snake, and in particular the snake which guarded the celebrated Oracle at Delphi."[22] Similarly, *Thayer's Greek-English Lexicon of the New Testament*, says that the word *python* in Greek mythology referred to the "Pythian serpent or dragon that dwelt in the region of Pytho at the foot of [Mt.] Parnassus in Phocis, and was said to have guarded the oracle of Delphi."[23] *The New International Dictionary of New Testament Theology* agrees: "The word python is connected with the Delphic oracle, Delphi being the place where Apollo slew the mighty serpent Python that guarded the oracle."[24] And *A Greek-English Lexicon of the New Testament and Other Early Christian Literature* says, "[T]he word came to designate a spirit of divination, then also a ventriloquist, who was believed to have such a spirit dwelling in his (or her) belly."[25]

In addition to these references, snakes/serpents have always had a long history of symbolism in occult tradition. Interestingly, in the Harry Potter series, Harry—who is portrayed as a "True Seer" possessing the gift of foretelling the future (i.e., divination)—can speak to snakes. This is but one of the "evil wizard" abilities that Harry received from Lord Voldemort when the wicked sorcerer first tried to kill him. Again, Rowling has infused her fantasy tales with some very intricate occultism.

ROWLING'S STARGAZERS

Although several forms of divination appear in the Harry Potter books, astrology is one of the more blatantly displayed practices (see Chapter 8). Perhaps the clearest biblical rebuke of astrology appears in Isaiah 47:13-15, which is a prediction of Babylon's demise due to its unrepentant use of magick/sorcery and astrology. In these verses, God actually challenges the astrologers, daring them to use their magickal abilities to save themselves. But they cannot even see their own destruction coming, let alone save those who are seeking answers from them:

> Let now the astrologers, the stargazers, the monthly prognosticators, stand up, and save thee from these things that shall come upon thee. Behold, they shall be as stubble; the fire shall burn them; they shall not deliver themselves from the power of the flame: there shall not be a coal to warm at, nor fire to sit before it. . . . [N]one shall save thee.

"Astrologers" comes from the Hebrew words *habar*, meaning "divide," and *shamayim*, meaning "the heavens" or "the sky." They attempted divination by accurately dividing up the heavens and looking for signs. "Stargazers" comes from the two Hebrew words *hozeh* ("seer" or "gazer") and *kokab* ("stars"). They would observe, contemplate and study the stars in hopes of foretelling the future or gaining otherwise unknowable information.

"MAGICKED" BY HARRY

Although both divination and magick are condemned in the Bible, there is a obvious distinction made between the two practices that must be noted. Whereas divination simply seeks to discover information, especially about the future, magick seeks to influence and manipulate future or current events. Magick serves as a foundational component of various contemporary forms of occultism, including Wicca, paganism and Satanism. Its connection to the Harry Potter series lies in the basic thrust of the plot.

Scripture refers numerous times to magick, often using different words. One such term, *kashap*, can be found in Exodus 7:11 and 22:18, as well as in Deuteronomy 18:10, Daniel 2:2 and Malachi 3:5. It means to practice magick or sorcery, use witchcraft, or enchant. It is the feminine form of *kashap* that appears in Exodus 22:18, the well-known verse in which God tells Israel that the penalty for being a witch is execution. Obviously, practicing magick/sorcery/witchcraft must be an extremely profane activity to God. Consider the following passage about King Manasseh:

> [H]e caused his children to pass through the fire in the valley of the son of Hinnom: also he observed times, and used enchantments, and used witchcraft, and dealt with a familiar spirit, and with wizards: he wrought much evil in the sight of the LORD, to provoke him to anger. (2 Chronicles 33:6)

Keshep, which is the corresponding noun form of the verb *kashap*, is another general term used for magick. The word means magick or magical arts, sorcery or sorceries, soothsayer, spell or witchcraft. God sternly condemns magick in several biblical passages (i.e., 2 Kings 9:22; Isaiah 47:9, 12; Micah 5:12), but His intense displeasure of *"keshep"* is especially apparent throughout His condemnation of Ninevah in Nahum 3:4-7:

> Because of the multitude of the whoredoms of the well-favoured harlot, the mistress of witchcrafts [*keshep*], that selleth nations through her whoredoms, and families through her witchcrafts [*keshep*]. Behold, I am

against thee. . . . I will shew the nations thy nakedness,
and the kingdoms thy shame. And I will cast abominable
filth upon thee, and make thee vile, and will set thee as a
gazingstock [i.e., a spectacle]. And it shall come to pass,
that all they that look upon thee shall flee from thee, and
say, Ninevah is laid waste.

In the New Testament, there is an equally strong emphasis
against magick. For example, Acts 8:9-24 speaks of Simon the sor-
cerer/magician who astonished the people of Samaria through his
magical arts. Although he appeared to be a convert to Christianity, the biblical account ends with him offering the apostles
money for the secret of their power and Peter rebuking him for
still living bound in his sins (8:23). There also is Acts 19:19, which
describes how Ephesian converts to Christianity gathered together and burned all of their books relating to magick.

Another relevant passage is Galatians 5:19-21, which places
magick/witchcraft alongside the sins of adultery, fornication, hatred, strife, murder and drunkenness. Verse 21 reads: "[T]hey
which do such things shall not inherit the kingdom of God." Similarly, there is Revelation 9:20-21 and Revelation 18:23, both of
which describe magick/sorcery as sinful behavior. Clearly, the art
of magick—i.e., seeking to bring about change in accordance with
one's own will through various ceremonies, rites, rituals, spells or
charms—is resoundingly condemned by Scripture.

HERMIONE'S TALENT: SPELLCASTING/CHARMS

Although a variety of Old Testament words apply to
spellcasting or charming (i.e., enchantments), the two most common ones would be *chabar* and *cheber*. Both of these Hebrew
terms communicate the idea of magick being used in order to
bring about a desired result through charming, enchanting or in-

fluencing another individual by magick. A concise explanation of this activity and how it relates to Scripture appears in *Witchcraft: Exploring the World of Wicca*:

> Associated with enchantment is the concept of charming. Charm (the noun) is defined in part as "the chanting or reciting of a magic spell: incantation" and "a practice or expression believed to have magic power." ... Thus, a charmer would be an enchanter or magician. ... "[T]his term appear[s] in a verbal form to express the idea of charming, i.e., casting a spell or tying up a person by magic." *The New Brown-Driver-Briggs-Gesenius Hebrew and English Lexicon* ... says its meaning in Deuteronomy 18:11 is "tie a magic knot or spell, charm." [Charming] is set forth as "an idolatrous act and diametrically opposed to receiving revelation from God through his appointed prophets (Deut. 18:15)." The nominal form of *habar* is *heber*. ... "The usual translation is 'enchantments' referring to the means the charmers employed to influence people or the result of their charming efforts (Deut 18:11). All aspects were divinely forbidden to covenant people." The occult practices of charming, enchanting, or spell casting are condemned, and those who attempt such spells are held in contempt by God.[26]

J.K. Rowling makes it obvious throughout her Harry Potter novels that one of her lead characters, Hermione, is an extremely clever and gifted witch with a special talent for casting enchantments/spells/charms. Not only are each of these activities prohibited by God, but they would also fall under the general category of magick, which also is condemned by Scripture.

TRELAWNEY'S MEDIUMSHIP

A medium, according to *The International Standard Bible Encyclopedia*, is anyone who contacts the dead for the purpose of learning about past, present or future events. The Hebrew word *ob*—translated as medium, wizard or necromancer throughout the Old Testament—is applied in multiple passages to individuals who speak to a "familiar spirit" (a demonic entity), regularly consult the dead or communicate with ghosts (Deuteronomy 18:11; 2 Kings 23:24; 2 Chronicles 33:6; Isaiah 19:3).[27]

Although no one knows for certain exactly how the term *ob* originated, many scholars believe that in ancient cultures it referred to the common medium ability to "produce a deep, husky voice, apparently not their own, which represented the spirit of the dead person speaking through, or from within, them."[28] Notice the similarity between this explanation and how J.K. Rowling described what happened to Professor Trelawney in *Harry Potter and the Prisoner of Azkaban* when the teacher suddenly entered a trance and brought forth a prophecy:

> [A] loud, harsh voice spoke behind him. "IT WILL HAPPEN TONIGHT."
>
> Harry wheeled around. Professor Trelawney had gone rigid in her armchair; her eyes were unfocused and her mouth sagging. . . .
>
> Professor Trelawney didn't seem to hear him. Her eyes started to roll. Harry sat there in a panic. She looked as though she was about to have some sort of seizure. . . .
>
> [T]hen Professor Trelawney spoke again, in the same harsh voice, quite unlike her own.[29]

Clearly, this scene is depicting mediumship. Rowling is describing real-world occultism; a form so abhorrent to God that in the Old Testament anyone found guilty of mediumship was to be stoned (Leviticus 20:27). God's people were repeatedly warned to stay far away from mediums, as the following passages show:

> Regard not them that have familiar spirits, neither seek after wizards, to be defiled by them: I am the LORD your God. (19:31)

> And the soul that turneth after such as have familiar spirits, and after wizards, to go a whoring after them, I will even set my face against that soul, and will cut him off from among his people. (20:6)

> [H]e made his son pass through the fire, and observed times, and used enchantments, and dealt with familiar spirits and wizards: he wrought much wickedness in the sight of the LORD, to provoke him to anger. (2 Kings 21:6)

Perhaps the most tragic example of how mediumship can destroy an individual can be found in First Samuel 28:7-19, which tells the story of King Saul's reliance on the witch of Endor to contact the spirit of Samuel the prophet.[30] But because such practices are forbidden by God, Saul paid the ultimate price: "Saul died for his transgression which he committed against the LORD, even against the word of the LORD, which he kept not, and also for asking counsel of one that had a familiar spirit, to enquire of it; And enquired not of the LORD: therefore he slew him, and turned the kingdom unto David" (1 Chronicles 10:13-14).

FOR OUR OWN GOOD

Why would God prohibit the many varied forms of occultism? This question must be answered in order to gain a fuller understanding of God's character and the appropriateness of Christianity's position. Also, Christians should be prepared to demonstrate why God forbids occultism when occultists sincerely want to know the justification for each biblical statement made against their practices. There are several reasons why God condemns occultism.

First, divination is an extremely unreliable method of obtaining accurate information about the world, ourselves, others and the future. For example, famed psychic Gordon-Michael Scallion claims to average nearly ninety percent accuracy with his predictions.[31] But out of sixty-six predictions made for 1995, only a few came to pass and all of those were either so vague that it would have been difficult for them *not* to come true, or simply the obvious continuation of an ongoing trend (e.g., UFO sightings will increase, herb sales will soar, media programming on metaphysics and the world of the spirit will expand).[32]

The renowned psychic Edgar Cayce (a.k.a. the Sleeping Prophet) has an equally dismal record. His countless failed predictions include: the complete geographical annihilation of Japan, America and the Arctic sometime between 1958-1998; the destruction within "one generation" of 1941 of New York City, Los Angeles and San Francisco; the appearance of the mythical continent of Atlantis by 1968/1969; and worldwide devastation via a "pole shift" in the year 2001.[33]

Astrologers have not fared any better at predicting the future. Consider the results from the following studies that have been done on this form of divination:

- A 1979 advertisement in *Ici Paris* offered a free horoscope, and those who responded were asked to judge how accurate they and their friends thought it was. Of the first 150 people who replied, ninety-four percent said it was accurate along with ninety percent of their friends and family. It was later revealed that the respondents all received the *same* horoscope—that of a notorious mass murderer.

- In 1982, the Australian Skeptics organization compared the horoscopes from thirteen different newspapers for the same week and found that they gave a wide variety of *differing* predictions for the *same* astrological sign. After rating the predictions for such topics as health, luck, relationships and finance, the researchers concluded that "most signs had a fairly even spread so, for instance, you could find one paper telling you it would be a lucky week and another saying the opposite."
- In 1989, in response to a $100,000 TV challenge, an astrologer cast the charts of twelve people after being given their birth information. Then he interviewed the twelve and attempted to match them to their horoscopes. He did not get a single one right.
- In 1994, six astrologers and psychics were challenged by the Melbourne *Sunday Age* to predict the winner of the Melbourne Cup. Not one of them came close.[34]

Obviously, the so-called vast storehouse of "knowledge" available to occultists is a poor substitute for what God offers: absolute truth. The only source of trustworthy information is the Lord (Isaiah 8:19-20). This fact is evident from the confrontation between the prophet Daniel and the Babylonian astrologers (Daniel 1:20; 2:13, 18-19; 5:7-17). There is no reason to be in awe of occultism—or, as Jeremiah 10:2 puts it, "Thus saith the LORD, Learn not the way of the heathen, and be not dismayed at the signs of heaven."

Second, occultism tends to pull people away from God, as Deuteronomy 4:19 warns of astrology: "[Beware] . . . lest thou lift up thine eyes unto heaven , and when thou seest the sun, and the moon, and the stars, even all the host of heaven, shouldest be driven to worship them, and serve them." Consequently, since it is God's desire for people to know and love Him, the Lord forbids occult activity, knowing that it will only be a hindrance to people's search for spiritual fulfillment and eternal joy in the afterlife.

Third, with regard to mediums and necromancy, God condemns such activity because there is no reason for people to consult with the dead (Isaiah 8:19). In this passage, God makes it clear that the realm of the dead is not where individuals will find a way to living a joy-filled life, nor will they find eternal life in the world of the departed. They need to turn to God (Matthew 22:31-32), through the person of Jesus Christ, in whom life itself resides (John 5:26; 10:10, 28). It is to Christ that spiritual truth-seekers must look. Occultism presents nothing but a distraction.

Fourth, occultism provides access to certain powers that are demonic in nature and as such are spiritually deadly (Exodus 7-8). As well, these powers of darkness, according to Scripture, are no match for God's omnipotence (8:19). Consequently, there is simply no reason to waste one's time on them. Why would anyone settle for inferior spiritual power when the most potent of spiritual power rests with God the Creator, with whom anyone can have a relationship?

Fifth, practically every form of occultism, when boiled down to its irreducible minimum, is merely a different vehicle through which one may obtain power through magick. Magick—defined as any spiritual technique designed to harness either supernatural forces or the secret power of nature in order to influence events for one's own purposes—is a direct affront to God's sovereignty. The personal Creator God of the universe is the one whom individuals should seek out for assistance in this life. Attempting to control one's own destiny and the environment through occult means is the equivalent of making oneself into a god, which interestingly is one of the main tenets promoted in occultism: man is god.

Sixth, most occult practices involve entering an altered state of consciousness (ASC) wherein one's normal everyday awareness (or consciousness) is replaced by an alternate (or altered) awareness. An ASC is induced when anything interrupts or brings to a halt "the normal patterns of conceptual thought without extinguishing or diminishing consciousness itself."[35] A hypnotic trance, for example, is an ASC.

This is problematic because during an ASC persons cannot separate fact from fiction. They function under a confused sense of reality. This in turn opens a doorway to the mind through which demonic forces may funnel information in hopes of leading someone away from God. Demonic entities might even take the form of deceased relatives, friends or religious figures in order to add credibility to their messages. Consider the following report from occultist Robert Monroe concerning one of his "out-of-body" excursions that he claims enabled him to travel to higher realms of spiritual existence:

> I started out carefully—and felt something climb on my back! I remembered the little fellow from before, and certainly didn't want to try to go somewhere with him hanging on my back. I let the vibrations continue, and reached down my side to get hold of his leg. . . . I was quite surprised when my hands did touch something! The consistency felt much like flesh, normally body warm, and somewhat rubbery; it seemed to stretch. . . . I finally pulled what I thought was all of it off my back. . . . It got to be quite a struggle . . . and I was getting a little panicky . . . as I was trying to hold off the first, a second climbed on my back! Holding the first off with one hand, I reached back and yanked the second off

me, and floated over into the center of the office, holding one in each hand, screaming for help. I got a good look at each, and as I looked, *each turned into a good facsimile of one of my two daughters*. . . . I seemed to know immediately that this was a deliberate camouflage on their parts to create emotional confusion in me and call on my love for my daughters to prevent my doing anything more to them. The moment I realized the trick, the two no longer appeared to be my daughters [emphasis added].[36]

Finally, the various theological doctrines and overall worldview normally associated with occult practices are decidedly unbiblical. They include: the inherent divinity of all human beings; reincarnation; relativism (i.e., your truth is not my truth and my truth is not your truth); denial of Jesus' fully divine and fully human nature; denial of God's personal nature; denial of salvation by grace alone through faith alone in Christ; and acceptance of all religions as equally valid.

Some people argue that occult practices such as Tarot card reading, palmistry and astrology are, at best, harmless amusements and, at worst, scams that can be used by unscrupulous individuals to bilk trusting customers out of hard-earned cash. But as we have seen, occult involvement invites negative spiritual forces into one's life. Yet, the popularity of occultism in America continues to grow at an alarming rate. As we shall discover in the next chapter, this is one of the main reasons why the Harry Potter series has garnered so much attention and acceptance.

ENDNOTES

1. Sean Sellers, *The Confession of My Crimes*, available online at www.seansellers.com/confess.html.
2. Sean Sellers, public letter to Michael Stackpole, February 5, 1990, available at www.rpg.net/252/quellen/stackpole/pulling_report.html#App1,
3. Sean Sellers, quoted in Jerry Johnston, *The Edge of Evil* (Dallas: Word, 1989), 18.

4. Vicki L. Dawkins and Nina Downey Higgins, *Devil Child* (New York: St. Martin's Press, 1989), 58. Quoted in Bob and Gretchen Passantino, *When the Devil Dares Your Kids* (Ann Arbor, MI: Servant Publications, 1991), 44-45.

5. Sellers, letter to Stackpole, available online at www.rpg.net/252/quellen/stackpole/pulling_report.html#App1.

6. Sellers, quoted in Johnston, 18.

7. Sellers, *The Confession*.

8. Arthur Lyons, *Satan Wants You* (New York: Mysterious Press, 1988), 11.

9. Sellers, quoted in Johnston, 20-21.

10. Quoted in Johnston, 18.

11. Sellers, *The Confession*.

12. Sean Sellers, quoted in John Trott, "About the Devil's Business," *Cornerstone*, Vol. 19, issue 93, 10.

13. Sellers.

14. Passantino, 159.

15. Sellers, quoted in Johnston, 19.

16. Sellers, *The Confession*.

17. Statements available at www.seansellers.com.

18. Lori Gray, "Preventing Violence," *Education Report*, January 6, 1998, available online at www.dnj.com.

19. Norvin Richards, quoted in "Satanic Crimes on the Rise in Alabama," available online at www.sounddoctrine.com/ptimes/satanic.htm.

20. Lawrence O. Richards, *Expository Dictionary of Bible Words* (Grand Rapids: Zondervan, 1985; 1991 edition), 232.

21. *Qesem* appears in Deuteronomy 18:10; Numbers 22:7; 23:23; First Samuel 15:23; Second Kings 17:17; Jeremiah 14:14; and Ezekiel 13:6, 23; 21:21-22.

22. I. Howard Marshall, *Tyndale New Testament Commentaries* (Grand Rapids: Eerdmans, 1980), 268.

23. Joseph Henry Thayer, trans. and ed., *Thayer's Greek-English Lexicon of the New Testament* (Grand Rapids: Zondervan, 1978), 557. Cited in Craig Hawkins, *Witchcraft: Exploring the World of Wicca* (Grand Rapids: Baker Books, 1996), 103. This endnote, along with the following two citations, refer to a series of references that mirror those references found on page 103 of Hawkins' book *Witchcraft: Exploring the World of Wicca*. Credit for the research behind this particular information (i.e., regarding the word *python*) and the order of its presentation belongs solely to Hawkins.

24. See Hawkins, 103.

25. Hawkins.

26. Hawkins, 104-105.

27. Geoffrey W. Bromiley, gen. ed., *The International Standard Bible Encyclopedia* (Grand Rapids: Eerdmans Publishing, 1986; 1990 edition), 3:306.

28. Bromiley, 3:307

29. J.K. Rowling, *Harry Potter and the Prisoner of Azkaban* (New York: Scholastic Press, 1999), 324.

30. This particular *ob* was more of a necromancer (one who contacts the dead), rather than a medium (one who becomes possessed by a spirit).

31. Gordon-Michael Scallion, cited in Richard Abanes, *End-Time Visions: The Road to Armageddon?* (New York: Four Walls Eight Windows, 1998), 53.

32. Abanes, 53-55.

33. Abanes, 57.

34. Roland Seidel, "Astrology Overview," *The Skeptic*, available online at www.skeptics.com.au/journal/astrol.htm.

35. Elliot Miller, *A Crash Course on the New Age Movement* (Grand Rapids: Baker Books, 1989), 36.

36. Robert Monroe, *Journeys Out of the Body* (New York: Doubleday, 1971; Anchor Books edition, 1977), 138-139.

ELEVEN

BEYOND FANTASY:
AN AMERICAN TALE

*Parents have little time for their children, and a great vacuum
has developed, and into that vacuum is going to move some
kind of ideology.*

Billy Graham[1]
Evangelist

The release of J.K. Rowling's fourth novel, *Harry Potter
and the Goblet of Fire*, created a worldwide wave of
consumerism hysteria the likes of which had never before been seen in the book-buying community. Even prior to the
release date of July 8, 2000, advance orders taken by Barnes and
Noble and Amazon.com exceeded a combined total of more than
600,000 copies—six times the prepublication sales record that had
been set by John Grisham's *The Brethren*. Lyn Blake (general
manager of Amazon's bookstore) commented: "I haven't seen a
book like this ever. This is over seven times the largest pre-order
we've ever had."[2]

Some publishing industry watchers attributed the madness to
Rowling's public relations campaign, which had succeeded in creating a deluge of newspaper, magazine and TV stories about Potter as early as June 1999. Then, as the release of Book IV drew
nearer, Rowling's publisher pumped up reader anticipation even
higher by not releasing any information about the novel. No one

even knew its title, until it was strategically "leaked" to the press shortly before going on sale. Only six people reportedly had read the manuscript, which was kept in a locked safe in the publisher's office in London before it went to print.

Booksellers were made to sign contracts "agreeing not to open their boxes of Harry Potter IV until 12:01 a.m. on July 8. (The penalty for violating this agreement was a complete cutoff of future supplies.)"[3] Sheila Egan, manager of the "A Likely Story" bookstore (Alexandria, Virginia), reported that she had never seen such tight security over a book. "We signed an affidavit that we will not reveal anything about it. No employee is to have access to it."[4] At a Barnes and Noble in Fairfax, Virginia, one manager (who refused to be identified for fear of reprisal) revealed, "We're under severe pressure not to talk about it. We've all been threatened so bad."[5]

Other publicity stunts included the publicized revelation that a main character would be killed in Book IV. There were also planes pulling banners emblazoned with Harry Potter advertisements. And bookstores were shipped Harry Potter stickers and party planner kits. These acts of pure capitalism enraged some commentators, such as biographer and literary critic Anthony Holden. In reference to Rowling's British publishers, Holden wrote, "Haven't Bloomsbury sold enough copies of J.K. Rowling's three volumes so far without resorting to advance hype worthy of the Wonderbra?"[6]

The hype worked. Nightfall on July 7, 2000 found both children and adults waiting in long lines to obtain a copy of Rowling's work. The *New York Times* reported that the onslaught of excited children "created bedlam at bookstores."[7] Children were crying, store clerks were cursing and numerous scuffles broke out between enraged customers wrestling over the last remaining copies. Bay Anapol, the Harry Potter party organizer for a Borders bookstore in Sante Fe, New Mexico, described it all very well: "It's that cabbage patch doll mentality all over again. People have been calling panic-stricken over not being able to get a book."[8]

At one store in England, where J.K. Rowling appeared, police had to be called in to control the mayhem that included fathers fighting to secure a closer spot from which to view Rowling.[9] A similar situation arose at a Borders store in New Jersey when Rowling showed up in October 1999 to promote her third book, *Harry Potter and the Prisoner of Azkaban*. Police were summoned when the estimated crowd of 2,000 became unruly and practically rioted because Rowling had to leave early. "It was a total fiasco, really ugly," said Matthew Demakos, who witnessed the scene. "Irate parents were screaming; people who had bought books were demanding their money back." The store's manager was reportedly "bitten and punched" by angry Potter fans.[10]

Book IV's success will probably never be duplicated, except perhaps by Book V of the Potter series (reportedly entitled *Harry Potter and the Order of the Phoenix*), scheduled for release near the end of 2001. Astoundingly, advance orders for this volume began adding up only days after *Goblet of Fire* went on sale. In fact, by August 2000, it already ranked fifty-fifth on Amazon.com's (United Kingdom) best-seller list, the highest spot ever reached by a novel not yet written.[11]

WELCOME TO POST-CHRISTIAN AMERICA

Given America's religious climate, the phenomenal popularity of Rowling's Harry Potter series comes as no surprise. For many years now, a virtual tidal wave of religious fervor has been sweeping across the United States. Rowling's books, although categorized as children's fantasy, fit very well into the current atmosphere of "spirituality" where occult-related ideas and values

not only are accepted, but also often are viewed far more positively than Christian-based beliefs and concepts of morality.

Early indications of America's renewed interest in religion appeared as early as 1987 in a *Better Homes and Gardens* survey of
more than 80,000 readers. Sixty-two percent of those polled said
that in recent years they had "begun or intensified personal spiritual study and activities."[12] The informal study also found that
fifty percent of the respondents thought spirituality was gaining
influence "on family life in America." Interestingly, New Age
spiritualists and Christians—despite their widely differing beliefs—both perceived "a growing spiritual undercurrent in America today."[13] Other findings were equally significant:

- ninety-six percent believed in God (although their inter-
  pretations of "God" varied);
- eighty-nine percent looked forward to an "eternal life";
- eighty-one percent felt they would be reunited with
  loved ones after death.[14]

By 1993, spirituality was "in" and atheism/agnosticism was
"out." Church historian and University of Chicago professor
Martin Marty observed: "[S]pirituality is back, almost with a
vengeance.... I find myself treating the concern for spirituality
as an event of our era."[15] On the heels of Marty's remarks appeared countless secular articles in mainstream publications
that confirmed his perceptions—articles bearing titles like: "In
Search of the Sacred," "The New Spin Is Spirituality," "The
Power of Faith" and "Desperately Seeking Spirituality."[16]

Even more telling were figures from a 1994 *Newsweek* poll,
which revealed that fifty-eight percent of Americans at that time
felt "the need to experience spiritual growth." The eye-opening
data further shows that a third of all adults reported having had a
mystical or religious experience, twenty percent said they had re-

ceived a revelation from God within the prior year, and thirteen percent claimed to have "seen or sensed the presence of an angel."[17]

As we enter the twenty-first century, these types of responses to religious polls and surveys remain unchanged. The years 1994-2000 saw a steady ninety-five percent to ninety-six percent of the American public believing in God (although definitions of "God" varied).[18] A 2000 Gallup Poll also found that "54 percent of Americans say they are religious, 30 percent spiritual and 6 percent both."[19] And according to this same research, more than eighty percent of Americans desire to grow spiritually.[20]

The many Americans craving spiritual fulfillment are simply seeking to answer those questions that have always plagued the human soul: What is the meaning of life? Is there an afterlife? Does God exist? But unlike in decades past, today's spiritually starved seekers are searching for spiritual relief through a variety of nontraditional groups, doctrines and rituals: Transcendental Meditation, Hinduism, Buddhism, Taoism, Shamanism, astral travel, numerous meditative arts, neopaganism, witchcraft, Satanism and occultism. All of these have become an established part of the American religious scene.[21]

Donald G. Bloesch, professor of theology emeritus at Dubuque Theological Seminary in Iowa, concisely notes the underlying doctrines promoted by America's alternative routes to spiritual fulfillment:

> What makes the current fascination with spirituality significant is that much of it reflects the largely secular flavor of our time rather than the Bible or church traditions. . . . [E]stablished religion has been unable to assuage the anxieties that cripple people today. . . . Spirituality has become for many a technique for tapping into the "reservoir" of un-

limited power within us. . . . The new spirituality represents a kind of naturalistic mysticism, a re-emergence of the ancient religion of the Earth Mother. . . . All nature is seen to be alive, filled with divine energy. It is not simply the handiwork of God, but the very body of God. . . . The new mysticism does not emphasize self-denial, but self-affirmation and self-esteem. It prizes growth and change more than repentance and service. . . . Our vocation is no longer to be pilgrims in a vale of tears, nor witnesses to what God has done for us in history. Instead, we are to be gods on earth. . . . The new secular spirituality represents a descent into worldliness under the guise of holiness.[22]

Thomas C. Oden, theology professor at Drew University, critically observes that in this day and age almost everything is being termed spirituality: "One can study the daily horoscope and call it spirituality. One can study women's outrage and call it spirituality. One can offer educational videotapes on techniques of masturbation and call it eroto-spirituality. Only in America."[23] Oden goes on to give a patently negative, and rather ominous, assessment of today's "great awakening":

The evidences of a new spiritual hunger are usually painted with a good or bad face. The happy face: Angels have made a comeback. Prayer is alive again in a popular culture. The ugly face: Witches are claiming equality under religious-freedom rulings. Neo-pagan feminism has substituted Sophia [a feminine personification of wisdom] for Jesus in the Eucharist. The demonic is hidden in every sociological or psychological equation but seldom recognized as such.[24]

The findings of both Oden and Bloesch are easily substantiated. For example, there may now be up to 1 million practicing neopagans in America, 100,000-200,000 of whom practice witchcraft/Wicca (arguably the fastest growing religion in the U.S.).[25] Moreover, recent surveys indicate that nearly half the U.S. population believes in ghosts and more than a quarter think modern-day witches may have mystical powers.[26] Consider how dramatically American views have changed regarding various aspects of occultism since just 1976.

Which if any of the following do you believe at least to some degree?		
BELIEF	1976	1997
Spiritualism (i.e., communication with the dead)	12%	52%
Astrology	17%	37%
Reincarnation	9%	25%
Fortune-Telling	4%	14%
(Margin of error= +/- 3-5%)[27]		

Other surveys show that nearly half of all middle-aged Americans now consider "all faiths equally good and true."[28] How are these beliefs and their supportive rituals reaching the population at large? Many alternative forms of religious expression are gaining converts through one of the oldest and most common ways of communication: books.

SPELLBOUND: A NEW GENERATION

Literature endorsing occultism used to be a rare thing in "Judeo-Christian" America. Today, however, occult books are no longer confined to the dirty back shelves of libraries and occult curiosity shops. In fact, marketing executives at Barnes and Noble, the "World's Largest Bookseller Online," have estimated that approximately 10 million book-buyers in America regularly purchase pagan/neopagan literature (regardless of their personal religious beliefs).

Simply put, the buying and selling of occult books has become a multimillion-dollar industry. Those who doubt this need only go the Amazon.com retail site and enter the word "divination" in its search engine. Within seconds this request will pull up more than 1,300 divination-related books, including *Crystal Balls & Crystal Bowls: Tools for Ancient Scrying & Modern Seership* (1995), *The Illustrated Encyclopedia of Divination: A Practical Guide to the Systems That Can Reveal Your Destiny* (1997), *Palmistry Revealed: A Simple Guide to Unlocking the Secrets of Your Hands* (1997) and *Secrets of the Runes: Discover the Magic of the Ancient Runic Alphabet* (1999).

Several books with a similar theme have become *New York Times* best-sellers. The year 1994, for instance, saw the publication of James Redfield's *The Celestine Prophecy*, a spiritual adventure novel that had a sold-out first printing of 250,000 copies. Then, between 1996-1998, Putnam Publishing Group released three volumes in Neale Donald Walsch's *Conversations with God* series, which allegedly contain the very words of God that came to the author through the occult practice of automatic writing. More recently, James Van Praagh—an occult medium who claims he can talk to the dead—has written several best-sellers, most notably *Talking to Heaven: A Medium's Message of Life After Death* (1998/1999), which made him a nationwide sensation.

Individuals wanting to find occult information presented in a more informal fashion simply travel to a nearby newsstand, grocery market magazine rack or bookstore. These locations abound in occult and alternative spirituality periodicals, such as: *Common Boundary, New Age: The Journal for Holistic Living, Alternate Perceptions Journal* and *Fate* magazine. The articles in these publications, along with those that have appeared in more mainstream magazines, have produced some lasting effects on America's youth. For example, after the teen magazine *Bliss* published a report that included the address of the international Pagan Federation, the occult organization "received more than one thousand letters in one month."[29] Pagan Federation spokesperson Andy Norfolk had this to say about the surge of inquiries and its relation to the current abundance of occult literature:

> I am sure that some of the increase in interest is because some of the films and books show young glamorous women using magic to beat evil. These fantasies provide a role model for some young women who would like to emulate their heroines, and so, [they] start to find out about contemporary paganism.[30]

Since the early 1990s major publishers have released a steady stream of occult-glamorizing fiction geared to young people. In 1994, for instance, Dial Books for Young Readers produced *The War of the Wizards* (ages 4-8), which displayed a five-sided pentagram inside its front cover. In 1999, Magic Carpet Books released *Wizard's Hall* (ages 9-12), a novel about a young boy at a school for wizards-in-training. Even more popular has been Diane Duane's "young adult" wizard series, which follows the adventures of a teenage witch and her wizard boyfriend: *So You Want to Be a Wizard* (1996), *Deep Wizardry* (1996), *High Wizardry* (1997) and *A Wizard Abroad* (1999).[31]

Nonfiction volumes promoting occultism also have targeted America's youth. These books, designed to teach *real* witchcraft to children/teens, include *To Ride a Silver Broomstick: New Generation Witchcraft* (170,000 copies sold), which is described as "the definitive Wicca 101 book" and the soon-to-be-released *The Young Witches Handbook* (HarperCollins), which includes spells for passing exams and attracting a partner.[32] Perhaps the most prominent indoctrination work has been *Teen Witch: Wicca for a New Generation*, by well-known witch Silver RavenWolf. Her book, with a cover illustration depicting five provocatively dressed adolescents (four girls and one boy) standing in sexually suggestive poses, is aimed directly at young audiences. An advertisement for the "how-to" manual reads:

> Be a Witch 24/7. *Teen Witch!* is the book you've been waiting for! Written for teens between the ages of 13 and 18, this terrific book is designed "just for you." Complete with serious explanations on techniques used by today's practicing Wiccans, this innovative book is packed with useful spells and rituals to help any teenage Witch spread his or her wings into the world of magick. From cell phone magick to learning how to work enchantments with your friends—you'll love this down-to-earth book.[33]

The Harry Potter series is but one more example of how publishing houses are marketing works that not only feed into, but also perpetuate, the current obsession with occultism prevalent among young people. Predictably, Rowling's publisher in England (Bloomsbury Press) sought to repeat its Harry Potter success via a new book written for children ages eleven and up: *Witch Child*, the story of Mary—granddaughter of a witch trying to avoid persecution in seventeenth-century New England.

It is undeniable that children, teens and young adults are turning to occultism with ever-increasing frequency. This may be due, in part, to the current openness to occultism more than in previous generations. A 1999 Scripps-Howard News Service poll found that among adults eighteen to twenty-four years old, "63 percent said ghosts could be real, compared to only 22 percent of adults 65 and over."[34] More significant was the survey's discovery that young adults are more inclined than ever to view as "harmless" books, TV shows and movies dealing with "vampires, witches, and other supernatural creatures."[35]

Such findings coincide with the observation of University of Houston philosophy professor Cynthia A. Freeland (author of *The Naked and the Undead: Evil and the Appeal of Horror*), whose research indicates that "films about the supernatural—an ever growing genre in Hollywood—are almost exclusively watched by teenagers and young adults."[36]

Media Magick

In addition to books and magazines, the television and film industry has undoubtedly persuaded countless young people to delve into occultism. Several occult-based television programs have enjoyed immense popularity: *PSI Factor: Chronicles of the Paranormal* (CBS); *Poltergeist: The Legacy* (Fox); *Millennium* (Fox); *The X-Files* (Fox); *Profiler* (NBC); *Charmed* (WB); *Sabrina, the Teenage Witch* (ABC) and *Buffy: The Vampire Slayer* (WB).

The last two programs have been the most successful shows by far. In the fall of 1997, *Sabrina* was watched weekly by nearly 8 million households, and the week of November 30-December 6, 1998 saw *Buffy* receive a 3.7 Nielsen rating (approx. 3,677,800 households). These shows have continued to grow steadily in popularity, especially through the Internet where nearly 15,000 web sites are dedicated to *Sabrina*, while some 71,000 web sites are devoted to *Buffy*. The storylines to these two programs are simple enough:

- *Buffy: the Vampire Slayer*: [O]nce each century a single teenaged, female warrior (called a "Slayer" ...) is born to combat vampires, demons and other supernatural beings. . . . Buffy Summers, the series' heroine, is the current Slayer. . . . [She] and a small group of friends live in the suburban town of Sunnyvale, which also happens to be the mouth of Hell. Each week is thus spent with the group battling demons, vampires, werewolves, and other creatures. . . .

The early episodes were a commentary on the social life of American teenagers: an unpopular student who is rejected as a cheerleader uses supernatural powers to exact her revenge. . . .

In the last two seasons, however, the series has taken a much darker twist. After a sexual encounter with Buffy, Angel is stricken by an old curse that destroys his soul. [Though Angel is freed from this curse,] Buffy kills Angel and sends him to Hell in order to save her friends. . . . It is also revealed that one of the recurring villains, a vampire named Drusilla, was turned into the undead in the Middle Ages by Angel, who killed her entire family and attacked her on the day that she was to take her final vows as a nun.[37]

- *Sabrina, the Teenage Witch*: Sabrina is highly reminiscent of the program *Bewitched*, in which a well-meaning domestic witch dealt with her supernatural extended family while using her magic to harmlessly assist her mortal husband. Sabrina is a teenager who, on her sixteenth birthday, learns that she (as well as her mother and live-in aunt) is a witch. She's welcomed into the family coven with the gift of a black cauldron, to which she responds, "A black pot? Doesn't anyone shop at the Gap anymore?" In addition to her family, Sabrina is tutored in the art of witchcraft by Salem, a warlock doing penance as a black cat.

Early episodes involved Sabrina's inability to control her magic leading her into zany situations. She turned a rival into a pineapple; she made her boyfriend pregnant, turned him into a bowling pin, and also into a frog.[38]

But the degree of influence that TV has had over the way people view occultism is nothing compared to how dramatically Hollywood movies have altered America's overall perceptions of the occult. For many years now Hollywood has been producing a steady stream of pictures that portray occultism in a positive way (e.g., *Ghost* [1990] and *Phenomenon* [1996]).

Some films have specifically targeted younger audiences. Columbia Pictures' *The Craft* (1996), for instance, tells the tale of four attractive high school girls who mischievously use witchcraft in order to achieve their every desire. Some may believe such films are innocent fun, but occultists plainly recognize the proselytizing value in them. In reference to this particular movie, the occult publication *New Worlds of Mind and Spirit* stated,

> Whether you loved it or hated it, *The Craft* created a surge of interest in magick, the occult, and Witchcraft. New students and interested seekers are flocking to bookstores, people are looking for or establishing covens. There is an intense interest in Wicca reminiscent of the late sixties.[39]

Currently, the seven films based on Rowling's Harry Potter books are scheduled to be released annually from 2001-2007 at the rate of one per year. They will no doubt receive much attention.

POISONED FROM WITHIN

The occult influences in our society are innumerable, from the lucrative "psychic hotline" industry fueled by endorsements from numerous celebrities (e.g., Dionne Warwick and Billy Dee Williams) to public school educational programs built around New

Age meditation techniques.[40] Sales of occult paraphernalia are booming. New Age energy crystals and an unprecedented variety of tarot/divination card decks have literally flooded the marketplace. Some New Age stores report that as much as ten percent of their business comes from such occult tools. They can even be purchased at mainstream stores like B. Dalton's or Target.[41]

And, of course, the Internet is being used to advocate occultic involvement. In early 1997, for instance, I signed on to America Online only to be met with an official AOL "TAROT TO GO" button, accompanied by the promise: "Your future is available today." The selections at this AOL-advertised site included "1997 Predictions" and "Your Weekly Horoscope." Also, there are numerous occult-based role-playing games into which countless teens/young adults are immersing themselves: *Dungeons & Dragons*, *Magic the Gathering* and *Vampire: The Masquerade*.

As disturbing as all of this may be, a deeper anguish fills the hearts of many evangelicals, who for the first time are beginning to see occultism worm its way into the Christian church. This tragedy perfectly illustrates the warning found in Acts 20:17-31, where the apostle Paul tells leaders of the Ephesian church that there would eventually arise *from within* their congregation wolves in sheep's clothing, "speaking perverse things" to draw people away from God.

Paul's prophetic words are no less applicable today than they were in his day. Indeed, such warnings actually may be more poignant now due to the doctrinal lukewarmness permeating many Christian denominations. Heretical concepts based on occultic notions (usually pagan/Wiccan) have infiltrated the Christian community in no small way, especially with regard to radical feminist theology that seeks to replace God the Father and Jesus with images of "the goddess" worshiped by neopagans.

Mary Daly, who calls herself a "Christian feminist," makes clear the desire held by a growing number of like-minded individuals: "To put it bluntly, I propose that Christianity itself should be castrated."[42] In the *SCP Journal* article "Goddess Worship," Tal Brooke and Russ Wise explain further by quoting the views of yet another "Christian feminist," Susan Cady:

> Susan Cady, pastor of Emmanuel United Methodist Church in Philadelphia and co-author of *Sophia: the Future of Feminist Spirituality*, illustrates the direction that Daly and others are taking the church. In *Sophia*, Cady and her co-authors state that "Sophia is a female, goddess-like figure appearing clearly in the Scriptures of the Hebrew tradition."
>
> *Wisdom Feast*, Cady's latest book, presents Sophia as a separate goddess, with Jesus as her prophet, hence replacing Jesus with the feminine deity Sophia.[43]

Surprisingly, a growing number of women throughout various denominations are embracing this new feminist/pagan theology while maintaining their denominational affiliation. The result has been the appearance of pagan/Wiccan gatherings held at denomination-affiliated locations. One such seminar, sponsored by the Perkins School of Theology at Southern Methodist University, took place in February 1990 at the Highland Park United Methodist Church in Dallas. This "Women's Week" conference featured Linda Finnell, a Wiccan, who spoke on the subject of "Returning to the Goddess through Dianic Witchcraft."[44] During the event—which promoted tarot cards, channeling energy and communication with spirit guides— Finnell actually built an altar to the goddess Diana.[45]

At a 1998 "Feminist Retreat"—sponsored by the Dakota Conference of the United Methodist Church—the guest speaker was

Judith Duerk, a favorite lecturer at neopagan/Wiccan/feminist gatherings. Participants were given drums to facilitate meditative states wherein they contemplated the powers of their femininity.[46] Her book, *Circle of Stones*, is often listed among standard works on Wicca, feminist spirituality and paganism. One review stated: "*Circle of Stones* by Judith Duerk creates the female space for women to think of their present lives from the eyes of women's ancient culture and ritual. . . . In *Circle of Stones*, women will find a guide for attending to the Goddess within."[47]

Markedly more disturbing than these incidences, however, have been the two "Reimagining" Women's Conferences held in recent years. The first gathering, which occurred in Minneapolis in 1993, drew more than 2,000 participants from twenty-seven countries, forty-nine states and fifteen denominations. Not only was it fully sanctioned and financially sponsored by denominations (e.g., Presbyterian Church USA and United Methodist Church), but also dozens of high-ranking denominational officials attended the event. The twenty-seven speakers included lesbians, radical feminists and neopagans. The purpose of the conference turned out to be an organized attempt to fit ("reimagine") Scripture, the church and theology into feminist/pagan ideals.

One of the main speakers was Korean radical feminist Chung Hyung Kyung, who "drew substantially from New Age and animistic religions, expressing God as an all-encompassing energy force in nature."[48] Kyung repeatedly led women in *prana* (psychic energy) exercises and often referred to the Gnostic Gospels, a set of occultic texts rejected as heretical by the church centuries ago. Statements made by various other key figures at the conference also were highly revealing:

- Francis Wood (National Council of Churches) and Elizabeth Bettenhausen (Evangelical Lutheran Church in

America) both promoted abortion rights and homosexuality.

- Virginia Mollenkott (National Council of Churches) claimed that women are equal with Jesus, and that His death was not a blessing, but "the ultimate in child abuse."

- Aruna Gnanadson (World Council of Churches) and Dolores Williams (professor at Union Theological Seminary in New York) both painted the idea of Christ's atonement as an abusive patriarchal system with the comment, "I don't think we need folks hanging on crosses dripping blood and weird stuff."

- Chinese feminist Kwok Pui-Lan (World Council of Churches) explained that the Chinese reject the sinfulness of humans and dismissed Christ in favor of Confucius, who emphasized "the genuine possibility for human beings to achieve moral perfection and sainthood." She also rejected the doctrine of the Trinity.[49]

According to a detailed account of the event published by Watchman Fellowship (a counter-cult organization), "[t]here were regular convocations during the conference to the goddess Sophia, the source of everyone's divinity, the creator god who dwells within all, instead of God the father."[50] The conference concluded with a perversion of the Lord's Supper: In a ritual called "Milk and Honey," participants were asked to pray that "oppression of women would cease. The chant was repeated, 'Our Maker Sophia, we are women in your image, with the hot blood of our wombs we give form to new life . . . with nectar between our thighs we invite a lover . . . with our warm body fluids we remind the world of its pleasure and sensations.' "[51]

In 1998, the Conference was held again, this time with nearly 1,000 in attendance. Again, participants "shared milk and honey in a communion-like ritual affirming the sensuality of women." They spoke of savoring "the life-giving juices of our bodies and the planet" and prayed to "Sophia," who was identified as the Goddess of Wisdom. The 1998 event began as follows: "Participants . . . began in a darkened room with primal fires and beating drums to summon the 'First Woman'." The Reimaginers then called up spirits of the dead under the guise of "praying."[52]

Just how far will churches stray from Christian orthodoxy? That is something which remains to be seen. September 2000 saw the first instance of a church adapting its services to fit Rowling's Harry Potter novels. This radical departure from Christian tradition, which took place at the Church of England's All Saints parish (Guildford, Surrey), was dubbed by church leaders as a weekend of special "Harry Potter" family services.

Banners representing Hogwarts' four dorms decorated the church sanctuary (including one flag displaying a serpent for the House of Slytherin). The Vicar of All Saints, the Rev. Brian Coleman, wore wizard's robes and a wizard's cap so he could deliver his "service of the word" as the Harry Potter character of Albus Dumbledore. A whole new "Harry Potter Liturgy" was written featuring Hogwarts teachers, a sorting ceremony drama, "Muggle Songs" (i.e., hymns) and a concluding game of Quidditch.[53] The first weekend in September was designated because the church's liturgical calendar listed James 1:17-27 as the scheduled New Testament reading, which church officials viewed as "particularly appropriate themes of Harry Potter."[54]

To illustrate the biblical passage, which speaks of how God blesses His people with good gifts, Reverend Coleman drew comparisons between God's blessings to us and three blessings to Harry: 1) a flying broomstick; 2) an "invisibility cloak"; and

3) a cleverly crafted magical candy. Coleman told *The Times* of London, "[The Harry Potter books] are about loyalty, standing up for friends, standing up for good against evil. That is exactly what the passage in James is about."[55]

This significant show of support for the Rowling books shocked and appalled England's Evangelical Alliance, an umbrella organization for evangelical Christians. The Rev. Paul Harris, an Anglican clergyman who chairs the alliance's panel on cults and spirituality, could hardly believe Coleman's actions: "We do encourage clergy to connect with contemporary culture. But it is going too far to use images from Harry Potter. There is a risk that children are going to be very confused by the use of symbols associated with evil."[56] Despite such objections, the information about Coleman's service was posted on the Internet and was immediately "welcomed by other clergy who wished to adapt it for their churches as well."[57]

WHAT'S THE ATTRACTION?

What kind of people are being drawn toward occultic beliefs? Christian writer W. Elwyn Davies, in his book *Principalities and Powers*, identifies the types of individuals who are consistently interested in occult phenomena:

- *The curious*, who experiment with demonic forces without having a fully formed system of religious beliefs. A number of teenagers, for example, get involved in the occult due to nothing more than curiosity.
- *The dissatisfied*, "whose religious experience has left him unfulfilled and skeptical."
- *The bereaved*, "whose bereavement inclines him toward anything that offers knowledge of the dead."

- *The psychically inclined*, "who wants to develop suspected latent powers."
- *The rebellious*, "who recoils from the status quo in the church and in society, and seeks a viable alternative elsewhere."
- *The credulous*, who are ready to believe just about anything and everything.
- *The conformist*, who looks at his or her peers and says, "'Everyone does it,'" and decides "to be another who 'does it.'"
- *The children* of practicing occultists, "who are conditioned from childhood."[58]

As we have seen, the ongoing positive portrayals of occultism in society has had a profound effect on people. A 1997 Purdue University study found that "exposure to paranormal phenomena on television affected belief in such things as unidentified flying objects, ghosts, devils and extra-sensory perception."[59] According to Glenn Sparks, professor of communication, "Television may explain 10 percent of the belief in the paranormal."[60] Particularly susceptible to media influences are those persons who have no prior personal experiences with the paranormal (e.g., children).

"We are hoping to draw attention to the ways in which people arrive at their beliefs about the nature of the world," Sparks said. He also noted that charges about the media not exercising enough caution in disseminating information about paranormal events may be justified if it can be proven that the media have undue influence in shaping society's beliefs.[61] In other words, the media may be desensitizing the public to the very real dangers of occultism, especially when they are presented in connection to fashionable religious belief systems such as witchcraft/paganism.

This is not to say that followers of Christ should have absolutely nothing to do with imagination, fantasy, witches or even "magic." The crucial question is: How is it presented? Such topics are acceptable in *some* novels (e.g., C.S. Lewis' *Narnia* novels and J.R.R. Tolkien's *The Hobbit*). An extremely important distinction must be made between these works and J.K. Rowling's Harry Potter books. Consequently, my next chapter will be devoted to exploring the world of fiction that is safe and edifying for Christians.

ENDNOTES

1. Billy Graham, quoted in Edythe Draper, ed., *Draper's Book of Quotations for the Christian World* (Wheaton, IL: Tyndale House, 1992), 460.
2. Lyn Blake, quoted in Kristen Gerencher, "There's Something About Harry," *CBS MarketWatch*, July 6, 2000, available online at www.cesnur.org/recens/potter_029.htm. The audio version of Book IV also broke several records. For example, Listening Library originally shipped 180,000 copies of Rowling's fantasy, the largest first installment of a children's audio title ever distributed. These were sold in less than one week, forcing three more printings of 110,000 copies. This brought a stunning pronouncement from *Publishers Weekly* on July 24: *Goblet of Fire* had become "the fastest selling audio book ever—in the children's or adult category" (Shannon Maughan, "All Ears On Harry," *Publisher's Weekly*, July 24, 2000, available online at www.publishersweekly.com/index_articles/20000724_88176.asp).
3. Laura Miller, "Harry Potter Rumor Watch," Salon.com, July 6, 2000, available online at www.salon.com/books/log/2000/07/06/potter_rumors/.
4. Sheila Egan, quoted in Michael D. Shear, "Magic Day for Harry Potter Fan," *Washington Post*, July 1, 2000, A01, also available at http://washingtonpost.com/wp-dyn/articles/A29734-2000Jun30.html.
5. Anonymous, quoted in Shear.
6. Anthony Holden, "Why Harry Potter Doesn't Cast a Spell Over Me," *The Observer (London)*, June 25, 2000, available online at www.observer.co.uk/review/story/0,6903,335923,00.html.
7. David D. Kirkpatrick, "Harry Potter Magic Halts Bedtime for Youngsters," *New York Times*, July 9, 2000, available online at www.nytimes.com, also available at www.cesnur.org/recens/potter_036.htm.
8. Bay Anapol, quoted in Kirkpatrick.
9. Amelia Hill, "Harry Potter and the Small Snubbed Fans," *The Observer (London)*, July 9, 2000, available online at www.observer.co.uk.
10. Shannon Maughan, "Keeping Up With Harry," *Publishers Weekly*, November 1, 1999, available online at www.publishersweekly.com/articles/19991101_82411.asp.
11. "Potter Still Selling Strong," *Library Journal*, July 31, 2000, available online at www.ljdigital.com; Bill Hoffman, "Harry Potter and the Unwritten Best-seller," *New York Post*, July 24, 2000, available online at www.nypost.com.

12. Kate Greer, "Are American Families Finding New Strength in Spirituality?," *Better Homes and Gardens*, January 1988, 16-19.

13. Greer, 16, 19.

14. Greer, 16, 25.

15. Martin Marty, quoted in Timothy Jones, "Great Awakenings," *Christianity Today*, November 8, 1993, 24.

16. Barbara Kantrowitz, "In Search of the Sacred," *Newsweek*, November 28, 1994, 55; Bob McCullough, "The New Spin Is Spirituality," *Publishers Weekly*, May 16, 1994; Francine Prose, "The Power of Faith," *Redbook*, December 1994, 47-48, 50; and Eugene Taylor, "Desperately Seeking Spirituality" *Psychology Today*, November/December 1994, 57.

17. Kantrowitz, 54.

18. David Gibson (Religious News Service), "Is the New Christianity No Longer About 'We' and All About 'Me'?," *Salt Lake Tribune*, January 15, 2000. Surveys have consistently "put the level of Americans' belief in some higher power at close to 95 percent" available online at www.adherents.com; cf. similar statements in the following:

   • "A Harris poll taken in July 1994 revealed that 95 percent of those surveyed believed in God" (Thomas C. Reeves, *Twentieth Century America* [New York: Oxford University Press, 2000], 284).

   • "As the millennium approaches, the experiential, individualistic thread remarked so long ago by Emerson runs brightly through America's religious fabric. Among nations, only India is demonstrably more spiritual. Ninety-five percent of Americans say they believe in God" (Winifred Gallagher, *Working on God* [New York: Random House, 1999], 16).

   • "Nor is the hotel industry intentionally discriminatory. It regards itself as faithfully assisting the 96% of the populace who profess belief in God with a volume of that seemingly deepens that faith" (Gerald L. Zelizer, *USA Today*, 1 July 1999, 15A).

19. Cecile S. Holmes (Religious News Service), "Seeking Spirituality, Americans Are Picking and Choosing Their Religion," *Salt Lake Tribune*, February 12, 2000, citing George Gallup, Jr. and D. Michael Lindsay, *Surveying the Religious Landscape: Trends in U.S. Beliefs* (Ridgefield, CT: Morehouse Publishing, 2000).

20. Holmes.

21. Taylor, 64.

22. Donald G. Bloesch, "Lost in the Mythical Myths," *Christianity Today*, August 19, 1991.

23. Thomas C. Oden, "Blinded by the Lite," *Christianity Today*, September 12, 1994, 14.

24. Oden.

25. Wren Walker and Fritz Jung, "Welcome Members of the Press," *Witches' Voice Website*, October 1, 1999, available online at www.witchvox.org: "How many Witches, Wiccans and pagans are there? . . . Our best estimate here at The Witches' Voice is about 1 million in the U.S."; cf. Catherine Edwards, "Wicca Casts Spell on

Teen-Age Girls" *Insight* online magazine (Vol. 15, No. 39), October 25, 1999. Estimates cited by Helen Berger (associate professor of sociology at the University of Westchester in Pennsylvania) and Christian apologist Craig Hawkins in his book *Witchcraft: Exploring the World of Wicca* puts the U.S. witch population at the 150,000 to 200,000 mark. "In May, 1998, the *Chicago Tribune* reported that, though difficult to quantify due to lack of formal organization, neo-paganism is the fastest-growing religion in North America with the Internet being the prime means of proselytizing."

26. Thomas Hargrove and Guido H. Stempel, "Ghosts, Ghouls, and Goblins Haunt Americans' Imaginations," *San Francisco Examiner*, October 27, 1999, available online at www.examiner.com. The public's belief in ghosts has steadily increased over the last twenty years. In the 1980s only about twenty-five percent gave credence to the idea of spirits, according to the Index of American Public Opinion. Then, three separate polls in the early 1990s found that thirty-nine percent accepted ghosts as real. Now, nearly fifty percent believe in ghosts (see Hargrove and Stempel).

27. "Belief in the Beyond," *USA Today*, April 20, 1997, quoted in Matt Nisbet, "New Poll Points to Increase in Paranormal Belief," *Skeptical Inquirer* (vol. 22 no. 5, 1998), available online at www.csicop.org/articles/poll/index.html. Another study indicated that one out of five persons believed in reincarnation (John P. Newport, *The New Age Movement and the Biblical Worldview: Conflict and Dialogue* [Grand Rapids: Eerdmans, 1998], 46).

28. Winifred Gallagher, *Working on God* (New York: Random House, 1999), 148. Original source, Robert Wuthnow, *Sharing the Journey: Support Groups and America's New Quest for Community* (New York: The Free Press, 1994).

29. Patrick Goodenough, "Paganism Finds Growing Interest Among UK Children," August 25, 2000, *CNSNews.com*, available online at www.mcjonline.com/news/006/20000828b.htm.

30. Andy Norfolk, quoted in Goodenough.

31. A thirteen-year-old avid reader of the series posted the following opinion of these novels on Amazon.com: "*So You Want to Be a Wizard* is the beginning of an exciting and tantalizing series where wizardry and life in the city are a little too close for comfort. Nita, an intelligent but physically unendowed 13-year-old, finds refuge in the kid's section of the library after a particularly bad beating by a group of school bullies—and finds a book that not only tells her that there *is* magic, but how to get it, why to get it, and how to use it.

Kit, a 12-year-old Hispanic boy with school troubles similar to hers, teams up with her in a wizardly ordeal to gain their powers. Shifted 'sideways' into an alternate Manhattan, they discover both their wizardly talents and find friends in each other."

32. Goodenough; also see Silver RavenWolf, *To Ride a Silver Broomstick: New Generation Witchcraft* (St. Paul, MN: Llewellyn Publications, 1993).

33. Advertisement for *Teen Witch*, statement available at www.silverravenwolf.com/enchantm.htm.

34. Hargrove and Stempel.

35. Hargrove and Stempel.

36. Hargrove and Stempel.

37. Jason Barker, "Youth Oriented TV and the Occult," *Watchman Expositor* (vol. 15 no. 6, 1998), 8, also available at www.watchman.org/occult/youthandoccult.htm.

38. Barker.

39. *Llewellyn's New World*, September/October, 1996, 6.

40. *Watchman Vantage Point*, April 1999, 6-7; and *Watchman Vantage Point*, November 1998, 5. Even the U.S. government has had its hand in the occult cookie jar. Documents declassified in the 1990s revealed that during the last twenty years of America's cold war with the Soviet Union, the CIA and Pentagon spent $20 million investigating ESP and other psychic phenomena "in an effort to determine whether these forces of the paranormal world could somehow be put to use by espionage experts in the natural world." Not only were the results dismal, but the program was also marked by bizarre, and in some ways, humorously silly episodes:

    Newsweek also reported that, as if the early years of the program weren't bad enough, it became even worse in the mid-1980's. A senior general would call subordinates together for spoon-bending sessions. One "psychic" wrote a long paper predicting a huge air attack on Washington during a Reagan State of the Union speech. The program offered several suggestions about capturing Saddam Hussein during Desert Storm, and all of them proved utterly useless. And one of the "remote viewers" left the army because he was convinced there was a Martian colony beneath the New Mexico desert (David Bloomberg, "Psychic Spies!," *Themestream*, September 1, 2000, available online at www.themestream.com).

41. U.S. Games Systems has sold more than 15 million divination decks since 1968. A sample of the new systems is "Medicine Cards," a $29.95 deck inspired by Native Americans, which has sold more than 300,000 copies since 1988. Harper San Francisco's "Sacred Path Cards" has sold more than 100,000 copies. "Twenty-five years ago we were selling the decks to people in the occult and in underground types of stores," says Stanley Kaplan, president of U.S. Games Systems. "But today, they're at the front counter at the Waldenbooks and B. Dalton stores" (*Christian Research Journal*, Spring 1997).

42. Mary Daly, quoted in Russ Wise & Tal Brooke, "Goddess Worship," *SCP Newsletter* (vol. 23:2, Winter 98/99), available online at www.spc-inc.org and www.worthynews.com/goddess.htm.

43. www.spc-inc.org and www.worthynews.com/goddess.htm.

44. Russ White, "The Goddess and the Church," *Probe Ministries Leadership U*, available online at www.leaderu.com.

45. James Walker, "Can a Christian Church Be a Cult?," *The Watchman Expositor* (vol. 11, no. 5, 1994), 3.

46. Information available online at the "Unofficial Confessing Movement" web site, www.ucmpage.org/news/neopaumcl.html.

47. Meris Morrison, "Woman's Journey to Herself," information available online at www.state.vt.us/libraries/b733/BrooksLibrary/reviews2.htm#womans.

48. Walker, 5.

49. Walker., 5-6.

50. Walker, 6.

51. Walker.

52. "1998 Reimagining Revival," *The Watchman Expositor* (vol. 15 no. 4, 1998), 3.

53. Ruth Gledhill, "Church to Lure Young With Harry Potter," *The Times (London)*, September 1, 2000, available online at www.times-archives.co.uk/news/pages/tim/2000/09/01/timnwsnws01005.html.

54. Gledhill.

55. Rev. Brian Coleman, quoted in Gledhill.

56. Rev. Paul Harris, quoted in Gledhill.

57. Gledhill. Interestingly, secular columnist Rod Dreher of the *New York Post* wrote a scathing opinion piece on the "Harry Potter" church services. It read, in part, as follows:

> According to the report, the parish priest, whose British brain has apparently gone as soft as his British teeth, intended to don wizard's robes as Albus Dumbledore, the Hogwarts headmaster. Banners from the four Hogwarts houses, including the serpentine standard of evil Slytherin, were to be hung from the rafters. The special service was to end with worshippers chasing a yellow rubber ball around the church in an attempt to play Quidditch, the popular wizard's game in the best-selling children's-book series. Oh, dear. The thought of a church full of mad Englishmen pursuing a rubber ball around the sanctuary in a desperate attempt to be culturally appealing is simply beyond parody. Monty Python, thou shouldst be alive at this hour. Some clergy from the Church of England's evangelical wing have protested, saying importing occult symbols into Christian liturgy is a terrible idea that can confuse children. They're right—and I say that as someone who adores the Harry Potter books—but the real error here has nothing to do with the misuse of our beloved Harry. The real offense here is the profane notion that sacred liturgy can or should be made a slave of entertainment-driven faddishness. What's next, a "Survivor" service, with the minister as God (Jeff Probst), a deacon as Lucifer (Richard), and a congregant as the Christian innocent (Dirk) fighting to keep from being booted off the island for reading his Bible too much? Don't laugh: Somewhere in America, a suburban megachurch is surely hatching this idea. Never underestimate the clueless idiocy of those who, having shed the timeless structures of traditional religion, fall for anything that seems "relevant." . . . Nobody respects a religious institution willing to compromise willy-nilly with the secular culture on a fool's quest for popularity. A church that will try anything stands for nothing. The ancient churches trading their birthright for a pot of pop-culture message bring to mind that gruesome grandmother who used to roller-skate around Studio 54 in its heyday. How desperately the daft old bird needed someone to say to her, "Please, dear, remember your

dignity. You're embarrassing yourself." So, too, do those hopelessly unhip churchmen trying to drag Hogwarts' star pupil into their dorky services. Harry Potter, God bless 'im, has many virtues, but dying for England's sins is not one of them" (Rod Dreher, "England's 'Potter' Parish Isn't Hip To Changing Culture," *New York Post*, September 5, 2000, available online at www.nypost.com).

58. Adapted from W. Elwyn Davies, *Principalities and Powers* (Minneapolis, MN: Bethany House, 1976), 303-304; cf. Josh McDowell and Don Stewart, *Handbook of Today's Religions* (San Bernardino, CA: Here's Life Publishers, 1983; 1992 edition), 153.

59. "Never Seen a Ghost? Then TV May Be Your Teacher," *Purdue News*, October 17, 1997, available online at www.purdue.edu/UNS/html4ever/971017.Sparks. survey.html.

60. Glenn Sparks, quoted in "Never Seen a Ghost?"

61. "Never Seen a Ghost?"

TWELVE

BEYOND FANTASY:
TOLKIEN, LEWIS AND ROWLING

Stop comparing Harry Potter to The Lord of the Rings. . . .
*Rowling's series is elitist kiddie fare that serves to make modern
American children even more narcissistic than they are, and
Tolkien's is a masterpiece and—this is crucial—a completely
adult tragedy with profound moral and religious implications.*

Mark Gauvreau Judge[1]
commentator, *Baltimore City Paper*

In an effort to deflect concerns about Rowling's books, Potter supporters have consistently likened the Harry Potter series to the works of J.R.R. Tolkien and C.S. Lewis. This has been done continuously through an unending stream of news stories, interviews and book reviews. The following statement by Judy Corman, spokesperson for Scholastic Press (J.K. Rowling's U.S. publisher), is typical: "There's something these parents are missing, which is it's a magical book. It takes its place along the best in classic literature for children, along with . . . *The Chronicles of Narnia* [C.S. Lewis] and *The Lord of the Rings* [J.R.R. Tolkien]."[2] A similar comment appeared in a Knight-Ridder News Service story: "Rowling's books are not so much anti-Christian as they are fully Christian, drawing on the legacy of fellow British writers C.S. Lewis and J.R.R. Tolkien, whose popular children's tales about the magical lands of Narnia and Middle Earth were written as Christian allegory."[3]

But such a position is seriously flawed, most obviously because the fantasy tales of Tolkien and Lewis fall within the category of mythopoetic literature, meaning that they take place in worlds disassociated from the real world in which we live. As Dr. Curt Brannan of Washington's Bear Creek School District observes: "[In Lewis' and Tolkien's works] there is no confusion in the child's mind . . . that these are mythical characters in a mythical place."[4]

But the Harry Potter books are not mythopoetic. Unlike Lewis' and Tolkien's creations, Rowling's fantasy is set in our twenty-first-century world, complete with contemporary forms of occultism (e.g., astrology and divination) and references to persons and events from our own human history (e.g., Nicholas Flamel, Hand of Glory, Witch Hunts). Rowling's novels also use a vastly different definition of "magic" than the one used by Lewis and Tolkien. Furthermore, the Harry Potter series promotes a concept of right and wrong that is radically altered from the one presented by Lewis and Tolkien.

REMEMBERING TOLKIEN

English literature professor John Ronald Reuel Tolkien (1892-1973) is commonly viewed as the father of contemporary fantasy. Although he authored a number of brilliant works, his most famous ones are *The Hobbit* and The Lord of the Rings epic trilogy (*The Fellowship of the Ring*, *The Two Towers* and *The Return of the King*). All of these tales interconnect with one another and occur in "Middle-Earth," a complex world Tolkien created with his commanding knowledge of linguistics, history and mythology.

The Hobbit, originally published in 1937, tells the story of Bilbo Baggins, who is a "hobbit." According to Tolkien, hobbits are

> little people, about half our height. . . . There is little or no magic about them, except the ordinary everyday sort which helps them to disappear quietly and quickly when large stupid folk like you and me come blundering along, making a noise like elephants which they can hear a mile off. They are inclined to be fat in the stomach; they dress in bright colours (chiefly green and yellow); wear no shoes, because their feet grow natural leathery soles and thick warm brown hair like the stuff on their heads (which is curly); have long clever brown fingers, good-natured faces, and laugh deep fruity laughs (especially after dinner, which they have twice a day when they can get it).[5]

Bilbo's adventures begin with a visit from a powerful wizard named Gandalf. He reveals that Bilbo's destiny is to travel with a group of thirteen dwarves to a Mountain where Smaug, an evil dragon, dwells. The group's goal will be to slay the dragon and capture his treasure, which rightfully belongs to the dwarves. Throughout this quest they face numerous hardships (e.g., storms, hunger, fatigue, etc.) and dangers (e.g., trolls, goblins, evil wolves and giant spiders). Additionally, when Bilbo becomes separated from the group, he confronts an especially evil creature named Gollum. Eventually, Bilbo escapes Gollum, reunites with the dwarves and Smaug is slain. Bilbo then returns home with a number of treasures, including a magic ring with which he can become invisible and a sword that glows when goblins are near.

Tolkien's The Lord of the Rings trilogy begins sixty years after the conclusion of *The Hobbit*, and finds Bilbo making preparations for his 111th birthday. It will be a special birthday in that Bilbo plans to use the occasion to leave the Shire (where hobbits live) and bequeath all of his possessions, including his house, to his nephew, Frodo. His hope is to do some peaceful traveling and visit the mountains one last time before he dies. And so, at the conclusion of his party, he slips on his magical ring and disappears right before everyone's eyes. Frodo moves into Bilbo's home, and among all of his inherited possessions is the left-behind magic ring, which Gandalf the wizard now suspects is a very dangerous item.

As the trilogy progresses, Gandalf reveals that Bilbo's ring, which now belongs to Frodo, is the magical ring that originally belonged to the Dark Lord, Sauron, who had tried in ages past to conquer all of Middle-Earth. Sauron was eventually forced into hiding after being vanquished by an army of Elves and Men, but in *The Fellowship of the Ring*, he has risen again and is seeking the ring in order to fully restore his former powers. The only way dwellers of Middle-Earth will ever defeat Sauron is if Frodo destroys the ring by throwing it into the volcanic fires of the Crack of Doom in which it was forged, in the depths of Orodruin, beneath the Fire Mountain.

The remainder of the trilogy follows Frodo and his three hobbit companions (Sam, Merry and Pippin) on their mission to destroy the ring. Along the way, they are separated, forced to flee evil "Black Riders" (deadly phantoms); fight Orcs and evil wolves; evade a traitorous wizard named Saruman; and battle internal psychological stresses caused by the ring.

By the time Frodo reaches the Crack of Doom, Sauron's evil Hordes have converged on the last stronghold of the forces of good, and a final Armageddon-like battle ensues. Fortunately, the ring is destroyed just when all hope seems lost. Sauron's power is broken once and for all, the forces of good triumph and Middle-Earth is saved from the Dark Lord's tyranny. But it is a bittersweet victory. Although Sauron has been defeated, the destruction of the ring marks the beginning of the end of Middle- Earth, the allotted time for which has passed. The world of Hobbits, Dwarves and Elves must give way to the time of Men.

This brief summary of *The Hobbit* and The Lord of the Rings trilogy cannot begin to do justice to the masterful tale Tolkien weaves using his expansive imagination and brilliant mind. He was truly one of the most gifted writers of the last 200 years, easily on the level of Dickens, Jane Austen or Mark Twain.[6] *The Hobbit* and The Lord of the Rings trilogy, because of their superior literary quality, unique storylines and timeless nature, certainly deserve a place among the classics.

Now compare Tolkien's work with the Harry Potter books. According to a number of insightful reviewers, the Potter books are little more than occult-glamorizing, morally bleak, marketing sensations filled with one-dimensional characters and a hero who is, to borrow the words of Rowling's Professor Snape, "a nasty little boy who considers rules to be beneath him."[7]

For example, British commentator Anthony Holden, judged her books to be "not particularly well-written."[8] Roger Sutton, editor of *The Horn Book* (a seventy-five-year-old children's literary digest in Boston), has described the Potter books as a "critically insignificant" series, adding that as literature, they are "nothing to get excited about."[9] And in his article for ScienceFictionFantasy.net, Sherwood Smith observed: "The adults are conveniently stupid when needed to keep the kids in the action, refusing to listen just when any other adult would see alarms. The headmaster, supposedly benevolent and omniscient, seems content to permit the beginners to face death over and over, sure they will somehow win. But of course they do."[10] An even more caustic review has come from renowned literary critic Harold Bloom, who made scathing remarks about Rowling's works on the PBS interview program, *Charlie Rose*: "[T]here's nothing there to read," Bloom asserted. "They're just an endless string of clichés. I cannot think that does anyone any good. That's not *Wind in the Willows*. That's not *Through the Looking Glass*.... It's really just slop."[11]

It seems apparent that J.K. Rowling is no J.R.R. Tolkien. But if there is such a disparity between Rowling's novels and Tolkien's classics, why are they still being compared to each other? It may stem from the fact that both include: 1) a struggle between good and evil; 2) use of the word "magic"; and 3) "wizard" characters. These superficial similarities, however, do not justify putting both writers in the same league. In fact, upon close examination, the "similarities" do not really exist.

First, the struggle between good and evil in *The Hobbit* and The Lord of the Rings trilogy relies heavily on, and is rooted in, Tolkien's devout Christian faith. His good characters are truly good. His evil characters are truly evil. And when any good character commits an evil deed, he suffers as a result of his actions, or at the very least, he must do something to atone for his behavior. Tolkien's stories also do not include episodes of good characters doing bad things (e.g., lying to friends or stealing from authority figures) in order to accomplish a good task.

Furthermore, Tolkien's moral boundaries are clearly drawn with "good" and "evil" characters behaving in a manner that corresponds to their identities in Middle Earth: Orcs, Trolls and Sauron are evil; Gandalf, Hobbits, Elves and Dwarves are generally good. In Rowling's novels, however, moral ambiguity and relativism abound, while at the same time no one really seems to know exactly who is and who is not evil. In the Harry Potter series, one's best friend might turn out to be an enemy, while an enemy might actually be one's closest ally.

Second, the "magic" most often seen in Tolkien's novels is not the kind of occult-based/contemporary-pagan magick Rowling employs. In fact, Tolkien disliked the word "magic," but was forced to use it because he could find no other word closer to the meaning he intended. He attempted to fix this problem in Middle-Earth by including strict limitations on magic, its nature, who has it, how it is used and why it is used. Even so, Tolkien often complained that the word "magic" failed to adequately, or accurately, explain his meaning.

Various letters written by Tolkien make it clear that his definition of "magic" in the context of Middle-Earth does not include any kind of supernatural power. It is a natural ability given *only* to Elves. No other race—including Orcs, Trolls, Dwarves, Hobbits and others—has magical capabilities. In Letter #155, published in *The Letters of J.R.R. Tolkien*, Tolkien writes: "[A] difference in the use of 'magic' in this story is that it is not to come by [i.e., acquired] by 'lore' or spells; but is in an inherent power not possessed by Men as such."[12]

For Elves, however, "magic" is as natural as singing or drawing. In fact, Tolkien actually described it simply as "Art" without human limitations.[13] The source of it rests within Elves themselves. It depends on no external power, nor can it be learned or enhanced. The very term "magic" is perplexing to Elves when they hear it being used by mortals to describe their abilities. This is apparent in *The Fellowship of the Ring*, when Galadriel (Elven "Lady of Lorien") shows Frodo her "magic" mirror, saying: "For this is what your folk would call magic, I believe; though I do not understand clearly what they mean. . . . But this, if you will, is the magic of Galadriel."[14]

The other kind of magic that exists in Middle-Earth is magic within various objects (e.g., weapons, rings, helmets, mirrors, etc.). But these items, too, hold a different type of magic than the objects in Rowling's works (e.g., Mr. Weasley's Flying Car, Harry's Marauder's Map and his invisibility cape). The items on the Harry Potter series are bewitched or enchanted. However, the objects in Tolkien's fantasy receive special qualities through "lore," which Tolkien likened to technology and science. They are created in accordance with the laws of nature as found in Middle-Earth.[15]

Interestingly, drastic and negative consequences always result in Middle-Earth when its non-magical dwellers (non-Elves) get too close to magic. For example, nine Men, each of whom are given magical rings by the dark wizard Sauron, eventually turn into evil phantoms (i.e., ringwraiths) enslaved by Sauron. The one ring Bilbo possesses begins to corrupt him, just as it had corrupted its previous owners. Frodo, after his long journey with Bilbo's magical ring, is never physically or psychologically the same. He tells Gandalf he has been forever "wounded" by the ordeal.[16] And every year on the anniversary of the ring's destruction, he becomes bedridden with nausea.[17] Obviously, the properties of "magic" are very different in Middle-Earth.

But what about Tolkien's many "wizards" (e.g., Gandalf and Sauron)? Do these characters not mirror the kind of wizards that are in Harry Potter? In a word, no. Any argument to the contrary exposes a superficial understanding of the nature of magic in Tolkien's novels. Alan Jacobs of Wheaton College, for instance, although a well-respected literature professor, has on numerous occasions put forth this groundless argument:

> I was eagerly describing Harry Potter to a good friend of mine . . . [A]nd he said, "You know, I'm a little nervous about this. I mean, you know, witches, wizardry, magic. I don't know whether I want to read a book like this to my kids." And I said, "Well, doesn't your family enjoy *The Lord of the*

Rings?" And he said, "We revere *The Lord of the Rings*." . . .
And I said, "But, isn't there a lot of magic, and isn't Gandalf a
wizard?" And he said, "Yeah, I guess that's right."[18]

Jacobs' analogy is faulty because Rowling's wizards are human,
whereas Tolkien's "wizards" are not human at all. Gandalf is a
"Maia"—i.e., an angelic-like being that has taken on human form.
Sauron, the evil wizard in The Lord of the Rings trilogy, is also a
Maia, albeit a fallen one. According to Tolkien, the Maiar (plural for
Maia) were sent into Middle-Earth by the Valar (an even higher or-
der of angelic beings) to render assistance to Elves and Men.[19]

Gandalf and Sauron, along with every other wizard in Middle-
Earth (e.g., the evil Saruman, another Maia) are, in essence, illustrations of good angels and evil angels (or demons). Hence, their
powers are part of their nature and not obtained through occultism. This also would hold true for the evil Melkor—perhaps the
most powerful of all the Valar—who tried to subjugate Middle-
Earth in direct rebellion against the creator of all things, Eru, also
known as the One or Ilúvatar (i.e., God).

In Tolkien's writings Elves, the Maiar and Valar are simply
exercising their God-given abilities when they do "magic," either for good or for evil. In J.K. Rowling's world, however, wizards are human and their magickal powers are tapped/increased
through occultism. Furthermore, *there is no Ilúvatar (i.e., God)
overseeing the battle between good and evil*. This is by far the
most profound difference between Rowling's books and the
works of Tolkien.

Beyond a limited number of vague similarities, Tolkien's
works and those of J.K. Rowling are vastly different. The chasm
that separates their fantasies was concisely expressed by Mark
Gauvreau Judge in a June 12, 2000 *Baltimore City Paper* article
titled "The Trouble With Harry":

[T]he power of *The Lord of the Rings* is the heavy under-current of tragedy and loss that runs through the story. Tolkien's masterwork is about growing up, the loss of en-chantment, and the Christian paradox of salvation through suffering and painful death. . . .

These themes are expressed in the trilogy's central conun-drum: If Hobbit Frodo, thrust by circumstance into the role of Ring-Bearer, fails in his mission, evil overwhelms the world. If he succeeds, he unravels his own world. As the an-gelic Elf Queen Galadriel tells him, "Do you not see where-fore your coming to us is the footstep of doom? For if you fail, then we are laid bare to the Enemy. Yet if you succeed, then our power is diminished, and [our kingdom] will fade, and the time and tides will sweep it away."

In other words, like mortal life, this Ring business is a no-win situation. Indeed, the heroic Ring-Bearer never re-covers from his mission. . . . Frodo sacrifices everything for the world because he answered to the higher calling of con-science and duty, even if that meant enduring the slings and arrows of the world's Muggles. Would Harry and his pals do the same?[20]

Would Harry and his pals do the same thing? Probably not. In *Harry Potter and the Sorcerer's Stone*, we learn how wizards/witches feel about helping others (specifically, Muggles) with their magic. On page 65 of Book I, Harry asks Hagrid why wiz-ards do not tell Muggles about their existence. In his reply, Hagrid explains that Muggles would just keep bothering wizards/witches for assistance with their problems, then he concludes: "Nah, we're best left alone."[21]

This is a far cry from the kind of response Frodo gives after Gandalf tells him he has two choices set before him: 1) take on the terrible burden of destroying the ring to help save others from Sauron, and in so doing, leave his beloved home at Bag End, in the Shire; or 2) give the responsibility to someone else. Frodo exhibits a very un-Harry-Potter-like sense of duty, sacrificing his own life and concerns for those of his neighbors:

> "As far as I understand what you have said, I suppose I must keep the Ring and guard it, at least for the present, whatever it may do to me. . . . [I]n the meanwhile it seems that I am a danger, a danger to all that live near me. I cannot keep the Ring and stay here. I ought to leave Bag End, leave the Shire, leave everything and go away." He sighed. "I should like to save the Shire, if I could—though there have been times when I thought the inhabitants too stupid and dull for words, and have felt that an earthquake or an invasion of dragons might be good for them. But I don't feel like that now. I feel that as long as the Shire lies behind, safe and comfortable, I shall find wandering more bearable: I shall know that somewhere there is a firm foothold, even if my feet cannot stand there again. Of course, I have sometimes thought of going away, but I imagined that as a kind of holiday, a series of adventures like Bilbo's or better, ending in peace. But this would mean exile, a flight from danger into danger, drawing it after me. And I suppose I must go alone, if I am to do that and save the Shire. But I feel very small, and very uprooted, and well—desperate. The Enemy is so strong and terrible."[22]

The most critical difference between Rowling and Tolkien is the spiritual perspectives from which they created their stories. Tolkien was unabashedly Christian. In one of his letters, he wrote: "With regard to The Lord of the Rings . . . I actually intended it to be consonant with Christian thought and belief, which is asserted elsewhere."[23] In Letter #310, he openly declared:

> So it may be said that the chief purpose of life, for any one of us, is to increase according to our capacity our knowledge of God by all the means we have, and to be moved by it to praise and thanks. To do as we say in the Gloria in Excelsis . . . "We praise you, we call you holy, we worship you, we proclaim your glory, we thank you for the greatness of your splendour."[24]

To date, Rowling's only public statements of any spiritual significance is a brief and rather flippant remark made during a 1999 interview, in response to a question about her personal beliefs: "Well, as it happens, I believe in God, but there's no pleasing some people!"[25]

A Look at Lewis

English scholar Clive Staples Lewis (1898-1963), who was a close friend of Tolkien, authored numerous books explaining and defending Christianity: *The Screwtape Letters* (1942), *Miracles* (1947) and *Mere Christianity* (1952), to name but a few. He also excelled at writing both fantasy and science fiction. Perhaps his most famous work is The Chronicles of Narnia series of seven volumes, which for the most part, detail the adventures of four children surnamed Pevensie: Peter, Susan, Edmund and Lucy.[26]

The stories take place in Narnia, a land reached by way of a secret multidimensional doorway located, of all places, at the back of a common wardrobe. Lucy is the first to discover the hidden passageway, but she is soon followed by her sister and brothers. All of them eventually become entangled in a great Narnian conflict between forces of good and evil. This war places the armies of a wicked White Witch against the followers of the Great Lion, Aslan, the son of the Emperor Beyond the Sea.

It all began when the White Witch seized control of Narnia and turned the once beautiful land into a dreary world where it is always winter, but never Christmas. Eventually, the Witch is defeated, Aslan's loyal subjects are freed, spring returns to Narnia and the four children are crowned as kings and queens. The four children return to our world, but throughout successive books revisit Narnia to live out more adventures with Aslan.

In a news article covering the controversy over using the Harry Potter books in public schools, Children's Librarian Stephanie Bange expressed the following sentiment: "[N]obody makes a fuss about C.S. Lewis' The Chronicles of Narnia series, which are based on Christian theology, but there are also witches and the dark side."[27] Although this type of analogy seems logical and applicable on the surface, closer examination reveals that it is flawed in three ways.

First, the "Christian theology" in Lewis' fantasy is veiled beneath various characters (e.g., Aslan the Lion). Consequently, there is no *direct* association that can be made between the books and any contemporary religion. In Harry Potter, however, a *direct* link to paganism/witchcraft is made via the presentation to readers of current occult beliefs and practices.

Second, there is indeed a witch in the *Narnia* series, but she is evil and based on age-old and widely accepted symbols and illustrations of evil. In contrast, the witches and wizards in Harry Potter are children who have numerous characteristics in common with young readers, including age, attitudes, thoughts, feelings and experiences. Consequently, Rowling's line between fantasy and reality is extremely thin, as evidenced by her own admission that many children believe Hogwarts is a real place (see Rowling quote in Chapter 8).

Third, Lewis does not present a conflict between good and evil based on any "dark side" concepts of power. This "dark side" versus "light side" battle, popularized by "the force" concept in George Lucas' *Star Wars*, is built around the existence of a neutral "power" that has a dark and light side. Conflict arises when persons drawn to the force's dark side ("evil") seek dominion over those who remain faithful to the light side ("good"). Both sides, although they may certainly have different goals, are drawing upon the same "power." The outcome of their battle depends solely on how adept each participant has become at controlling "the force" (i.e., magic). Although a similar "dark side"/"light side" battle exists in the Harry Potter series, it cannot be found in Lewis' novels.

In The Chronicles of Narnia series, the conflict involves two opposing forces (i.e., kinds of magic) of entirely different origins. The one source of magic (Aslan's deep magic) is "good" because it comes from, is controlled by and operates through the One who has legitimate authority over all things (i.e., the Emperor Beyond the Sea). The other source of magic is "evil" because it springs from an illegitimate authority that has usurped control over Narnia (i.e., the White Witch). This clearly distinguishes Lewis' fantasy books from those authored by Rowling.

Closely tied to this issue is the method by which evil is conquered in Lewis' story as opposed to how it is overcome in Rowling's books. Lewis' good characters (e.g., Peter, Lucy, Susan) do not overcome witchcraft by learning more witchcraft. Instead, they respond to evil by becoming servants of the good character, Aslan, who ultimately vanquishes the White Witch. Rowling's good characters, however, seek to overcome evil by using the same dualistic magical power employed by Lord Voldemort and his Death Eaters. In fact, every good witch and wizard has been trained by the same kind of institution that instructed Voldemort and his followers.

Additionally, it must be mentioned that Rowling's works, unlike those of C.S. Lewis, are completely dependent on magick. It is central to her story, whereas Lewis uses magic sparingly and in a highly stylized manner that does not connect with the real world. But the magickal arts used by Harry and his friends are available to children in the occult section of any nearby bookstore or at any number of Internet web sites. As one newspaper columnist observed, "Lewisian magic seems a bit pale and remote compared with Rowling's; it is far easier to imagine a Harry Potter fan thinking: 'Wow, that sounds like fun! If only I could find a way to . . .' "[28]

Another difference between Lewis' books and those produced by Rowling lies in the ultimate meaning of the works. As journalist Alan Cochrum noted in his *Fort-Worth Star Telegram* article, Rowling's novels seem to have no grander purpose than to "provide a rollicking good time."[29] Consequently, her stories are filled with crude jokes, crass remarks, gratuitous violence, gore, juvenile antics and just about every other ploy used in today's action-packed PG-13 films and video games. Lewis' novels, however, offer an immeasurably deeper gift to readers, as Cochrum notes:

> Lewis' books have a very different goal; the British scholar does hope that his readers come away with a good time, and much more as well. His question is: "What would the story of the Bible (Creation, Incarnation, Death-and-Resurrection, Redemption, Revelation) look like in another world?" The answer, in a word, is Aslan—the leonine Christ figure of Narnia.[30]

It also must be recognized that in the works of Lewis and Tolkien issues of "morality and integrity are at stake and dealt with as important and significant concerns."[31]

Tolkien, for instance, illustrates right and wrong, good and evil not only through the choices his characters make, but how those choices affect others. His stories raise issues involving the consequences of disobedience, the merits of self-sacrifice, the detrimental effects of negative emotions (e.g., pride, greed, lust, unforgiveness, etc.) and the need to fulfill one's responsibilities for the benefit of others, even when those responsibilities are difficult and painful.

Lewis' tales offer similar morality lessons. The most obvious example involves the disobedience of Edmund Pevensie, a little boy whose errant ways subject him to the power of the wicked White Witch. To rescue Edmund, Aslan offers himself as a sacrifice on the ancient Stone Table. Although he is killed, Aslan rises again through a "deeper" magic unknown to the witch. This sacrificial love convicts Edmund of his evil ways, and he repents of his sins. Ultimately, the once mischievous Edmund is transformed by Aslan's love into Narnia's "King Edmund the Just."

In the Harry Potter series, however, morality is presented inconsistently. Though there are examples of true, admirable courage and loyalty, in too many instances the ethics are muddied. Bad characters turn out to be good. Good characters turn out to be bad. Misbehavior is condoned as long as the eventual outcome is either fun or rewarding (e.g., Harry's lying and disobedience). Good deeds bring about evil results (Harry shows mercy by sparing Pettigrew's life, but this eventually leads to the rising of Voldemort and the murder of Cedric). Harmful deeds are committed to bring about positive results (e.g., Sirius Black, while in the form of a dog, drags Ron into a secret corridor beneath a tree, breaking Ron's leg in the process, in order to get Harry to follow and learn the truth about Peter Pettigrew). In short, Rowling's moral universe is a topsy-turvy world with no firm rules of right and wrong or any godly principles by which to determine the truly good from the truly evil.

ENDNOTES

1. Mark Gauvreau Judge, "The Trouble With Harry," *Baltimore City Paper*, July 12-18, 2000, available online at www.citypaper.com/2000-07-12/feature2.html.

2. Reuters, "Muggles Seek to Muzzle Harry Potter In Schools," October 13, 1999, available online at www.cesnur.org/recens/potter_04.htm#Anchor-42728.

3. Richard Scheinin, "Harry Potter's Wizardly Powers Divide Opinion," Knight-Ridder News Service, December 3, 1999, available online at http://arlington.net/news/doc/1047/1:FAITH2/1:FAITH2120399.html.

4. Curt Brannan, "What About Harry Potter," available online at www.tbcs.org/.

5. J.R.R. Tolkien, *The Hobbit* (New York: Ballantine Books, 1937; 1982 revised edition), 2.

6. Dozens of books have been written about Tolkien the man, his work and his message. The titles of these study volumes, many of which deal with the unbelievably complex and detailed descriptions of Middle-Earth and its "history," hint at the literary genius they discuss: *J.R.R. Tolkien: Man of Fantasy*; *J.R.R. Tolkien: Myth Maker*; *Between Faith and Fiction: Tolkien and the Powers of His World*; *Tolkien's Legendarium: Essays on the History of Middle-Earth*; and *Recovery and Transcendence for the Contemporary Mythmaker: The Spiritual Dimension in the Works of J.R.R. Tolkien*.

7. J.K. Rowling, *Harry Potter and the Goblet of Fire* (New York: Scholastic Press, 2000), 516.

8. Anthony Holden, quoted in Sarah Lyall, "Wizard vs. Dragon: A Close Contrast, but the Fire-Breather Wins," *New York Times*, January 29, 2000, available online at www.nytimes.com.

9. Roger Sutton, quoted in Elizabeth Mehren, "Wild About Harry," *Los Angeles Times*, July 28, 2000, available online at www.latimes.com.

10. Sherwood Smith, "The Harry Potter Phenomenon," *Science Fiction Fantasy*, available online at www.sff.net.

11. Harold Bloom, quoted in Jamie Allen, "Harry and Hype," July 13, 2000, CNN Online, available online at www.cnn.com/2000/books/news/07/13/potter.hype/.

12. Humphrey Carpenter, *The Letters of J.R.R. Tolkien* (New York: Houghton Mifflin, 1981; 2000 edition), Letter, 155.

13. Carpenter, Letter #131.

14. J.R.R. Tolkien, *The Fellowship of the Ring* (New York: Ballantine Books, 1955; 1982 edition), 427.

15. Carpenter, Letter #153.

16. J.R.R. Tolkien, *The Return of the King* (New York: Ballantine, 1955; 1982 edition), 299.

17. Tolkien, *The Return of the King*, 341.

18. Alan Jacobs, interview on *Mars Hill Audio* (vol. 40, September/October 1999), audio cassette, side 2.
19. See the Tolkien Archives available online at www.tolkien-archives.com/racehistories.shtml.
20. Judge, available online at www.citypaper.com.
21. J.K. Rowling, *Harry Potter and the Sorcerer's Stone* (New York: Scholastic, 1997), 65.
22. Tolkien, *The Fellowship*, 88-89.
23. Carpenter, Letter #269.
24. Carpenter, Letter #310.
25. J.K. Rowling, interview with America Online, May 4, 2000, available at http://www.geocities.com/harrypotterfans/jkraolchat.html.
26. This plot is primarily the storyline in Book II of Lewis' series, although the remaining volumes (III-VII) continue following the adventures of the four children. Book I, however, is somewhat of a precursor to the rest of the volumes, and deals with two other children—Digory Kirke and Polly Plummer—and their struggles against the White Witch, who is known as Jadis in Book I. (Editor's note: The publisher of the Lewis books has in recent years renumbered the books in the series; the endnote above refers to the new numbering scheme.)
27. Stephanie Bange, quoted in Mary McCarty, "Potter's Pouters Puzzling," *Dayton Daily News*, November 3, 1999.
28. Alan Cochrum, "Harry Potter and the Magic Brew-haha," *Fort-Worth Star Telegram*, December 18, 1999, available online at www.fwst.com.
29. Cochrum.
30. Cochrum.
31. Brannan, available online at http://www.tbcs.org/vision/article04.htm.

THIRTEEN

LESSONS LEARNED:
COMMENTS AND CONTROVERSIES

Mimicking the paranoid Chicken Little, a fictional character who assumes the sky is falling when an acorn hits him, the anti-Potter parents are forming illogical conclusions similar to those of generations of book censors before them.

Elizabeth D. Schafer[1]
author, *Exploring Harry Potter*

The controversy surrounding J.K. Rowling's Harry Potter series, especially for use in public school class-rooms, has evolved into nothing less than a bitter war of words. The majority opinion belongs to pro-Potter journalists, educators, religious liberals and freedom of speech advocates. The minority consists of a coalition of Harry Potter critics comprised of Christian parents, teachers, pastors from diverse churches and counter-cult ministry workers.

Unfortunately, some Christians have added unnecessary fuel to this fire by accusing Rowling of *deliberately* seeking to draw children into black magic/occultism/witchcraft, which is an unprovable charge. Others have made rash and unjustified criticisms of her novel's contents. (e.g., Some preachers have claimed that the S-shaped lightning bolt scar on Harry's forehead actually stands for Satan.)

Making matters worse has been the media. Rather than representing both sides fairly or, at the very least, consistently quoting well-reasoned Christian responses, journalists have taken great pains to paint Harry Potter critics as ignorant Bible-thumpers whose objections are inconsistent, illogical and groundless. A number of news articles have even resorted to mocking Christians as "narrow-minded moralists."[2] Other stories have labeled as "paranoid" anybody daring to raise objections against Rowling's novels.[3] A *London Review of Books* article went so far as to label parental objections to the Harry Potter series as a stupid and childish fight, specifically referring to "born-again" Christians.[4]

A particularly nasty *Jewish World Review* article titled "Casual Censors and Deadly Know-Nothings" called Rowling's critics "Barbarians" whose attacks amounted to "ignorance parading as piety."[5] Equally caustic was a story from Scripps Howard News Service, which dubbed the conservative Family Friendly Libraries a "House of Slytherin" organization and called Lindy Beam of Focus on the Family a "squib." (i.e., In the Harry Potter series, a non-magical person resulting from a genetic abnormality and who, as a result if their non-magicalness, tends to be resentful, bitter and bad-tempered.)[6]

There also was a scathingly sarcastic commentary posted to the CBS-News Channel 4000.com web site, which misrepresented an evangelical critique of Rowling. The author of this CBS opinion piece, Betsy Gerboth, lambasted the evangelical analysis, alleging that it not only condemned children's "imagination," but also put forth the idea that "[c]hildren who are unhappy should just put up or shut up." After implying that concerned parents are illiterate, Gerboth added some patently anti-Christian comments:

> Have you ever noticed that the longer you let these people spout their sanctimony, the less sense they make? . . .

I'm sure a lot of you are even now leaping head-first into your e-mail programs to tell me that . . . I am not only an idiot, but also condemned for all eternity to burn in the fiery pit of hell. Or something like that. . . .

The books are fantasies. Don't understand the word? Look it up.

Perhaps what the anti-Harry factions are most frightened of is that their children will read books like Rowling's, develop their own imaginations—and learn to make up their own minds—and reject the fanatical teachings of those who would like to decide what *every* child should and shouldn't read, based on their own narrow beliefs.[7]

Such venomous barbs mimic a kind of intolerance expressed by some of the Harry Potter characters toward non-magical folk (i.e., Muggles). Even some of the "good" characters have a superior attitude toward Muggles. As Mr. Weasley says about Muggles on page 38 of *Chamber of Secrets*, "[T]hey'll go to any lengths to ignore magic, even if it's staring them in the face." In reference to Rowling's depiction of Muggles, *The New American* noted: "The magical world is exciting, compassionate, and full of lovably unconventional characters, while the world of conventional, button-down, working stiffs is populated by dysfunctional families full of narrow-minded bigotry and pathological pettiness."[8]

Rowling's anti-Muggle slant is easily translated to the real world by faithful Potter supporters who are finding new and colorful ways to attack Harry Potter detractors. A September 19, 2000 Reuters newswire story, for example, compared anti-Potter parents in Canada to "Muggles—those pesky non-magical people."[9] Consider, too, the following statement by Dr. Elizabeth Schafer, author of *Beacham's Sourcebooks for Teaching Young Adult Fiction: Exploring Harry Potter*, a teaching guide for public school educators: "Like the boorish non-wizard Muggles in the Harry Potter novels, most censors lack imagination. Unable to separate reality from fantasy, they are oblivious to the books' theme of love conquering evil."[10]

This is only one of many instances in which Christians and concerned parents have been depicted as "Muggles." The implied meaning behind "Muggles" is even clearer through recent translations of Rowling's novels into other languages: *babboni* (Italian, sounds like "babbioni," meaning idiots) and *dreuzel* (Dutch, sounds like "dreutel," slang for a clumsy person).[11] Compare these definitions with how "Muggle" is used similarly in a July 25, 2000 Amazon.com "Wizard Toy" advertisement: "Harry Potter fans can hone their wizardry and magical skills with these toys that will help them break free from their humdrum Muggles-existence!"[12]

Rowling herself admits that the word "Muggle" has now evolved from meaning just a non-magical person to someone "fairly dull and unimaginative."[13] The derogatory nature of "Muggle" is clear, and yet the word is now being routinely used by the media in reference to Christians and other conservatives voicing concerns over the Harry Potter books. This is not to say that every Harry Potter supporter has resorted to name-calling. In fact, there have been sincere attempts made to address concerns about Rowling's books. The following pages list the most common pro-Potter arguments, and also provide a Christian rebuttal:

Argument #1: The magic used in Harry Potter has "complex moral rules . . . moral rules dictating when to use, and when not to use, magic."[14]

Rebuttal: Although there are indeed "rules" about magic and its uses, these rules are regularly broken by Harry and his companions, usually with no negative consequences. Ultimately, the use or nonuse of magic is completely dependent upon subjective determinations of right and wrong made by individual characters. Therefore, the so-called "moral" rules of magic in Rowling's stories are insignificant.

Argument #2: "[F]or the most part, Christian experts agree that the world of wizards and spells created by Rowling is not the same as the occult-type practices Scripture condemns."[15]

Rebuttal: There is no documentation to support the contention that a majority of "Christian experts" on occultism believe the wizards and spells in Rowling's novels are altogether different than actual occultism. The media has repeatedly quoted only three Christian sources presenting such a sentiment, and *none* of them are "experts" on occultism: 1) Chuck Colson, who is primarily a social commentator and evangelist to prisoners; 2) Alan Jacobs, a literature professor at Wheaton College; and 3) *Christianity Today*, a social-cultural magazine specializing in topics relating to the Christian community. The fact is that numerous knowledgeable Christian experts on occultism have objected to the books and continue to do so.

Argument #3: If you ban all books with witchcraft and supernatural, you'll ban three-quarters of children's literature" (J.K. Rowling, *Washington Post*).[16]

Rebuttal: This is a strawman argument (i.e., arguing against a position by creating a different, weaker or irrelevant position and refuting that new position instead of the original). No one is advocating banning all books with witchcraft or the supernatural. Concerned parents and Christians are arguing that the Harry Potter books have no place in public schools and are inappropriate for children because a great deal of the "magick" in Harry Potter mirrors real occultism as practiced within neopaganism/Wicca, which are contemporary religions (unlike the fairy tale "witchcraft" found in stories such as *Hansel and Gretel* or *Sleeping Beauty*).

Argument #4: Harry Potter does not teach witchcraft/Wicca, a neopagan religion in which the Goddess (Mother Earth) and her male consort (the Horned God) are worshiped. In Rowling's books, "there are no celebrations of the turning of the seasons, no Full Moon or New Moon rituals, and certainly no invocation of Goddess or God."[17]

Rebuttal: It is true that Harry Potter does not present the formal doctrines of contemporary witchcraft/Wicca. However, as noted in previous chapters, Rowling's novels do glamorize various occult practices currently used by Wiccans/witches/pagans as part of their religion (e.g., scrying, fortune-telling, mediumship/channeling, astrology, numerology, etc.).

Argument #5: Even if the Harry Potter books do contain "occultism," that does not mean the contents should not be discussed in public school classrooms. The novels are just fantasy.

Rebuttal: Unlike the bulk of fantasy stories read by students in public schools, Rowling's works tread well within the realm of religion because the world of Harry Potter includes actual forms of religious expression (i.e., occult practices). These practices are then discussed in a positive light and used as the basis for children's activities. This violates public school policies. According to the Anti-Defamation League's "ABC's of Religion in the Curriculum," religion in public schools "must be discussed in a neutral, objective, balanced and factual manner. . . . A public school's curriculum may not be devotional or doctrinal. Nor have the effect of promoting or inhibiting religion."[18] Clearly, some of the classroom projects and discussions taking place do not adhere to this condition. Simply reading the novels in a classroom setting might easily encourage a student to pursue activities like astrology, numerology and scrying, which are religious practices performed by pagans/witches and other occultists.

Argument #6: "[R]estricting the use of books that kids want to read violates their First Amendment rights and helps produce an illiterate society."[19]

Rebuttal: This statement is not only illogical, but also legally inaccurate. First, children already are restricted from reading and purchasing materials that state and local governments have ruled as obscene, adult and/or inappropriate for children. Second, it is logically absurd to assert that widespread illiteracy among our nation's youth will be the end result of not allowing children to read a relatively small amount of material amid the thousands of volumes unanimously viewed as appropriate for children.

Argument #7: According to the newly formed Free Expression Network (a coalition comprised of People for the American Way, the American Civil Liberties Union and The National Council of Teachers of English), restricting the Harry Potter books from public schools would create "a veritable avalanche of school-based censorship."[20]

Rebuttal: These same organizations fully support book censorship in schools when it relates to volumes they judge as inappropriate for children.[21]

Argument #8: It is wrong to restrict reading material from children; parents should "just . . . let them go do what they need to do" (J.K. Rowling, *USA Weekend*).[22]

Rebuttal: Children need guidance when it comes to literature. Why? According to child psychologist Bruno Bettelheim, author of *The Uses of Enchantment: The Meaning and Importance of Fairy Tales*, children do not analyze literature or fictional characters as adults do. Although children may engage in "seeking meaning and crafting a moral philosophy of life" from stories (even more than adults), they do so via an indirect method: "The question for the child is not, 'Do I want to be good?' but 'Who do I want to be like?'."[23] Consequently, a clear delineation between good and evil *must* be present for children to nurture within themselves a moral center of being. This, however, does not occur in the Harry Potter series. Rowling's fantasy presents a morally confusing world where good characters (e.g., Harry, Ron, Hermione, Lupin, etc.) consistently resort to unethical behavior (e.g., lying, cheating, stealing, deception) to further their own goals that are supposedly "good."[24]

Argument #9: The Harry Potter books should be read by children and used in public schools because they are reintroducing children and teens to the joy of books, getting young people away from watching television and showing our youth that reading can be more rewarding that noneducational video games. As one parent commented in a *New York Times* news story, "Harry Potter really got my daughter reading—she didn't read books before and now she loves it."[25]

Rebuttal: Just because children are reading *more*, does not mean that *what* they are reading is emotionally, psychologically, morally or spiritually beneficial for them. Moreover, if a child has not been reading books at all before Harry Potter, they are certainly in no position to: 1) identify poor literature when they read it, or 2) comprehend the destructive nature of some of the messages being presented in the stories they are reading.[26]

Oddly, many avid supporters of the Harry Potter books have remained relatively unfazed by these reasonable rebuttals to their pro-Potter arguments. This unwillingness to acknowledge the obvious problems in Rowling's novels may stem from nothing more than a lack of desire to ruin a good thing. It seems that most people do not want to think very much about the series, but rather, just enjoy it, even if it means overlooking various problems with the characters and underlying messages.

One Harry Potter fan admitted as much in a message posted on September 26, 2000 at the online "Harry Potter Opinion Board." A web surfer named "Flo" posted her (or his) opinion in response to an earlier post I had made, wherein I pointed out some of the many problems in Rowling's books. Flo began by saying, "I do agree with you on some things," then continued:

> Harry is really sort of a brat. He is always breaking the rules and is very disrespectful to some of the teachers. I never have talked to adults the way he has. But I still like him. It would just be better if he was corrected by Dumbledore and not treated with kid gloves all the time. I have noticed Hagrid seems to have a drinking problem!!!!

In concluding, Flo unwittingly went on to reveal what may be the psychological process whereby so many people have accepted the Harry Potter series without concern over its many spiritual and moral failings: "I guess when you read these books you just have to put your mind in neutral and enjoy."[27]

ENDNOTES

1. Elizabeth Schafer, "The Bad Boy Censors Want to Kick Out of School," *ThomasPaine.CommonSense*, November 18, 1999, available online at www.tompaine.com/history/1999/11/18/index.html.
2. Julia Keller, "Should Harry Potter Be Expelled from the Classroom?," *The Holland (West Michigan) Sentinel*, November 28, 1999, available online at www.thehollandsentinel.net/stories/index.html.
3. Schafer.
4. Wendy Doniger, "Spot the Source: Harry Potter Explained," *London Review of Books*; reprinted in *The Guardian*, February 10, 2000, available online at www.guardian.co.uk/lrb/articles/0,6109,135352,00.html.
5. Suzanne Fields, "Casual Censors and Deadly Know-Nothings," *Jewish World Review*, December 7, 1999, available online at www.jewishworldreview.com/cols/fields120799.asp.
6. David Waters, "Not Every Christian Horrified by Harry Potter," Scripps Howard News Service, July 5, 2000, available online at www.cesnur.org/recens/potter_039.htm.

7. Betsy Gerboth, "Feeling Demonic? It's Harry Potter's Fault," CBS News, available online at www.channel4000.com/sh/entertainment/cultureshocked/stories/cultureshocked-20000606-151157.html.

8. Steve Bonta, "Harry Potter's Hocus Pocus," *The New American*, August 28, 2000, available online at www.thenewamerican.com/tna/2000/08-28-2000/vo16no18_potter.htm.

9. Reuters, "Harry Potter Wins Round Against 'Muggles'," September 19, 2000, available online at www.foxnews.com.

10. Schafer.

11. John Kelly, "A Muggle's a Dreuzel as Rowling Fans Clamor for Translated Tome," *Chicago Sun Times*, July 9, 2000, available at www.northernlight.com.

12. "Wizard Toys" section, www.amazon.com, last viewed on July 25, 2000.

13. J.K. Rowling, interview with Margot Adler, "All Things Considered," National Public Radio, December 3, 1998, real audio available at www.npr.org.

14. Doniger.

15. Lisa Jackson, "The Return of Harry Potter," *Christian Parenting Today*, May 2000, available at www.christianityonline.com/cpt/2000/005/4.44.html.

16. J.K. Rowling, quoted in Linton Weeks, *The Washington Post*, October 20, 1999, C01, available online at www.washingtonpost.com.

17. Okelle, "Harry Potter and the Witch Conspiracy," About.com, available online at www.paganwiccan.about.com.

18. "ABC's of Religion in the Curriculum," Anti-Defamation League, available online at www.adl.org.

19. "Purpose Statement," Muggles for Harry Potter Website, available online at www.mugglesforharrypotter.org/.

20. Jonathan Zimmerman, "Harry Potter and His Censors," *Education Week*, August 2, 2000, available online at www.edweek.org.

21. One example would be *Little Black Sambo* (published 1899), a book that presents the "shiftless, carefree African clown of American folklore" (see Zimmerman). Although not a perfect analogy, it shows that book suppression/censorship is admissible when the political climate is correct.

22. J.K. Rowling, quoted in Michele Hatty, "Harry Potter Author Reveals the Secret to Getting Kids to Read As Children's Book Week Kicks Off," *USA Weekend*, Nov. 14, 1999, available online at www.usaweekend.com/99_issues/991114potter.html.

23. Bruno Bettelheim, *The Uses of Enchantment: The Meaning and Importance of Fairy Tales* (New York: Vintage, 1989 edition), 10; cf. Alison Lentini, "Harry Potter: Occult Cosmology and the Corrupted Imagination," *SCP Journal* (vols. 23:4-24:1), 26.

24. It is understandable that Rowling would raise an argument promoting the letting loose of children to "do what they need to do." Her sentiment perfectly mirrors the level of guidance the adult characters in her Harry Potter novels give to Harry and his companions—virtually none. Nowhere, for example, does any adult even suggest that lying and disobedience are wrong. On the contrary, such actions are looked upon as a means of accomplishing good deeds and receiving rewards. Ultimately, some children might create within themselves a skewed perception of right and wrong, believing that they are being "good" by emulating Harry.

25. Lorraine Stern, quoted in David D. Kirkpatrick, "Harry Potter Magic Halts Bedtime for Youngsters," *New York Times*, July 9, 2000, available online at www.nytimes.com; cf. Art Toalson, "Latest 'Harry Potter' Book Meets Cautionary Response From Christians," *Baptist Press*, July 13, 2000, available online at www.cesnur.org/recens/potter_036.htm.

26. It may be that a significant number of parents simply do not take or have the time it takes to guide their children through good books, and as a result are simply allowing them to, as Rowling has put it, go "do what they need to do."

27. Flo, "Response to Convincing Muggles," September 26, 2000, posted at "Harry Potter Opinion Board," available online at http://members.boardhost.com/harrypotter1/msg/203.html.

FOURTEEN

If a child's reading is habitually in the area of the supernatural, is there not a risk that he will develop an insatiable appetite for it, an appetite that grows ever stronger as it is fed? Will he be able to recognize the boundaries between spiritually sound imaginative works and the deceptive ones? Here is another key point for parents to consider: Are we committed to discussing these issues with our children? Are we willing to accompany them, year after year, as their tastes develop, advising caution here, sanctioning liberality there, each of us, young and old, learning as we go? . . . Are we willing to sacrifice precious time to pre-read some novels about which we may have doubts? Are we willing to invest effort to help our children choose the right kind of fantasy literature from library and bookstore?

Michael O'Brien[1]
author, *A Landscape With Dragons*

More than twenty-five years ago, child psychologist Bruno Bettelheim severely criticized children's literature for its lack of psychological meaning. Exempt from his criticism, however, were fairy tales, of which he stated, "More can be learned from them [i.e., fantasies] about the inner problems of human beings and of the right solutions to their predicaments in any society than from any other type of story within a child's comprehension."[2]

If Bettelheim is correct, then today's young readers will certainly not benefit, morally and spiritually speaking, from having read Harry Potter. At the very least, they will not have received positive guidance either from J.K. Rowling or her boy-wizard protagonist. Indeed, the novels actually are filled with potentially harmful messages exalting occultism and moral relativism.

This remains a problem, despite protests to the contrary by J.K. Rowling, her publicists, the media and various Christians (e.g., Alan Jacobs and *Christianity Today*). In *A Landscape With Dragons: The Battle for Your Child's Mind*, Michael O'Brien voices the inescapable fact that children are vulnerable to powerful images "precisely because they are at a stage of development when their fundamental concepts of reality are being formed. Their perceptions and understanding are being shaped at every moment, as they have been in every generation, through a ceaseless ingathering of words and images."[3]

What do the words and images in Rowling's Harry Potter series communicate? There may indeed be a few "good" messages scattered throughout the books, such as: 1) remain loyal to your friends; 2) do not commit murder; and 3) share your snacks. But the underlying lessons communicated through Rowling's novels are far from positive:

- Lying, stealing and cheating are not only acceptable, but can also be fun.
- Astrology, numerology, casting spells and performing "magick" can be exciting.
- Disobedience is not very serious, unless you get caught.
- Being "special" means you deserve to escape punishment for behaving badly.

- Adults just get in the way most of the time.
- Rules are made to be broken.
- Revenge is an acceptable course of action.

O'Brien astutely notes the problem with today's children's literature, a problem painfully apparent in the Harry Potter series:

> [A]uthentic literature is slowly disappearing from public and school libraries and being replaced by a tidal wave of children's books written by people who appear to have been convinced by cultic psychology or converted in part or whole by the neopagan cosmos. Significantly, their use of language is much closer to the operations of electronic culture, and their stories far more visual than the thoughtful fiction of the past. They are evangelists of a religion that they deny is a religion. Yet, in the new juvenile literature there is a relentless preoccupation with spiritual powers, with the occult, with perceptions of good and evil that are almost always blurred and at times downright inverted.[4]

Equally applicable to the Harry Potter series are O'Brien's concerns about the violence and gore in today's literature for children, which is accented by the complete absence of any heroes or heroines as previously defined by classic fantasy tales. As an illustration, he points to R.L. Stine's gruesome *Goosebumps* series, which has sold more than 100 million copies. An excerpt from one of these books reads, "And then the heads. Human heads. Hair caked with dirt. Skin loose, hanging from their skulls. They stared at me with pleading eyes, faces twisted, mouths hanging open in pain. 'Take me with you,' one of them called in a dry whisper."[5] Interestingly, the publisher of these grisly volumes—the newest titles of which include *Headless Halloween*, *Scream School* and *Return to Horrorland*—is none other than Scholastic, the U.S. publisher of Harry Potter. O'Brien makes these observations about the books, which in many ways are very similar to Rowling's novels:

> For sheer perversity these tales rival anything that has been published to date. Each is brimming over with murder, grotesque scenes of horror, terror, mutilation (liberally seasoned with gobbets and gobbets of blood and gore). Shock after shock pummels the reader's mind, and the child experiences them as both psychological and physical stimuli. These shocks are presented as ends in themselves, raw violence as entertainment. In sharp contrast, the momentary horrors that occur in classical tales always have a higher purpose; they are intended to underline the necessity of courage, ingenuity, and character; the tales are about brave young people struggling through adversity to moments of illumination, truth, and maturity; they emphatically demonstrate that good is far more powerful than evil. Not so with the new wave of shock-fiction. Its "heroes" and "heroines" are usually rude, selfish, sometimes clever (but in no way wise), and they never grow up. This nasty little world offers a thrill per minute, but it is like a sealed room from which the oxygen is slowly removed, replaced by an atmosphere of nightmare and a sense that the forces of evil are nearly omnipotent.[6]

O'Brien's words easily fit the Harry Potter books. Nevertheless, despite their dismal depictions of morality, blatant occultism and gratuitous gore, Rowling's series continues to be used by educators in public schools. Complicating this problem are the many teacher's guides based on Rowling's books. Some of these manuals seem to be written with the intention of introducing students to occultism, while simultaneously prejudicing them against Christianity.

One of the most egregious examples is Dr. Elizabeth Schafer's *Beacham's Sourcebooks for Teaching Young Adult Fiction: Exploring Harry Potter*. This educator's guide not only includes chapters covering the history of real magick and occult practices such as alchemy,[7] but also attempts to get students to research these practices and the personalities associated with them through the online companion resources page, accessed through Beacham's web site.[8] Consider these assignments:

- "Investigate and write a paper about alchemy. When and why did humans begin to practice alchemy? What did different metals such as gold symbolize to alchemists?"
- "Look up the names mentioned on the wizard cards [in *Sorcerer's Stone*] . . . and list whether they are real or fictional. If they are historical figures, write a paragraph about each magician, witch, or wizard."
- "Learn about the role of witchcraft [i.e., real witchcraft] in different cultures. Either make a costume for yourself . . . or use construction paper to design the attire of witches in a specific geographic location."
- "[W]rite a poem, short play, literary non-fiction, or other form of expression about magic or witchcraft."[9]

One can only wonder how many public schools in America would permit Schafer projects if they were to be Christianized in the following manner:

- "Investigate and write a paper about Christian prayer. When and why did people begin to pray to Jesus?"
- "Look up the names mentioned in *Foxe's Book of Martyrs*. Write a paragraph about each apostle, Christian or church leader."

- "Learn about the role of Christianity in different cultures. Either make a costume for yourself . . . or use construction paper to design the attire of Christians in a specific geographic location."
- "[W]rite a poem, short play, literary non-fiction or other form of expression about Jesus Christ or Christianity."

Such activities probably would elicit strong protests from numerous organizations such as American Atheists and the American Civil Liberties Union. But because occultism/paganism has become the fashionable religion of our era, Rowling's Harry Potter series and the educational lessons based on it continue to go largely unchallenged. Beacham's online companion site to Schafer's book even recommends that children read books like *The Encyclopedia of Celtic Wisdom* which, according to Schafer/Beacham, "[d]iscusses subjects noted in the Harry Potter novels such as prophecy, divination, quests, initiations, shapeshifting, and ancestral worship."[10]

Under "Reading for Research," Schafer/Beacham lists *Drawing Down the Moon: Witches, Druids, Goddess-Worshippers and Other Pagans in America Today* by well-known advocate of neopaganism/Wicca Margot Adler. Also recommended is Lewis Spence's *An Encyclopedia of Occultism*, which Schafer describes as a "reprint of a classic encyclopedia source listing information about alchemy, the Philosopher's Stone, and the real Nicholas Flamel."[11]

Web sites listed by Schafer/Beacham include www.astrology.about.com, www.celticcrow.com (The Witches League for Public Awareness web site), www.theystica.com ("On-line Encyclopedia of the Occult, Mysticism, Magic, Paranormal, and More" web site), www.witchvox.com (a Wiccan web site) and www.druidry.org

(neopagan web site of the Druidism-promoting Order of Bards, Ovates and Druids).[12]

Other learning projects encourage children to research anti-Christian books that include misleading and inaccurate information about Christianity, such as *The Power of Myth* by Joseph Campbell, who referred to Judeo-Christian worship as "monkey-holiness."[13] A 1997 *WORLD* magazine article on Campbell concisely described his views:

> Combining Jungian psychology and New Age philosophy, Mr. Campbell's ambition was to construct a global theology based on the world's common mythological motifs. According to his theories, all human civilizations have told the same "myth," with only minor differences in the details.
>
> As he says in *The Hero with a Thousand Faces*, "The heroes of all time have gone before us; the labyrinth is thoroughly known; we have only to follow the thread of the hero-path. And where we had thought to find an abomination, we shall find a god; where we had thought to slay another, we shall slay ourselves; where we had thought to travel outward, we shall come to the center of our own existence; where we had thought to be alone, we shall be with all the world."
>
> For all of his universalism, Mr. Campbell had little regard for the non-mythological religions of Christianity and Judaism. "Whenever the poetry of myth is interpreted as biography, history, or science, it is killed," he says, attacking the biblical insistence on historicity. "Such a blight has certainly descended on the Bible and on a great part of the Christian cult."
>
> As for Judeo-Christian worship, "Such a monkey-holiness is not what the functioning world requires; rather, a transmutation of the whole social order is necessary, so that . . . the

universal god-man who is actually immanent and effective in all of us may be somehow made known to consciousness."

In an interview with *Omni* magazine shortly before his death in 1987, Mr. Campbell called for the "dissolution" of the three major religions of the West, namely Christianity, Judaism, and Islam. "The future, if there's going to be one, has to be a dissolution of those three systems and an opening up of the horizons to the planet." The clergy, he says, must "begin talking about humanity instead of their own little sect and, instead of saying, 'We have it,' say, 'It is through us, through our religion, that we realize that all people have it.' "[14]

In *The Power of Myth*, Campbell presents as fact various unbiblical and historically unverifiable notions:

1. the God of the Old Testament evolved over time from an angry tribal god into a savior deity;
2. there was no Garden of Eden, and the Genesis creation story is a myth;
3. Jesus did not rise from the dead or ascend to heaven bodily;
4. all humans are divine;
5. when Christ realized he and the Father were one, he was only recognizing the god within himself that all humans possess;
6. the gospel accounts are all contradictory; and
7. there is no personal God.[15]

In *Exploring Harry Potter*, Elizabeth Schafer appears to share many of Campbell's views since she favorably comments on his work (p. 130) and the work of psychologist Carl Jung (p. 160), whose theories about "collective unconscious" and "archetypes" heavily influenced Campbell's views of mythology and religion. Schafer, like Campbell, suggests that the Genesis creation account is a "primitive" myth which, when viewed by researchers, conflicts with "the logic of reason and history."[16] She even suggests that the entire Bible—its "demons and sorcerers, unexplained wonders, and brutal tortures and murders"—are merely "archetypal experiences."[17] In other words, Scripture is little more than a group of mythological stories that reflect or symbolize various truths (good, evil, suffering, etc.) embedded in society's collective unconscious. Schafer also implies that belief in an "invisible" God is similar to children who "often see things that aren't real."[18]

Additionally, Schafer poses extremely biased (i.e., pro-occult and anti-Christian) discussion questions pertaining to occultism in general, the controversies surrounding occultism, its relation to the Harry Potter books and other debates concerning religion in public schools. Some of these questions, comments and projects actually seem to be an attempt to influence public school policy and children's opinions in favor of occultism. Still others are plainly anti-Christian, such as the ones that compare today's conservative Christians to perpetrators of the murderous witch hunts that took place in the fifteenth to seventeenth centuries. Consider the following examples of both types of material found in her online resource companion:

- "Write a paper about how efforts to ban the Harry Potter novels because of their themes of evil, sorcery, or witchcraft, and to forbid children from wearing witch and devil costumes, resemble historic witch hunts."
- "Has your school or community ruled that children cannot wear witch or devil costumes at Halloween? . . . Write a letter to the editor of your school or local newspaper expressing your opinion about this."[19]

Finally, Schafer boldly offers comments, questions and projects that clearly delve into religiously based concepts of morality and ethics, which is an area that should be off-limits in public schools, unless the topics are presented in a fair manner. Some of her subjects actually bring into discussion the Bible, its worth as a historically reliable document and methods of biblical interpretation, even though there is no guarantee that any teacher leading the discussions will be qualified to deal with the issues with accuracy and objectivity. In fact, Schafer's book itself contains numerous errors relating to Christianity and the Bible. Consider the following examples:

> *False Schafer Statement:* "Marking people for death is an ancient rite, and whether readers recognize it through Passover, the holocaust . . . or branding cattle, the pain and power of the mark itself . . . becomes a fearsome symbol." (p. 127)

> *Biblical/Historical Account:* During the first Passover in the Old Testament, when lamb's blood marked the doorposts of the Israelites in Egypt, it did *not* mark the people for death. The blood marked the home and its inhabitants for life and forgiveness from God(Exodus 12:7-13)

> *False Schafer Statement:* "Joseph's magical coat from the Bible is a recognizable symbol for many people." (p. 157)

> *Biblical/Historical Account:* Joseph did not receive a "magical" coat from his father, Jacob. Joseph's garment was a full-length tunic similar to the kind a noblemen might wear. It signified Joseph's favored status in Jacob's eyes, which in turn incited Joseph's brothers to jealousy. (Genesis 37:1-4)

> *False Schafer Statement:* "Daniel slew the dragon Bel, a Babylon god described in the Apocrypha (early Christian texts not included in the New Testament)." (p. 168)

Biblical/Historical Account: The story to which Schafer alludes is contained in a second-century text known as *Bel and the Dragon*, which has been added to Roman Catholic Bibles as the fourteenth chapter of the Old Testament book of Daniel. Schafer's inaccurate statements are glaring: 1) "Bel" is *not* the dragon—a living reptile worshiped by the Babylonians— in *Bel and the Dragon*, but is the name of the clay/brass pagan idol worshiped by the Babylonians; 2) the Apocrypha has nothing to do with the *New* Testament, but is a collection of books accepted by *some* Christians as being part of the *Old* Testament; 3) the Apocrypha does not include any *Christian* texts, since all the writings (including *Bel and the Dragon*) were authored sometime between 300 B.C. and 30 B.C., before there even *were* any Christians!

False Schafer Statement: "The *Book of Revelations* [sic] chronicles Armageddon. . . . The narrative reveals that after one thousand years of peace, Satan will be freed but will die in a lake of fire before he can renew the conflict. . . . *Revelations* offers clues and symbols for readers." (p. 172)

Biblical/Historical Account: The last book of the New Testament is not "*Revelations*" (plural), as Schafer indicates. It is *Revelation* (singular), taken from the Greek word *apokalypsis*, which means "uncovering" or "unveiling." It refers to the final unveiling of Jesus Christ to the entire world. In addition, Satan, according to the Bible, does not "die" in a lake of fire. Revelation 20:10 says that Satan, the Antichrist (the beast), and the false prophet will be thrown into the lake of fire where they will be tormented forever.

In attempting to discuss biblical issues, Schafer obviously goes far outside her field of knowledge, which is primarily children's literature. Nevertheless, her online resource guide to *Exploring*

Harry Potter goes even further by including moral, ethical, theological and biblical discussion questions for use in public schools by teachers, many of whom are probably as ignorant as Schafer is about such issues. These are just a few of the questions:

- "Some parents have complained about Harry Potter novels on religious grounds. Explain how you think the novels do or do not parallel evil, violence and miracles in the Bible? [sic]"
- "Compare a Harry Potter character to a biblical character."
- "Can lies ever be created to achieve good goals or are they told for solely malicious intentions?"[20]

What is a parent to do about Harry Potter? There have been a number of suggestions made by various Christian leaders, counter-cult ministries, pastors and Christian educators. Ultimately, each parent will have to decide how their children will respond to the books. In order to do this, parents must have their facts straight concerning the novels so that appropriate questions can be raised about them. When it comes to the use of the Harry Potter books in public schools, Christian parents must be thoughtful about the decision they make regarding whether or not to allow their children to hear the series being read in class. A parent needs to discern what action will be more harmful—letting the child hear the stories or having their child bear the burden of feeling "left out," and perhaps even being ridiculed, as the only one to leave class.

Bear in mind that according to God's Word, the Holy Spirit dwelling in us is far more powerful than *any* force of darkness in the world (1 John 4:4). Moreover, no Christian should ever harbor fear regarding the contents of a book (1 John 4:18). God has not given us a spirit of fear or timidity, but one of power and love

(2 Timothy 1:7). So instead of being made to suffer the taunts of other children, perhaps a Christian parent could allow his or her child to remain in the classroom, but discuss the books each time they are read. A Christian child might benefit in several ways by hearing the books read to them in a classroom setting:

- During follow-up discussions at home, a Christian parent could demonstrate through Scripture where the Harry Potter series is in error regarding good and evil.
- Hearing the books read in class might ignite moral and ethical discussions between Christian parents and their children.
- The experience might open up witnessing opportunities for a child to share Christ's love with classmates.
- The presence of a Rowling's fantasy could be used as a means of introducing a child to godly fantasy such as C.S. Lewis' Narnia series or J.R.R. Tolkien's books about Middle-Earth.

The most important thing to remember, however, is that parents must be involved in this issue with their children. They should not simply tell their children, "It's about witchcraft, and that's against the Bible, so you can't read it." Such a rigid, noninformative approach may simply leave a child with no real answers for themselves or others. Parents should give examples of where the Harry Potter series is unbiblical and explain why God is against some of the things in Rowling's books, both from a spiritual and moral perspective.

GOOD ALWAYS TRIUMPHS

It is never easy to watch ungodly activity and unbiblical beliefs grow in popularity, nor is it ever comfortable to take a stand against such problems. Nevertheless, Christians are commanded by Scripture to "preach the word" and always be prepared to impart truth to others (2 Timothy 4:2). But equally important is the *manner* in which Christians are obedient to this command. The apostle Peter says it should be done with gentleness and reverence (1 Peter 3:15). Furthermore, Paul tells us that spreading truth involves great patience with a view toward instruction (2 Timothy 4:2).

Sharing Christian perspectives in such a manner not only demonstrates obedience to God, but also provides one of the most powerful and irrefutable proofs of God's love. Jesus said that proof of genuine Christianity is inextricably linked to how love is shown (John 13:35). Ephesians 4:15 clearly instructs Christians to speak the truth in love. Of course, it can be difficult to do so when talking about such emotional issues as the Harry Potter books. Fortunately, there are a number of ways a Christian can overcome negativity and hostility.

First, show respect to others. A Christian must make sure that he always communicates concern rather than condemnation. Don't resort to mockery or calling down fire and brimstone on people simply because they see nothing problematic with the Harry Potter books. The quickest way to destroy communication is by making someone feel attacked, which automatically causes walls of emotional protection to rise. Try to understand that many people have what they believe are good reasons for accepting the Harry Potter books as appropriate for children and schools. Even if a friend or family member chooses to ignore warnings about Harry Potter, let him know that he is still loved and accepted. In Second Timothy 2:24-26, Paul teaches that every ministering encounter is to be permeated with gentleness and kindness.

Second, respond to J.K. Rowling supporters with thoughtful answers that are prefaced by words of kindness, which show you respect their viewpoint. For example, before criticizing someone's view of the Harry Potter books, one could try saying: "You've made an interesting point, but have you thought of this?" or "That's certainly understandable, but I see a problem with looking at it like that."

Third, know that the enemy is not J.K. Rowling, the American public school system, Harry Potter fans, pro-Potter journalists or the publishers of the Harry Potter series. The true enemies are spiritual forces of darkness seeking to overshadow Christian values and virtues with occult myths, practices and morals. But this should come as no surprise. God warned believers long ago that there would appear many deceitful spirits and doctrines of demons to draw people away from truth (1 Timothy 4:1).

Fourth, Christians must get their facts straight regarding J.K. Rowling and her works. Accurate criticisms concerning the contents of Rowling's series will be far more effective than misrepresentations of her novels. Don't just repeat everything that is heard. Make sure that the objection over the book's contents is accurate, and not based on something taken out of context. Also, be ready to give examples of your objections to the Harry Potter books so that supporters of the series can clearly see the problem.

Fifth, remember that the battle being waged for the minds of today's children is a spiritual one, in which Christians are facing forces of darkness (Ephesians 6:12). Consequently, none of us can ignore the Bible's instruction to put on "the armor of God" (6:10-17). Only through God's power and strength will any of us be able to stand against the spiritual forces of darkness influencing our culture through the pagan practices and occult literature now so popular in America.

With the belt of truth (6:14) a Christian will be able to actively pursue the task of presenting with boldness the dangerous messages behind the seemingly harmless fantasy of Harry Potter. The breastplate of righteousness (6:14) will enable a believer in Christ to stand blameless and holy in front of a world that is clearly anti-Christian. God's spiritual footwear, the gospel of peace (6:15), symbolizes readiness of spirit and a commitment to share God's good news of salvation through whatever struggles arise. Behind the shield of faith (6:16) a Christian will be protected from the many fiery arrows of persecution that have already, and will continue to be, directed toward those expressing concerns over Harry Potter. Of course, a Christian's most potent weapon is God's Word, the sword of the spirit (6:17), which is able to divide truth from error in even the most confusing situations (Hebrews 4:12).

Finally, remember that God is in control. By maintaining a heavenly perspective (2 Corinthians 4:16-18) and trusting that at the end of the ages Christ will be victorious over everything that has exalted itself against God (10:4-5), Christians can confidently face something as temporal as the *Harry Potter* books and their influence on our culture. For the day will come when all those who have loved righteousness and hated evil will be able to sing a song similar to the one sung by the armies that defeated the evil Sauron near the end of Tolkien's The Lord of the Rings trilogy:

> Sing now, ye people of the Tower of Anor,
> for the Realm of Sauron is ended for ever,
> and the Dark Tower is thrown down.
> Sing and rejoice, ye people of the Tower of Guard,
> for your watch hath not been in vain,
> and the Black Gate is broken,
> and your King hath passed through,
> and he is victorious.
> Sing and be glad, all ye children of the West,
> for your King shall come again,

and he shall dwell among you all the days of your life.
And the Tree that was withered shall be renewed,
    and he shall plant it in the high places,
    and the City shall be blessed.
Sing all ye people![21]

ENDNOTES

1. Michael O'Brien, *A Landscape With Dragons* (San Francisco: Ignatius Press, 1998), 110-111.

2. Bruno Bettelheim, *The Uses of Enchantment: The Meaning and Importance of Fairy Tales* (New York: Vintage, 1989 edition), quoted in Richard Bernstein, "The Reality of the Fantasy in the Harry Potter Stories," *New York Times*, November 30, 1999, available online at www.nytimes.com/library/books/113099notebook-potter.html.

3. O'Brien, 61.

4. O'Brien, 65.

5. R.L. Stine, *Goosebump Series 2000 #10#0*, excerpt available online at www.scholastic.com/goosebumps/low/books/gb2ksums.htm#10.

6. O'Brien, 67.

7. Publicity Statement, Beacham Publishing, available online at www.beachampublishing.com.

8. Elizabeth D. Schafer, *Beacham's Sourcebooks for Teaching Young Adult Fiction: Exploring Harry Potter* (Osprey, FL: Beacham Publishing, 2000), 4, 8.

9. This document is entitled "Exclusive Download: Harry Potter," available at www.beachampublishing.com.

10. "Exclusive Download: Harry Potter," available at www.beachampublishing.com.

11. "Exclusive Download: Harry Potter," available at www.beachampublishing.com.

12. "Exclusive Download: Harry Potter," available at www.beachampublishing.com.

13. Joseph Campbell, quoted in Pamela Johnson, "Dark side of the force," *WORLD* Magazine, May 3/10, 1997, available online at www.worldmag.com/world/issues/05-03-97/cultural_2.asp.

14. Johnson.

15. Joseph Campbell, *The Power of Myth* (New York: Doubleday, 1988), 21, 42-51, 57, 174, 210, 211, 213.

16. Schafer, 128.

17. Schafer, 156-157.

18. Schafer, 164.

19. "Exclusive Download: Harry Potter," available at www.beachampublishing.com.

20. "Exclusive Download: Harry Potter," available at www.beachampublishing.com.

21. J.R.R. Tolkien, *The Return of the King* (New York: Ballantine, 1983 edition), p. 269.

OTHER BOOKS
BY RICHARD ABANES

Cults, New Religious Movements, and Your Family
Defending the Faith: A Beginner's Guide to Cults
Journey into the Light: Exploring Near Death Experiences
End-Time Visions: The Doomsday Obsession
Embraced by the Light and the Bible

Richard Abanes can be contacted on the web at:
www.abanes.com